SOCIAL PSYCHOLOGY
IN NATURAL SETTINGS

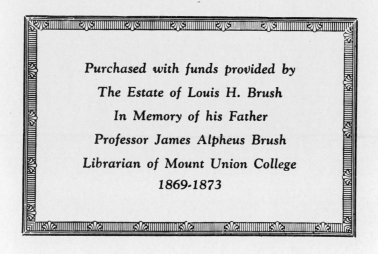

SOCIAL PSYCHOLOGY IN NATURAL SETTINGS

a reader in field experimentation

edited by
Paul G. Swingle

ALDINE PUBLISHING COMPANY
Chicago

About the Editor

Paul G. Swingle received his B.A. and M.A. from Hofstra
University and his Ph.D. from the University of Massachusetts.
He has taught at Dalhousie University, McGill University and
McMaster University, and is presently Professor and Chairman
of the Department of Child Psychology of the University of
Ottawa. He has also edited *Experiments in Social Psychology*
and *The Structure of Conflict*.

Consulting Editor
M. Brewster Smith

First published 1973 by
Aldine Publishing Company
529 South Wabash Avenue
Chicago, Illinois 60605

ISBN 0-202-25102-0 cloth
     0-202-25103-9 paper
Library of Congress Catalog Number 72-78223

Printed in the United States of America

Design by Christine Valentine

PREFACE

A question I am sure almost every student has asked and every professor has heard is, "What does social psychology have to do with real life?" An often-given answer to this question goes something like this: Experimental social psychology has been, and still is, largely a laboratory-based operation, because in the laboratory researchers can isolate variables of interest for close and highly controlled observation. The regularities thus observed then contribute to the development of social psychological theory, which (if it is good theory) should be applicable to natural social settings.

This answer, however, stresses the precision of laboratory procedures, and although such precision is of distinct value, it may contribute to the error of misplaced concreteness, as Whitehead termed it. That is, in laboratory situations researchers abstract those variables in natural environments that are of interest to them—but the effects of these variables when removed from their natural context may be pronounced, and may mislead theorists into attributing greater importance to them than they actually have in our everyday lives. Hence, although the need for refined laboratory research is compelling, the need for field experimentation is equally compelling, for only by it can the influence of variables be examined in their natural context.

The point, of course, is not that field experimentation should replace laboratory research, but that using both settings—laboratory *and* natural—researchers should proceed to develop as robust and relevant a science of social behavior as is possible.

This book is designed as a supplement to standard texts in experimental social psychology, most of which emphasize laboratory research. The articles in this book are reports of experimental social psychological studies conducted in natural settings, and although some of the studies use students as subjects, the experimental manipulations were accomplished in nonlaboratory situations. The orientation is scientific; that is, the focus is on consistencies between laboratory and field research, not inconsistencies. In addition, in the commentary preceding each chapter, I have emphasized methodological issues, since the most critical aspect of any research situation is the experimental design. Research can be an engaging and exciting activity when one has the methodological savvy needed to formulate experiments that provide answers to meaningful questions.

Articles were selected on the basis of both content area and measurement methodology. In field situations, the operationalization and measurement of the dependent variable with any reasonable level of precision is not easy, and many of the studies included in this book demonstrate particularly ingenious applications of experimental methodology to the study of social behavior in natural settings.

Some of the readings are abstracts or abridgements of the original experimental reports, and although I have attempted to retain the essential details of the original articles, abstraction and abridgement may have resulted in some shifts in emphasis. For any of these I apologize to the authors.

This book has benefited from the comments of many students and colleagues, and I thank them most heartily.

CONTENTS

SOCIAL PSYCHOLOGY IN NATURAL SETTINGS

■ INTRODUCTION

The study of human social behavior is an extraordinarily complex area of research. Among the many reasons, two are dominant. First, human social behavior obviously is affected by an enormous number of variables. To determine the relationship between a particular environmental or social variable and an individual's or a group's response, other influences on the behavior must be either eliminated or controlled. A most challenging task, therefore, is the design of adequate experiments that have the sophisticated controls necessary to increase the experimenter's confidence that a relationship between a particular stimulus in a social environment and a particular social response actually exists.

Second, human social behavior tends to be affected by the research process itself. That is, if an individual knows he is involved in an experiment he is likely to behave in a manner somewhat different from the way he would were he not apprehensive about being evaluated. The extent of this contamination is hard to assess. It may vary from the subject's simply being somewhat less active or more inhibited than usual in his behavior (the behavior in question being essentially the same) to a situation in which he acts in exact contradiction of his own personal beliefs in an attempt to behave in a manner he thinks is appropriate. Thus, an individual may act in a way he thinks the experimenter wants him to act, or in a way he feels normal people should act, but not the way he would behave were he unaware that his behavior was being observed.

A related problem is that the results of social research may have an effect on the behavior of the population in question. Let us assume that a researcher concerned with determining good indicators of conformity found that individuals who part their hair on the left side within two inches of the tops of their ears have a much higher probability of complying with requests than does the population at large. Should this information become public we might assume that individuals who did, in fact, part their hair in that fashion but also felt that being overly compliant was a negative personal characteristic might simply change their hairstyle. In short, the research process may have a reactive effect on the subjects in the research situation, be they individuals or groups of individuals.

Laboratory versus Field Experimentation

People have become overly concerned with the distinction between laboratory and field experimentation, and students frequently are expected to wade through the boring details of the essential differences between the two types of research. Much of the skepticism about laboratory-based studies of social behavior is the result of early self-report studies in which subjects were asked what they would do in various circumstances. Whenever data are limited to self-report, the researcher can never be quite sure that the reporter's statements are an accurate estimate of what he did or what he would do in various situations. Much data now available demonstrate quite conclusively that data derived from self-report frequently are at variance with the subject's actual behavior. Behavior is very much determined by the situation a person finds himself in. The prejudiced person may find it expedient to act as though he were extremely tolerant; the person who believes he is honest may feel compelled to be dishonest at certain times. It is important, therefore, to concentrate whenever possible on the actual behavior of subjects rather than on the subjects' self-reports, whether in the laboratory or in the field. However, when the experimenter is concerned with a person's aspirations or his confidence or his values, he generally must rely on what the subject tells him.

Advantages and disadvantages are, of course, associated with both laboratory and field research settings, and the advantages of one setting tend largely to reflect the weaknesses of the other. The laboratory might be thought of as the social psychologist's microscope. Artificial social cultures may be established and precisely controlled, and the independent variable can be manipulated with great precision and the dependent variable(s)—the subject's behavior—measured as frequently and as meticulously as the researcher deems appropriate. In the laboratory, however, subjects know they are being observed and evaluated. Their behavior may also be an artifact of the experimental setting such that the behaviors being studied may not be within the subject's normal range of behaviors.

In field settings the subject's behavior is natural, but the experimenter loses experimental precision and control. It is also difficult to find suitable field situations that can be experimentally manipulated for the purpose of studying a specific problem. Basically, one must consider only three things in evaluating a research project.

First, what is the likelihood that the subject was aware that his behavior was being observed and recorded? For instance, an experiment could easily be done on subjects walking through a building on the way to psychological experiments. In this situation it is very likely that the subjects would not be aware that their behavior was being observed. A long, detailed discussion about whether such an experiment would constitute a field or lab experiment seems to be a profound waste of time, but it is important to know whether a subject is aware of being observed, because his behavior may be affected by his awareness. Also to be considered is whether one is ethically and morally justified in interfering with a person's right to privacy in his normal day-to-day activities.

Second, if the subject is aware that his behavior is being systematically observed and recorded does he know what aspects of his behavior are being observed? In other words, is the experiment so transparent that the subject is not naïve? Subject's awareness of the behavior under investigation may be a serious contamination and may result in invalid data. In laboratory studies some sort of deception procedure usually is used to keep subjects unaware of the true purpose of the experiment, but in natural setting experiments transparency and subject naïveté usually are not serious problems.

Experimental Research

The third point to be considered in evaluating experiments is whether the data were collected in an experimental or in a non-experimental situation. Experimental social psychology refers to the deliberate manipulation of the independent variable and, concomitantly, controlled observation of the dependent variable. A few examples should clarify the distinction between experimental social psychology and other approaches to the study of social behavior.

One might be concerned, say, with the effects of heterosexual groups on the time required to solve a logical problem. The experimenter might ask four-person groups to solve a series of logical problems, taking measurements every 10 minutes to determine the number of problems correctly solved during that time unit. Three experimental conditions might be included: groups of four males, groups of four females, and groups of two males and two females. In this particular situation the experimenter has deliberately manipulated the independent variable—the sexual composition of the group—and is measuring the dependent variable—the number of logical problems solved during every 10-minute time block.

Another example is an episode staged by Allan Funt for the television show "Candid Camera," modified to study the effects of group size on conformity behavior in a field situation. When people enter an elevator they usually turn to face the door and almost never stand facing the back wall. People feel uncomfortable, however, when their behavior is at variance with that of other people in a situation. Thus, if experimental confederates enter the elevator just after the naïve subject enters and, rather than facing the door, face the back wall, a measure of yielding can be obtained. The experiment might involve groups of one, two, three, four, or five confederates who enter the elevator singly. Group size then would be the independent variable. The dependent measure of the naïve subject's conforming behavior might be whether or not he turned and faced the back wall within 30 seconds.

Endless examples, of course, could be offered. Most of the studies reported in this book involve manipulation of the independent variable and so can be referred to as experimental research. Again, the principal distinction between experimental and nonexperimental research is that in experimental research one deliberately manipulates the independent variable and determines the effect of this manipulation on the subject's (or group's) behavior —the dependent variable. Experimental studies of social behavior are our most powerful tool for developing an understanding of human social behavior, since this procedure facilitates the development of cause-and-effect hypotheses. If an experimenter has deliberately manipulated the independent variable and has observed a change in the subject's behavior, he can be more confident that there is a causal relationship between the independent and the dependent variables.

The many nonexperimental approaches to the study of social behavior include attitude surveys, content analyses, correlation procedures, and other techniques designed to examine behavior in highly controlled situations and to relate that behavior to correlated conditions. Any time one does not directly manipulate the independent variable, however, one must exercise extreme caution in making causal statements.

For example, suppose that all people who regularly attend church score very highly on scales of ethnic prejudice; that is, a high correlation exists between church attendance and prejudicial attitudes. Should one find such a relationship, it is not justified to state that church attendance leads to prejudicial attitudes, nor is it legitimate to say that ethnocentric attitudes lead to an affinity for organized religion, which reflects itself in high church attendance. Given the circumstances, one can say only that these two variables vary together. When a person tends to be high in one, he tends to be high in the other. It is entirely possible, for example, that both of these factors are related to a third variable, which results in both high prejudice and high church attendance. Possibly both correlate very highly with conformity, and compliant individuals comply with the community's social norms, which happen to be ethnocentrism and church attendance.

Ethical Considerations in the Conduct of Human Research

Man has the right to be left alone. He has the right to privacy. He has the right to protest individual surveillance of his behavior without his explicit permission. He has the right to know if his behavior is being manipulated, and if it is, why.

All of the above seems self-evident in any civilized free society. However, scientists with appalling frequency act in an unacceptably callous manner regarding physical and psychological hazards to their subjects. Beecher (1969) cites several disquieting experiments, such as the injection of live cancer cells into patients who were unaware of the type of cell being injected. Pappworth (1969) cites distressing examples of research conducted on human subjects; many violate ethical cannons of acceptability if not the law itself. Children have been exposed to harmful doses of chemicals without their parents' awareness and have been subjected to physically painful procedures unrelated to treatment for any existing malady.

In known cases subjects were exposed to unacceptable risks of pain or physiological injury in psychological experiments that involved electric shock and loud noise. In the noise cases the dangers resulted from the researchers' lack of knowledge about the stimuli they were using. Carrying out an experiment without being fully aware of the potential dangers to the subject is, of course, unethical as well as stupid.

Although the physical dangers to subjects are extremely important, they are more obvious than the psychological dangers, and regulating bodies therefore tend to notice them more rapidly. The psychological dangers to subjects are more insidious, less subject to regulation and control, but in general at least as dangerous to the subject as are the physical dangers. Subjects have been exposed to deceptive manipulations that have led them to believe that they had exposed a helpless person to extremely painful shock or loud noise, were homosexually aroused, had cheated, lied, or yielded. Persons have been observed to cheat, to open and keep lost mail, and to lie. Experimenters have joined groups and pretended to share the groups' norms and beliefs in order to observe the behavior of gangs, religious extremists, and work crews. Washrooms have been bugged, private conversations have been recorded, audiences in darkened theaters have been observed with infrared systems, and researchers have hidden under beds in students' dormitory rooms to record conversations during tea parties (Webb et al., 1966).

Scientists interested in the study of social behavior must therefore confront the serious conflict of concern for individual subjects in research situations against the scientist's obligation to develop an understanding of meaningful human social behavior and important social problems. Social psychologists are being encouraged to study the behavior of people in natural environments and to directly study urgent social problems. To accomplish this research, subjects may be exposed to deception, invasion of privacy, stress, embarrassment, restriction of personal freedom, and other indignities.

Professional associations have wrestled long with the problem of ethical standards for research. Codes of ethics have been developed for researchers who use human subjects, but the dilemmas scientists must face are extremely complex (APA, 1971). Some issues seem straightforward—for example, the right of any subject to refuse to participate in an experiment that involves risk of physical or psychological harm. However, this assumes that the experimenter can evaluate the risk, which may imply previous experimentation, and that prospective subjects are fully informed before they consent to participate. Children, mental patients, and persons highly dependent on the experimenter cannot give consent or may not be able to feel free to refuse participation. Consent of guardians is sometimes considered adequate if restricted to situations that have no risk to the subject or, if risks or discomfort are involved, to procedures that may benefit the subject. Further, in some situations informing the subject prior to the experiment would seriously contaminate the data, either because subjects would not act naturally or because many people would refuse to participate, which might leave a population of subjects who are unique, thereby limiting the extent to which the results could be generalized to the larger population.

One might argue that subjects could be informed after they had participated in an experiment and could be allowed to withdraw their data if they choose not to be included in the experiment. Once again the experimenter might be left with a unique population, perhaps limiting the usefulness of the findings. However, more serious issues are involved in the procedure of informing subjects after they have participated. It may be practically impossible to inform all participants, or, since psychologists frequently are interested in such important human behaviors as aggression, cheating, love, influenceability, and the like, informing the subject may create considerable stress, guilt, or embarrassment.

One could argue that protecting the subject's anonymity and not informing him of his participation would be the most ethically desirable procedure. The counterargument is that the indignities and invasions of privacy that unaware subjects are exposed to in experimental manipulation and scrutiny are legitimate because the scientists are well intentioned.

For man to learn something about himself, social research must be conducted. When risks are involved, the potential benefits from the results of the experiment must be weighed against the risks and costs to the participants. The question, of course, is: Who does the weighing? Researchers may be too concerned with continuing the project to deal objectively with the ethical issues; the agency or group that pays for the research may be too committed to deal effectively with them. One suggestion (APA, 1971) is that all research proposals dealing with human subjects be reviewed by a group of persons who represent different sensitivities and could advise the experimenter and assist him in developing the most ethically desirable procedures. A review board might include fellow social scientists, clergymen, lawyers, and representatives from the potential research population. Such review procedures are far from perfect, of course, and the responsibility for the research must remain solely with the experimenter.

It is obvious, then, that the problems of ethical standards in behavioral research are not at all simple. Even the seemingly straightforward issue of informed consent opens up into a myriad of complex and perhaps irreconcilable conflicts of values. Other problems of an ethical nature, including the selection of research topics and experimental populations and the final application of research findings, are likewise extremely complex and subject to marked differences of opinion. The interested student may want to read some of the many thorough treatments of these issues by such social scientists as Erikson (1967), Kelman (1968), Mead (1969), and Parsons (1969).

The following articles are reports of experimental manipulations of social behavior in nonlaboratory situations. Persons moving about in their day-to-day activities were the unknowing subjects observed by unobtrusive hardware or researchers. In some situations the subjects remained anonymously buried in larger groups of people. In others the person's manipulated behavior was individually recorded. Some of the experiments made use of naturally occurring manipulations of the independent variables; however, in most of the reported studies the experimenters deliberately manipulated the independent variable.

In a few of the studies the subjects were aware that their behavior was being recorded (e.g., when an experimenter asked questions) but were unaware of the independent variable manipulation. All of the experiments are highly ingenious applications of laboratory experimental techniques to society at large.

Finally, while reading the articles students should consider what advantages the field study had over laboratory-based experiments that dealt with the same issues. Since ethology has become fashionable, social psychologists have come under pressure to move into real-life situations. Critics of laboratory-based experimentation have argued that we now have a social psychology of college freshmen who are the traditional subjects in such studies. The assumption is that concepts uncovered in the laboratory lack the theoretical power to be applicable to the social behavior of the general population in natural settings. However, many of the experimental findings in field studies closely agree with laboratory findings. Of course, we cannot haphazardly generalize from laboratory to field or vice versa, but we can develop theoretical concepts whose probity is frequently as applicable in the laboratory situation as in natural life situations. It is most encouraging to find that the chasm between laboratory findings and natural field behavior is so easily bridged when aided by the development of theory.

Fad or fashion, of course, should not dictate research topics nor the experimental locale and methodology. The essential considerations in social science are the relevance of the research to the advancement of knowledge and the betterment of human welfare, and the ethical treatment of the subject population. In many areas of social research these values and obligations are in conflict.

As always, there is nothing quite so powerful as a good idea. The selection of the experimental locale for exploring good ideas should be guided by the scientist's consideration of both the conditions he needs for his work and the ethical questions associated with any type of research on human subjects.

REFERENCES

American Psychological Association. 1971. Ethical standards for psychological research. Washington, D.C.: APA.

Beecher, H. 1969. Cited in Academy conference on human research, part I. *The Sciences*. 9: 5–10.

Erikson, K. T. 1967. A comment on disguised observation in sociology. *Social Problems*. 14: 366–73.

Kelman, H. C. 1968. *A time to speak: On human values and social research.* San Francisco: Jossey-Bass.

Mead, M. 1969. Research with human beings: A model derived from anthropological field practice. *Daedalus* 98: 361–86.

Pappworth, M. H. 1969. *Human guinea pigs: experimentation on man.* Middlesex: Pelican.

Parsons, T. 1969. Research with human subjects and the "professional complex." *Daedalus* 98: 325–60.

Webb, E. J.; Campbell, D. T.; Schwartz, R. D.; and Sechrest, L. 1966. *Unobtrusive measures: nonreactive research in the social sciences.* Chicago: Rand McNally.

2 PERFORMANCE AND PARTICIPATION

We start with the consideration of a simple question. Can a person's ongoing behavior be altered quantitatively without his or her awareness by controlling the stimulus environment to which that person is exposed? It has been known for some time that people perform more rapidly when aroused—for example, when being observed by an audience. Laboratory studies have demonstrated that arousal enhances the probability of occurrence of the most probable response in a person's behavioral repertoire. This simply means that well-learned or simple motor behaviors are performed more rapidly or more frequently when the organism is activated. Arousal is curvilinearly related to most behaviors in that too much arousal reduces performance speed or efficiency. When exposed to extreme stress, for example, people may make many mistakes, and the less well learned the task, the greater the number of errors elicited by high levels of activation. It is also believed that even simple motor performance may also be suppressed at very high levels of activation.

Most of the experiments dealing with the relationship between arousal and performance have taken place in laboratory conditions. The first reading describes an experiment to demonstrate that increased background music in a supermarket increases shopper activity.

11 *Performance and Participation*

The second article describes an exploratory study in which course participants' activity was altered by experimenter manipulation of the social reinforcers. Many laboratory studies have supported the proposition that verbal behavior can be modified by controlling the reinforcement consequences of that behavior. Subjects' use of personal pronouns, statements of opinions, and specific grammatical form have been found to be influenced as an experimenter socially reinforces such behaviors with statements such as "um hum," "good," "right," and so on. Sarbin and Allen influenced the students' amount of verbal participation by differentially reinforcing the two initially highest and the two initially lowest participators whenever they made comments during the class discussions.

The authors comment on some of their problems in conducting this study. Such problems, quite common to natural setting research, include control of other (nonintended) influences on subject's behavior, experimenter error or bias, and lost data.

The Sarbin and Allen study brings to mind some interesting questions. Why do low participators miss so many meetings, whereas the high participators miss none? Is such absence influenced by the experimental procedure? How do other course participants perceive the high and low participators after the experimental treatment as compared with their initial impressions?

1. **"Arousal hypothesis" and the effect of music on purchasing behavior**   Patricia C. Smith and Ross Curnow

This study replicates, in a naturalistic setting, a prior finding that supported that portion of the "arousal hypothesis"

Abstracted from: Patricia C. Smith, and Ross Curnow, "Arousal hypothesis and the effect of music on purchasing behavior," *Journal of Applied Psychology* 50 (1966): 255–56.

which predicts that a certain degree of noise will actually increase activity. Music was varied from loud to soft in eight counterbalanced experimental sessions in two large supermarkets (N = 1,100). The "arousal hypothesis" seems to account for the results: significantly less time was spent in the markets during the loud session, although there was no significant difference in sales, nor in the customers' reported satisfaction.

Have you ever shopped in a store and found that almost everyone was in one section while the rest of the store was nearly empty? As population densities increase in our urban areas, environmental engineers are being asked to develop systems to cope with the larger numbers of people. Human traffic control offers an interesting example of the type of problems environmental engineers may be called on to deal with. If people spread out, in a supermarket, the store staff and facilities can handle many more people than is possible if everyone competes for service in a single section. In addition, simple shopping cart traffic jams increase the time required to shop and can be a source of frustration.

Smith and Curnow studied the effect of the loudness of background music on shopping behavior. During several Friday afternoon and Saturday morning hours the background music in two large supermarkets was set either loud or soft. The time shoppers spent in each market and the amount of each sale was recorded. Shoppers were then asked several questions to determine: (a) if the background music had been noticed; (b) if it was too loud, too soft, or just right; (c) how they rated its favorability.

Data collected on 1,100 shoppers revealed no differences in amount of money spent per person between the loud and soft music conditions ($9.81 versus $9.82, respectively). Amount of time shoppers spent when the background music was loud was about 5 percent less than when it was soft, as shown in Figure 2.1.

Although more people noticed the music in the loud condition, the numbers of shoppers who rated the music as favorable were virtually identical in the two conditions (89.5 percent versus 90.9 percent).

As background music becomes louder, the person's arousal or

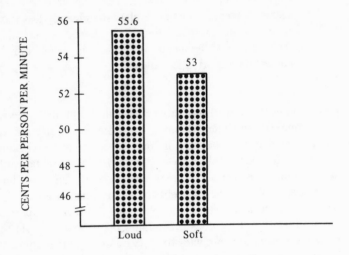

BACKGROUND MUSIC

Figure 1.1

activation level is increased, which in turn increases the speed of ongoing activity. That is, people do not buy more or less, just more rapidly. Any stimulation will increase arousal level. For example, people in brightly illuminated areas eat more rapidly than those in dimmer areas.

Could managers control traffic in their stores by controlling the level of stimulation to which their customers are exposed? A store might be divided into four quarters, each with independently controlled background music and overhead illumination. As the population density in any one quadrant of the store increased, the level of stimulation would increase to speed shoppers through that area. Should traffic be high in the canned goods section, one might slow shoppers down to keep them in the fresh fruit section until the canned goods section thinned out.

14 *Performance and Participation*

2. Increasing participation in a natural group setting: A preliminary report   Theodore R. Sarbin and Vernon L. Allen

An attempt was made in this exploratory study to influence amount of verbalization of group members by manipulating social reinforcement. Subjects were selected from nine members of a seminar that met two hours a week for an entire semester. During the first four meetings, operant levels of verbalization rate (participation) were determined for each member of the group. For the remaining eight two-hour sessions, two professors in the seminar gave the two lowest participators positive social reinforcement, and the two highest participators negative social reinforcement. Positive reinforcement included attention, nodding the head, and agreement; negative reinforcement included ignoring S, and giving indications of boredom. Low participators receiving positive reinforcement increased in participation during the first four reinforced sessions and remained at approximately the same level during the last four sessions. High participators receiving negative reinforcement showed a sharp decrease in participation during the first four negative reinforcement sessions, but during the last four sessions participation increased almost to the original operant level.

In those settings where decisions are made as the result of group discussion, one of the stumbling blocks to maximal performance is the nonparticipation of some members. On the assumption that all participants have the potential for offering contributions of value to the outcome of the conference, methods are continually being sought that would increase the verbal output of nonparticipants. If the aim of a group discussion is to discover creative solutions to

Reprinted by permission from the *Psychological Record*, 1968, 18, 1–7.

persistent and critical problems, then the informational, stimulational, and supportive contributions of every member of a group should be encouraged. This report illustrates a method for increasing the verbal output, and by extension, the participation of non-participants.

The method of increasing verbal output was adapted from the Skinnerian view of reinforcement. That is to say, we set up our procedures so that reinforcing stimuli could be emitted on schedule. A large number of research reports have demonstrated the utility of this method in increasing (or decreasing) verbal behavior. Aspects of verbal behavior that have been subjected to control by social reinforcement include verbal content (e.g., self-references), grammatical form (e.g., all nouns), and amount of speaking time regardless of content or form. If one assumes a direct relationship between verbalization and participation, then quantity of verbalization would appear to be a particularly important aspect of verbal behavior for social psychological study. Amount of verbalization has been shown to be related, for example, to leadership (French, 1950), interpersonal influence (Riecken, 1958), and group effectiveness (Knutson, 1960).

The reinforcement of verbal behavior through the use of "social" reinforcers may occur in a two-person or group setting, though the majority of experiments have taken place in the two-person situation [an experimenter (E) and a subject (S)]. Various degrees of structure have been used, ranging from a one-way communication, with the E verbalizing only the reinforcer, to interaction in an interview-like situation. Social reinforcement of verbal behavior in a group setting is probably more representative of real social situations than the restricted two-person situation. Unfortunately, there is a dearth of experimentation using social reinforcement of verbal behavior in groups. One series of experiments (Bachrach, Candland, and Gibson, 1961) used a three-person group, but two of the members were experimenters; therefore, only one S received reinforcement.

Isaacs, Thomas, and Goldiamond (1960), by using gum as a reward, reinstated verbal behavior in a mute schizophrenic in a therapy group. Several individuals who were not reinforced were present in the group. During the course of several meetings, these "free" *S*s, without prompting from *E*, began to reinforce the mute *S* by complimenting his performance on assigned tasks. The social reinforcement by the group members undoubtedly facilitated *E*'s efforts to reinstate verbal behavior in the mute *S*.

Reinforcement of verbalization in a group discussion has been reported by Cieutat (1959, 1962). In one experiment, a class of four *S*s was given four topics to discuss for about 10 minutes each. The *E* and an accomplice selectively attended two *S*s who were known to be low participators, and ignored the two high participators. Relative frequency of verbalization increased for the *S*s who were reinforced and decreased for the *S*s who were ignored. No "freely behaving" individuals were in the experiment: half the *S*s received positive reinforcement, and half received negative reinforcement. Unfortunately, the brevity of the discussion periods and the restriction on the group's interaction greatly limit generalizing from these results.

In view of the limited data available on social reinforcement in natural group situations, an exploratory study was designed to answer the following questions: (1) Will positive social reinforcement result in increased verbalization for low participating *S*s, and will negative social reinforcement result in decreased verbalization for high participating *S*s? (2) Is social reinforcement effective in the realistic setting of a two-hour seminar, meeting over an extended period of time?

Method

SUBJECTS

Subjects for the experiment were four male graduate students selected from eight males and one female who were enrolled in a graduate seminar.

PROCEDURE

The seminar met approximately 2 hours a week at the first author's residence for a total of 14 meetings. At the first meeting the instructor stated that he would like to have all meetings recorded on tape. The rationale for this procedure was that the instructor wanted to retain his lectures on the first two sessions as the basis of a future article, and that many original ideas arising during the seminar might be lost if sessions were not recorded. All the members of the seminar seemed to accept the explanation.

Lectures were given by the senior author during the first two meetings. Beginning with the third meeting, a student delivered a paper at each session. During these sessions, the student in charge usually gave a summary or a few comments on his paper, and free group discussion followed.

Average rate of students' participation for the third through the sixth meetings was used as the operant level. Two Ss having the lowest average operant verbalization rate on the four sessions were selected to receive positive reinforcement. Similarly, the two Ss having the highest operant verbalization rate were selected to receive negative reinforcement.

MEASUREMENT

After each seminar meeting the taped recordings were transcribed. A frequency count was made of the number of verbalizations (participations) made by each member of the group during the two hours of the seminar. (Verbalizations of a student were not included when he delivered a paper to the group.) One verbalization was counted as any spoken comment uninterrupted by anyone else, regardless of length of time of the verbalization. Exclamations or one-word comments ("Oh," "Yes") were not counted. The frequencies were converted to percentage of total verbalization in the group. In addition, amount of time spent talking by each person during a meeting was recorded to the nearest tenth of a minute.

REINFORCEMENT

Reinforcement was given by two persons, the instructor in charge of the seminar and a visiting professor from another university who attended the seminar. By employing two persons as reinforcers the situation was made more natural and realistic by the variation in source of reinforcement and by difference in specific reinforcer at any given instance. Appropriate reinforcement—positive or negative—was given immediately to the high and the low participators whenever they uttered a statement or asked a question.

Positive reinforcement, given to two Ss who had the lowest average operant level of participation on meetings three through six, included one or more of the following behaviors by one or both Es: looking directly at S, showing close attention, leaning forward in chair, nodding head in agreement, continuing the discussion in the direction taken by S, saying, "That's a good point," or rephrasing what S had said. Negative reinforcement, given to the two Ss who had the highest average operant level of participation on meetings three through six, included one or more of the following: averting eyes from the speaker, looking at other members instead of the speaker, and not continuing or rephrasing the comment of S. (In some contexts, what is here denoted as negative reinforcement would be called punishment.)

Appropriate reinforcement was given consistently to high and low participators at each two-hour meeting for a total of eight sessions.

Results

Percentage frequency and time in verbalizing were computed for the two Ss receiving positive reinforcement and the two Ss receiving negative reinforcement. Regularity of the change in participation over time, and the rather large change occurring are quite impressive.

Data in Table 1.1 show that operant level (average of four sessions) of the high and low participators were very different. High participators' verbalization rate was 29 percent as compared with low participators' rate of 5 percent. At the final reinforced session the high participators' verbalization rate was still far above the low participators' operant level, but the verbalization rate for one low participator was approximately the same as the operant level of the high participators.

Results of the low participators who received positive reinforcement will now be considered. Inspection of the data in Table 1.1 for person A indicates that at the first class meeting during which positive reinforcement was given, participation increased substantially above the operant level (from 6 percent to 34 percent). Percentage participation decreased for the next three meetings, but still remained above the operant level. For the last two meetings

Table 1.1
Verbalization of High Participators receiving Negative Social Reinforcement and of Low Participators Receiving Positive Social Reinforcement (Percent)

		Low Participators							
	Operant	Positive Reinforcement Sessions							
Person	Level	I	II	III	IV	V	VI	VII	VIII
A	06	34	25	17	11	16	17		28
B	03	08	—*	04	22*	—*	06		—*
Mean	05	21	25	11	17	16	11		28

		High Participators							
	Operant	Negative Reinforcement Sessions							
Person	Level	I	II	III	IV	V	VI	VII	VIII
C	29	18	27	11	11	32	27	24	29
D	29	08	10	04	24	30	17	26	08
Mean	29	13	19	07	18	31	22	25	19

*Subject absent from seminar.

participation again increased. The second low participator (B) who received positive reinforcement was absent from class for four of the eight class meetings during which reinforcement was given. The four meetings for which data are available also show enhanced participation. Participation was above the operant level on all reinforced sessions.

The two high participators who received negative reinforcement had similar operant levels and reinforcement data. As shown in Table 1.1, percentage of participation dropped considerably from the operant level during the first four meetings, then increased slightly above the operant level, only to go below the operant level during the last three meetings. At the third meeting the participation rate for one S was below the operant level of one of the low participators.

Mean verbalization for the first four reinforced meetings for the high participators was about half as high as their operant level (29 percent to 14 percent). An increase in participation is evident in the mean of the last four meetings, but does not reach the operant level. Low participators showed an increase over the operant level in the mean of the first four meetings, then a slight decrease in the mean of the last four. The average effect of positive reinforcement on the low participators was almost identical to the effect of the negative reinforcement on the high participators: high participators decreased about 15 percent, and low participators increased about 15 percent.

Percentage of total time the four experimental Ss spent in verbalization was also computed for each meeting. Data for percentage time and percentage frequency were highly correlated; therefore, the time data will not be reported.

Discussion

The present study was undertaken in an attempt to demonstrate the effects of positive and negative social reinforcement on participation in a natural group setting over an extended period of time. Results of the experiment offer tentative evidence that amount of participation in an informal discussion group may be influenced by social reinforcement from another person.

The two high participators who received negative reinforcement showed a substantial decrease in participation for the first four seminar meetings, then an increase during the last four meetings. It might be worthwhile to speculate about the causes of this behavior. Three factors may have been involved.

One important factor is that the Es found it more difficult in the later meetings consistently to maintain the negative reinforcement to high participators. Giving negative reinforcement to Ss conflicted with the professor's customary role of supporting and encouraging the students. On the other hand, giving positive reinforcement, being congruent with the professor's role, was much easier to maintain. During the last few meetings the Es often became so involved in the ongoing discussion that adherence to the negative reinforcement schedule was difficult or impossible. When the high participators made valuable contributions to the seminar, Es had difficulty in ignoring them.

A second possible factor contributing to increased verbalization of the negatively reinforced Ss during the last four meetings could be related to the high participators' past reinforcement history. It is likely that they have had a history of positive social reinforcement for high participation. Such reinforcement from others probably created strong preference for a high rate of participation. If this conjecture is correct, then the initial decrease in participation only represents a momentary "shock;" recovery soon occurs and S is not hesitant again to enter the discussions.

A third factor may be found in the nature of the group situation. Seven other graduate students were present in the seminar in addition to the two Es and the two negatively reinforced Ss. It is likely that student members of the group served as sources of reinforcement for the high participators. Our subjective impression is that other members did give these Ss social reinforcement (by attention, discussion, etc.) throughout the seminar. Probably for high participators the usual and most clearly perceived source of social reinforcement was the professor or high status person in the seminar. If social reinforcement is not forthcoming from this source, however, S may be more receptive and sensitive to social reinforcement from the group members. High participators might be more adept in their ability to substitute social reinforcement of the group for that of the professor. If such a substitution is achieved after several meetings, we should expect participation to increase.

A limitation of control of verbal behavior by reinforcement should be mentioned. It is necessary that the behavior one wishes to control manifests a frequency of occurrence high enough to be affected by social reinforcement. For example, the lowest participator spoke so rarely—sometimes only one comment for an entire meeting—that it was impossible to apply enough social reinforcement quickly to increase his participation. Salzinger and Pisoni (1958) found that a minimum number of social reinforcements were necessary before behavior could be influenced.

One low participator who received positive reinforcement confided that he enjoyed the seminar very much and was happy with his performance in the discussions. Perhaps positive social reinforcement increases morale of the person reinforced. Such a suggestion finds support from Leavitt's (1951) observation that persons in a position of high centrality in a communication network (i.e., persons who were in positions permitting high communication with others in the network) reported more satisfaction with their jobs and with the group. Positive social reinforcement of verbalization also creates in effect a condition of increased communication for the person receiving reinforcement; hence, an increase in morale seems reasonable.

An interesting problem for systematic exploration is the relation between social reinforcement received by an S and the quality of his contributions to the class. Subjective impressions of the authors were that the Ss who received positive reinforcement actually made many original and significant contributions. Riecken (1958) has found a tendency for group members to rank a high-talking member as having contributed more than a low-talking member; therefore, the authors' subjective impression may only reflect this tendency. It is plausible to hypothesize that members will tend not only to overevaluate contributions of Ss receiving positive reinforcement, but will also correspondingly underevaluate contributions of Ss receiving negative reinforcement. Apparent approval and disapproval of the positively and negatively reinforced Ss by the high status professor or group leader probably magnifies the effect.

It is possible that positive social reinforcement given by a group leader to low participating members may affect the entire group, as well as the low participators. Giving positive reinforcement is consonant with the group leader's role of social reinforcement dispenser for the entire group. Perception by group members that the group is a potent source in social reinforcement for themselves would increase the power of the leader.

REFERENCES

Bachrach, A. J.; Candland, D. K.; and Gibson, J. T. 1961. Group reinforcement of individual response experiments in verbal behavior. In *Conformity and Deviation,* eds. I. A. Berg and B. M. Bass. New York: Harper.

Cieutat, V. J. 1959. Surreptitious modification of verbal behavior during class discussion. *Psychological Reports* 5: 648.

Cieutat, V. J. 1962. Sex differences and reinforcement in the conditioning and extinction of conversational behavior. *Psychological Reports* 10: 467–74.

French, R. L. 1950. Verbal output and leadership status in initially leaderless discussion groups. *American Psychologist* 5: 310–11.

Isaacs, W.; Thomas, J.; and Goldiamond, I. 1960. Application of operant conditioning to reinstate verbal behavior in psychotics. *Journal Speech and Hearing Disorders* 25: 8–12.

Knutson, A. L. 1960. Quiet and vocal groups. *Sociometry* 23: 36–49.

Leavitt, H. J. 1951. Some effects of certain communication patterns on group performance. *Journal of Abnormal and Social Psychology* 46: 38–50.

Riecken, H. 1958. The effect of talkativeness on ability to influence group solutions to problems. *Sociometry* 21: 309–21.

Salzinger, K.; and Pisoni, S. 1958. Reinforcement of affect responses of schizophrenics during the clinical interview. *Journal of Abnormal and Social Psychology* 57: 84–90.

3 DISCRIMINATION AND STIGMATIZATION

We know that people are discriminated against for quite irrelevant and unfair reasons. Examples of discriminatory practices that are blatant and so absurd as to invite laughter are male-only lounges in university faculty clubs (a very prominent North American university maintained such a lounge until three years prior to this writing), Ladies-and-escorts-only rooms in taverns, and age-restricted motion picture entertainment. Some if not most discriminatory practices, of course, are blatant but not at all humorous and can be subtle and difficult to prove. All the studies in this section demonstrate discriminatory behavior of some persons toward others.

We are, of course, not surprised by data that indicate that stigmatization can lead to unequal and/or unfair treatment. We also tend to be more supportive of research projects that dig into society and drag out the evidence that people are not being treated the way they should be treated. However, the ethical and moral considerations experimenters must face in such research are the same as those of field experimenters with whose purposes we do not so readily sympathize.

The experiments in this section offer nice illustrations of bias problems particularly prevalent in field research. Of particular concern in such field studies is the behavioral consistency of the experimental confederates (people who act an assigned role unbeknown to naïve subjects in the experiment). As noted in the Heussenstamm study, for example, the experimental drivers may drive differently when they know the bumper stickers are on their cars. Similarly, the employment agent in the Schwartz and Skolnik study may make different appeals or react differently to questions when dealing with the different categories of applicants.

One method for handling these problems in more controlled experimental environments, such as laboratories, prisons, hospitals, and schools, is the *blind* method. The blind method involves keeping everyone associated with critical aspects of the study unaware of the experimental condition they are involved in. Thus, when testing a new drug against no drug (or placebo) the patient, the drug administrator, and the persons who evaluate the patient's behavior or illness are kept unaware of whether or not the tablet the patient received contained an active ingredient or an inert substance.

In the field, however, blind techniques are difficult to execute. Heussenstamm describes how her study could be conducted using blind techniques, but this method is not always possible. For example, the employment agent in the second experiment might be able to keep himself unaware of exactly which applicant file he was presenting to a prospective employer, but he would certainly have difficulty in remaining blind during any ensuing conversation.

In addition to its primary purpose of exploring those factors that affect discriminatory behavior, the last study in the section demonstrates that letters, telephone calls, and face-to-face encounters give rise to different results. The problem of keeping everyone blind in natural field experiments typically becomes more severe as one gets closer to observing subjects' actual behavior in their natural settings.

One method for estimating the extent of experimenter

(or confederate) bias is the use of multiple agents. The results obtained with one experimental agent (i.e., experimenter, confederate, observer, etc.) are compared with those obtained with a different agent to determine the extent to which the results are being influenced by the agents' behavior. The multiple agent method was used in the experiments included in Section VII.

3. **Bumper stickers and the cops**   F. K. Heussenstamm

During a discussion about a student group of Black Panther Party members who had received so many traffic citations that they were in danger of losing their licenses, it was discovered that all had Panther Party stickers glued to their bumpers. The Panthers' claims of police harassment were put to the test by having 15 drivers with no traffic violations for the preceding 12 months attach *Black Panther* stickers to the rear bumpers of their cars. With the bumper stickers on their cars, the students received a total of 33 citations in 17 days.

A series of violent, bloody encounters between police and Black Panther Party members punctuated the early summer days of 1969. Soon after, a group of black students I teach at California State College, Los Angeles, who were members of the Panther Party, began to complain of continuous harassment by law enforcement officers. Among their many grievances, they complained about receiving so many traffic citations that some were in danger of losing their driving privileges. During one lengthy discussion, we

Reprinted with permission of the publisher and author from *Transaction* 8 (1971): 32–33. Copyright © February, 1971, by Transaction, Inc., New Brunswick, New Jersey.

realized that all of them drove automobiles with Panther Party signs glued to their bumpers. This is a report of a study that I undertook to assess the seriousness of their charges and to determine whether we were hearing the voice of paranoia or reality.

Recruitment advertising for subjects to participate in the research elicited 45 possible subjects from the student body. Careful screening thinned the ranks to 15—5 black, 5 white, and 5 of Mexican descent. Each group included three males and two females. Although the college enrolls more than 20,000 students (largest minority group numbers on the west coast), it provides no residential facilities; all participants, of necessity, then, traveled to campus daily on freeways or surface streets. The average round trip was roughly 10 miles, but some drove as far as 18 miles. Eleven of the 15 had part-time jobs which involved driving to and from work after class as well.

All participants in the study had exemplary driving records, attested to by a sworn statement that each driver had received no "moving" traffic violations in the preceding 12 months. In addition, each promised to continue to drive in accordance with all in-force Department of Motor Vehicles regulations. Each student signed another statement to the effect that he would do nothing to "attract the attention" of either police, sheriff's deputies, or highway patrolmen—all of whom survey traffic in Los Angeles county. The participants declared that their cars, which ranged from a "flower child" hippie van to standard American makes of all types, had no defective equipment. Lights, horns, brakes, and tires were duly inspected and pronounced satisfactory.

The appearance of the drivers was varied. There were three blacks with processed hair and two with exaggerated naturals, two white-shirt-and-necktie, straight Caucasians and a shoulder-length-maned hippie, and two mustache- and sideburn-sporting Mexican-Americans. All wore typical campus dress, with the exception of the resident hippie and the militant blacks, who sometimes wore dashikis.

A fund of $500 was obtained from a private source to pay fines for any citations received by the driving pool, and students were briefed on the purposes of the study. After a review of lawful operation of motor vehicles, all agreed on the seriousness of receiving excessive moving traffic violations. In California, four citations within a 12-month period precipitates automatic examination of driving records, with a year of probation likely, or, depending on the seriousness of the offenses, suspension of the driver's license for varying lengths of time. Probation or suspension is usually accompanied by commensurate increases in insurance premiums. Thus, the students knew they were accepting considerable personal jeopardy as a condition of involvement in the study.

Bumper stickers in lurid day-glo orange and black, depicting a menacing panther with large BLACK PANTHER lettering, were attached to the rear bumper of each subject car, and the study began. The first student received a ticket for making an "incorrect lane change" on the freeway less than two hours after heading home in the rush hour traffic. Five more tickets were received by others on the second day for "following too closely," "failing to yield the right of way," "driving too slowly in the high-speed lane of the freeway," "failure to make a proper signal before turning right at an intersection," and "failure to observe proper safety of pedestrians using a crosswalk." On day three, students were cited for "excessive speed," "making unsafe lane changes" and "driving erratically." And so it went every day.

One student was forced to drop out of the study by day four, because he had already received three citations. Three others reached what we had agreed was the maximum limit—three citations—within the first week. Altogether, the participants received 33 citations in 17 days, and the violations fund was exhausted.

Drivers reported that their encounters with the intercepting officers ranged from affable and "standard polite" to surly, accompanied by search of the vehicle. Five cars were thoroughly gone over and their drivers were shaken down. One white girl, a striking blonde and a member of a leading campus sorority, was questioned at length about her reasons for supporting the "criminal activity" of the Black Panther Party. This was the only time that an actual reference to the bumper stickers was made during any of the ticketings. Students, by prior agreement, made no effort to dissuade officers from giving citations, once the vehicle had been halted.

Pledges to Drive Safely

Students received citations equally, regardless of race or sex or ethnicity or personal appearance. Being in jeopardy made them "nervous" and "edgy," and they reported being very uncomfortable whenever they were in their automobiles. After the first few days, black students stopped saying "I told you so," and showed a sober, demoralized air of futility. Continuous pledges to safe driving were made daily, and all expressed increasing incredulity as the totals mounted. They paid their fines in person immediately after receiving a citation. One student received his second ticket on the way to pay his fine for the first one.

No student requested a court appearance to protest a citation, regardless of the circumstances surrounding a ticketing incident. When the investigator announced the end of the study on the 18th day, the remaining drivers expressed relief and went straight to their cars to remove the stickers.

Some citations were undoubtedly deserved. How many, we cannot be sure. A tightly designed replication of this study would involve control of make and year of cars through the use of standard rented vehicles of low-intensity color. A driving pool of individuals who represented an equal number of both extreme-left and straight-looking appearance with matched age-range could be developed. Drivers could be assigned at random to preselected, alternate routes of a set length. Both left-wing and right-wing bumper stickers could also be attached at random after drivers were seated in their assigned vehicles and the doors sealed. In this way, no subject would know in advance whether he was driving around with "Black Panther Party" or "America Love It Or Leave It" on his auto. This would permit us to check actual driving behavior in a more reliable way. We might also wish to include a tape recorder in each car to preserve the dialogue at citation incidents.

No More Stickers

It is possible, of course, that the subject's bias influenced his driving, making it less circumspect than usual. But it is statistically unlikely that this number of previously "safe" drivers could amass such a collection of tickets without assuming real bias by police against drivers with Black Panther bumper stickers.

The reactions of the traffic officers might have been influenced, and we hypothesize that they were, by the recent deaths of police in collision with Black Panther Party members. But whatever the provocation, unwarranted traffic citations are a clear violation of the civil rights of citizens and cannot be tolerated. Unattended, the legitimate grievances of the black community against individuals who represent agencies of the dominant society contribute to the climate of hostility between the races at all levels and predispose victims to acts of violent retaliation.

As a footnote to this study, I should mention that Black Panther bumper stickers are not seen in Los Angeles these days, although the party has considerable local strength. Apparently members discovered for themselves the danger of blatantly announcing their politics on their bumpers and have long since removed the "incriminating" evidence.

4. A study of legal stigma   Richard D. Schwartz and Jerome E. Skolnick

The effects of legal accusation on a lower-class unskilled worker charged with assault were examined by having an experimenter who posed as an employment agent ask 100 employers if they could use a man described in one of four specially prepared employment folders. The employment folders described the same man save for the applicant's criminal court involvement. The results indicated that even when acquitted and holding a letter from the judge certifying the not guilty finding, men with any court involvement received far fewer job offers.

Reprinted with permission of the Society for the Study of Social Problems and the authors from *Social Problems* 10 (1962): 133–38.

Legal thinking has moved increasingly toward a sociologically meaningful view of the legal system. Legal sanctions (i.e., changes in life conditions imposed through court action) in particular have come to be regarded in functional terms. In criminal law, for instance, sanctions are said to be designed to prevent recidivism by rehabilitating, restraining, or executing the offender. They are also said to be intended to deter others from the performance of similar acts and, sometimes, to provide a channel for the expression of retaliatory motives. In such civil actions as torts or contract, monetary awards may be intended as retributive and deterrent, as in the use of punitive damages, or may be regarded as a *quid pro quo* to compensate the plaintiff for his wrongful loss.

While these goals comprise an integral part of the rationale of law, little is known about the extent to which they are fulfilled in practice. Lawmen do not as a rule make such studies, because their traditions and techniques are not designed for a systematic examination of the operation of the legal system in action, especially outside the courtroom. Thus, when extralegal consequences (e.g., the social stigma of a prison sentence) are taken into account at all, it is through the discretionary actions of police, prosecutor, judge, and jury. Systematic information on a variety of unanticipated outcomes, those that benefit the accused as well as those that hurt him, might help to inform these decision makers and perhaps lead to changes in substantive law as well. The present paper is an attempt to study the consequences of stigma associated with legal accusation.

From a sociological viewpoint, there are several types of indirect consequences of legal sanctions which can be distinguished. These include differential deterrence, effects on the sanctionee's associates, and variations in the degree of deprivation which sanction imposes on the recipient himself.

First, the imposition of sanction, while intended as a matter of overt policy to deter the public at large, probably will vary in its effectiveness as a deterrent, depending upon the extent to which potential offenders perceive themselves as similar to the sanctionee. Such "differential deterrence" would occur if white-collar antitrust violators were restrained by the conviction of General Electric executives, but not by invocation of the Sherman Act against union leaders.

The imposition of a sanction may even provide an unintended incentive to violate the law. A study of factors affecting compliance with federal income tax laws provides some evidence of this effect (Schwartz, 1959). Some respondents reported that they began to cheat on their tax returns only *after* convictions for tax evasion had been obtained against others in their jurisdiction. They explained this surprising behavior by noting that the prosecutions had always been conducted against blatant violators and not against the kind of moderate offenders which they then became. These respondents were, therefore, unintentionally educated to the possibility of supposedly "safe" violations.

Second, deprivations or benefits may accrue to non-sanctioned individuals by virtue of the web of affiliations that join them to the defendant. The wife and family of a convicted man may, for instance, suffer from his arrest as much as the man himself. On the other hand, they may be relieved by his absence if the family relationship has been an unhappy one. Similarly, whole groups of persons may be affected by sanctions to an individual, as when discriminatory practices increase because of a highly publicized crime attributed to a member of a given minority group.

Method

The subjects studied to examine the effects of legal accusation on occupational positions were lower class unskilled workers charged with assault. The project lent itself to a field experiment.

Four employment folders were prepared, the same in all respects except for the criminal court record of the applicant. In all of the folders he was described as a thirty-two year old single male of unspecified race, with a high school training in mechanical trades and a record of successive short-term jobs as a kitchen helper, maintenance worker, and handyman. These characteristics are roughly typical of applicants for unskilled hotel jobs in the Catskill resort area of New York State where employment opportunities were tested.

The four folders differed only in the applicant's reported record of criminal court involvement. The first folder indicated that the applicant had been convicted and sentenced for assault; the second, that he had been tried for assault and acquitted; the third, also tried for assault and acquitted, but with a letter from the judge certifying the finding of not guilty and reaffirming the legal presumption of innocence. The fourth folder made no mention of any criminal record.

A sample of 100 employers was utilized. Each employer was assigned to one of four "treatment" groups. To each employer only one folder was shown; this folder was one of the four kinds mentioned above, the selection of the folder being determined by the treatment group to which the potential employer was assigned. The employer was asked whether he could "use" the man described in the folder. To preserve the reality of the situation and make it a true field experiment, employers were never given any indication that they were participating in an experiment. So far as they knew, a legitimate offer to work was being made in each showing of the folder by the "employment agent."

The experiment was designed to determine what employers would do in fact if confronted with an employment applicant with a criminal record. The questionnaire approach used in earlier studies (Rubin, 1958) seemed ill-adapted to the problem, since respondents confronted with hypothetical situations might be particularly prone to answer in what they considered a socially acceptable manner. The second alternative—studying job opportunities of individuals who had been involved with the law—would have made it very difficult to find comparable groups of applicants and potential employers. For these reasons, the field experiment reported here was utilized.

Some deception was involved in the study. The "employment agent"—the same individual in all 100 cases—was in fact a law student who was working in the Catskills during the summer of 1959 as an insurance adjuster. In representing himself as being both an adjuster and an employment agent, he was assuming a combination of roles which is not uncommon there. The adjuster role gave him an opportunity to introduce a single application for employment casually and naturally. To the extent that the experiment worked, however, it was inevitable that some employers should be led to believe that they had immediate prospects of filling a job opening. In those instances where an offer to hire was made, the "agent" called a few hours later to say that the applicant had taken another job. The field experimenter attempted in such instances to locate a satisfactory replacement by contacting an employment agency in the area. Because this procedure was used and since the jobs involved were of relatively minor consequence, we believe that the deception caused little economic harm.

Results

As mentioned, each treatment group of 25 employers was approached with one type of folder. Responses were dichotomized: those who expressed a willingness to consider the applicant in any way were termed positive; those who made no response or who explicitly refused to consider the candidate were termed negative. Our results consist of comparisons between positive and negative responses, thus defined, for the treatment groups.

Of the 25 employers shown the "no record" folder, 9 gave positive responses (see Figure 4.1). Subject to reservations arising from chance variations in sampling, we take this as indicative of the "ceiling" of jobs available for this kind of applicant under the given field conditions. Positive responses by these employers may be compared with those in the other treatment groups to obtain an indication of job opportunities lost because of the various legal records.

Of the 25 employers approached with the "convict" folder, only one expressed interest in the applicant. This is a rather graphic indication of the effect that a criminal record may have on job opportunities. Care must be exercised, of course, in generalizing the conclusions to other settings. In this context, however, the criminal record made a major difference.

Discussion

From a theoretical point of view, the findings lead toward the conclusion that conviction constitutes a powerful form of "status degradation" (Garfinkel, 1956), which continues to operate after the time when, according to the generalized theory of justice underlying punishment in our society, the individual's "debt" has been paid. A record of conviction produces a durable if not permanent

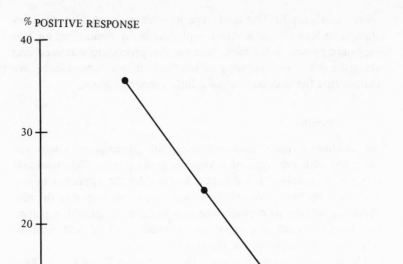

Figure 4.1
Effects of four types of legal folder on job opportunities.

loss of status. For purposes of effective social control, this state of affairs may heighten the deterrent effect of conviction—though that remains to be established. Any such contribution to social control, however, must be balanced against the barriers imposed upon rehabilitation of the convict. If the ex-prisoner finds difficulty in securing menial kinds of legitimate work, further crime may become an increasingly attractive alternative.

Another important finding of this study concerns the small number of positive responses elicited by the "accused but acquitted" applicant. Of the 25 employers approached with this folder, 3 offered jobs. Thus, the individual accused but acquitted of assault has almost as much trouble finding even an unskilled job as the one who was not only accused of the same offense but also convicted.

From a theoretical point of view, this result indicates that permanent lowering of status is not limited to those explicitly singled out by being convicted of a crime. As an ideal outcome of American justice, criminal procedure is supposed to distinguish between the "guilty" and those who have been acquitted. Legally controlled consequences that follow the judgment are consistent with this purpose. Thus, the "guilty" are subject to fine and imprisonment, while those who are acquitted are immune from these sanctions. But deprivations may be imposed on the acquitted, both before and after victory in court. Before trial, legal rules either permit or require arrest and detention. The suspect may be faced with the expense of an attorney and a bail bond if he is to mitigate these limitations on his privacy and freedom. In addition, some pretrial deprivations are imposed without formal legal permission. These may include coercive questioning, use of violence, and stigmatization. And, as this study indicates, some deprivations not under the direct control of the legal process may develop or persist after an official decision of acquittal has been made.

Thus two legal principles conflict in practice. On the one hand, "a man is innocent until proven guilty." On the other, the accused is systematically treated as guilty under the administration of criminal law until a functionary or official body—police, magistrate, prosecuting attorney, or trial judge or jury—decides that he is entitled to be free. Even then, the results of treating him as guilty persist and may lead to serious consequences.

The conflict could be eased by measures aimed at reducing the deprivations imposed on the accused, before and after acquittal. Some legal attention has been focused on pretrial deprivations. The provision of bail and counsel, the availability of habeas corpus, limitations on the admissability of coerced confessions, and civil actions for false arrest are examples of measures aimed at protecting the rights of the accused before trial. Although these are often limited in effectiveness, especially for individuals of lower socio-economic status, they at least represent some concern with implementing the presumption of innocence at the pretrial stage.

By contrast, the courts have done little toward alleviating the post-acquittal consequences of legal accusation. One effort along these lines has been employed in the federal courts, however. Where an individual has been accused and exonerated of a crime, he may petition the federal courts for a "Certificate of Innocence" certifying this fact.[1] Possession of such a document might be expected to alleviate post-acquittal deprivations.

Some indication of the effectiveness of such a measure is found in the responses of the final treatment group. Their folder, it will be recalled, contained information on the accusation and acquittal of the applicant, but also included a letter from a judge addressed "To whom it may concern," certifying the applicant's acquittal and reminding the reader of the presumption of innocence. Such a letter might have had a boomerang effect, by reemphasizing the legal involvement of the applicant. It was important, therefore, to determine empirically whether such a communication would improve or harm the chances of employment. Our findings indicate that it increased employment opportunities, since the letter folder elicited six positive responses. Even though this fell short of the nine responses to the "no record" folder, it doubled the number for the "accused but acquitted" and created a significantly greater number of job offers than those elicited by the convicted record. This suggests that the procedure merits consideration as a means of offsetting the occupational loss resulting from accusation. It should be noted, however, that repeated use of this device might reduce its effectiveness.

REFERENCES

Garfinkel, H. 1956. Conditions of successful degradation ceremonics. *American Journal of Sociology,* 61, pp. 420–24.

1. 228 United States Code, Secs. 1–195, 2513.

Rubin, S. 1958. *Crime and Juvenile Delinquency,* New York: Oceana. pp. 151–156.

Schwartz, R. D. 1959. The effectiveness of legal controls: factors in the reporting of minor items of income on Federal Income Tax Returns. Paper presented at the annual meeting of the American Sociological Association, Chicago.

5. Verbal attitudes and overt behavior involving racial prejudice Bernard Kutner, Carol Wilkins, and Penny Rechtman Yarrow

In this early experiment on discrimination, 11 restaurant managers received a letter requesting reservations for a social gathering of people, some of whom were black. After 17 days without a reply, each restaurant was called by telephone. The manager was reminded of the letter and asked for reservations. No manager accepted the telephone reservations for the racially mixed group, but one day later all managers took reservations from a control call made by the same person. Such blatant discrimination was not observed when 2 young white women and 1 black woman actually went to the same 11 restaurants. In all cases they received exemplary service.

The problem of explaining discrepancies between verbal attitudes and actual behavior relevant to these attitudes has been the subject of considerable theoretical thought (Chein et al., 1949). Empirical investigations of this problem have been exceptionally sparse. The classic study of LaPiere (1934) demonstrated that when an innkeeper was confronted with a white person and a Chinese couple

Reprinted from the *Journal of Abnormal and Social Psychology* 47 (1952): 649–52. Copyright 1952 by the American Psychological Association, and reproduced by permission.

"in the flesh," requesting lodging, the trio were almost never denied it. Yet when a mailed request was sent to the same innkeeper requesting lodging for himself and his Chinese companions there was an almost universal rejection of the request. What is the nature of the situation in each case that leads to such diametrically opposed behaviors? Put in another way our question is: Why is there a discrepancy between behaviors supposedly dependent upon the same constellation of attitudes?

Our procedure was as follows:

> Three young women, 2 white and 1 Negro, all well-dressed and well-mannered, entered 11 individual restaurants in a fashionable northeastern suburban community, Subtown. In each case, the white women entered first, asked for a table for three and were seated. The Negro woman entered a short while later, informed the hostess or headwaiter that she was with a party already seated, found her table and sat down. This procedure was repeated in each of the 11 restaurants and taverns.

In each case all three women were served in a manner in no wise different from the usual service accorded patrons at each establishment. At two places the group was taken unusual notice of by other patrons but in no instance was anything but exemplary service accorded them by the management, waiter, etc.

Two weeks following each visit, a letter signed with an assumed name was sent to each establishment. The return address was that of a cooperating resident of Subtown. The letter read as follows:

> Dear Sir:
>
> A group of friends and I are planning a social affair to be held in Subtown in the near future. I should like to make reservations to have them for dinner at your restaurant. Since some of them are colored, I wondered whether you would object to their coming.
>
> Could you let me know if the reservations may be made so that I may complete the arrangements as soon as possible?
>
> Yours truly,
M—— B——

Where appropriate, the term "beer party" was substituted for "social affair" and "tavern" for "restaurant."

Since no letters were returned by the Post Office,[1] it may be assumed that all were delivered. Seventeen days after the letters were sent out, no replies of any kind had been received. At this point each establishment was called by phone by one of the white women, and essential parts of the letter repeated. In each instance the manager or his representative answered the phone, and he was asked for reservations for the party. One day later "control calls" were made by the same person. She merely requested reservations for a party of friends to be held in the near future. Table 5.1 summarizes the nature of the responses to the letter and to each phone call.

It will be noted that no spontaneous replies to the letter were received, although two letters were received as a consequence of the first phone call. Three of the 11 managers admitted having received the letter; eight denied having received it.

With regard to reservations, except for Restaurant D (which has a "no reservation needed" policy), every control call terminated with a specific reservation. Ignoring Restaurant D, no manager accepted the phoned request for reservations when told that Negroes would be in the party. Three managers claimed that they do not take reservations; another said that he would accept a phoned reservation, but hung up before it could be made. Three maintained that they could make "arrangements" only if someone came in to the restaurant about it. One of the latter group suggested the possibility of a separate, private room for the dinner. Two managers suggested that we call back at another time. One of these managers went as far as to visit the address on our letter and demanded to know who the writer was and why she was causing a disturbance. During this visit he obtained the phone number and subsequently phoned back three times asking to speak to our fictitious writer.

Finally, one manager turned down the phoned request on the grounds that it was against the law to admit Negroes to his tavern.[2]

It is obvious from Table 5.1 that the managers were disturbed

---

1. As an added precaution, the local postman was requested to deliver to the address used any returned letters or regular mail bearing the fictitious name on the envelope.
2. A state law on discrimination does exist, but it *forbids* denial of service to a person in a public place on the grounds of race, religion, or creed.

Table 5.1
Summary of Responses to Letter and Phone Calls

RESTAURANT	RESPONSE TO LETTER	TELEPHONE CALL	CONTROL CALL
A	No reply	Didn't get any letter. We don't take large parties. We've got dancing after 6 P.M. [They actually don't.] Are you colored? [Yes.] I like everyone. My kitchen help are colored and they are wonderful people. But we have a certain clientele here. . . . This place is my bread and butter. Frankly I'd rather you not come. Try in T⎯⎯ [next town].	Took reservation.
B	No reply	I didn't get your letter. We can't have you. It's against the law.	Took reservation.
C	No reply	I got the letter. How many? [Negroes] I don't mind but customers might. In fact some of my help are colored. I had trouble about this before. Frankly I prefer you don't come but if you can't find another place we won't embarrass you here.	Took reservation.
D	No reply	We didn't get a letter. We don't take reservations. We take care of our regulars. A few Negroes come in just to eat. I *would* mind you coming.	Said they didn't take reservations but we should come in any time about them.
E	No reply	I didn't get any letter. Call any time to make reservation. [Hung up before reservations could be made.]	Took reservation.

Table 3.1 (Continued)

F	No reply	Yes, I got your letter. I refuse to discuss it on the phone. What is the purpose of your party? What school did you attend? Why are you never home when I call? How many Negroes are in the party? [5 out of 10] That's a large percentage isn't it? [Insisted he call us, instead of vice-versa.]	Took reservation.
G	Reply received 19 days after our letter was mailed.	A letter to you is in the mail. Reservations are available if you come in and make them.	Took reservation.
H	No reply	Didn't get letter. We have limited space. No reservations are taken. It's hard to answer you. You know Subtown. . . . We don't object but our patrons would. I won't answer on the phone. Come in about it.	Took reservation.
I	Reply sent as result of phone call.	Didn't get letter. [Hostess] We don't like that. Is it absolutely necessary to have them? [Manager]: if it's okay with you I guess it's okay with us.	Took reservation.
J	No reply	Didn't get letter. How many? [10] No reservations for more than 8 on weekends. I will mail you our menu for the following weekend. [Never received.] I'm too busy to look up reservation availability. [Asked on two occasions that we call back.]	Took reservation.
K	No reply	Didn't get letter. I'd think you'd want to come in to discuss something like that. Mixed group? How many people? We can't turn anyone away but never take reservations. You can have a separate room if you come in about it.	Took reservation.

by both the letter and the first call—they wished to avoid, if possible, having any Negro patrons but they also did not (for whatever reason) wish to give a categorical "No" to the request. To avoid the possibility of a charge of discrimination, they tried to dissuade the caller from coming to their restaurant, denied that they took reservations, requested a personal interview to discuss the matter, etc.

Nevertheless, five managers finally gave tentative approval for the party, two confirming the conversation with a letter. While none of these agreements was made unconditionally, tacit agreement was implied. Three others indicated that while they are unprejudiced themselves (Negro help in the kitchen, some Negroes eat there, etc.) they felt that it would be better if our assistant "listened to reason" and went elsewhere.

To call the behavior of the manager inconsistent with either their attitudes or their alleged previous behavior seems trite. The manager or owner of a business that depends on majority group patronage (which he may perceive, rightly or wrongly, as hostile to minority group "intruders") may nevertheless not object when a minority group member appears on the premises. Several hypotheses suggest themselves as possible explanations of his behavior:

1. He fears the consequences of violating the law forbidding discriminatory practices.

2. He may wish to avoid a scene that might not only be a disturbance of the peace but might also call particular attention to the presence of the unwanted guest.

3. Without consciously realizing what the rationale of his behavior may be, the reality situation moves him to adopt one of two competing motives: (*a*) to do nothing, thus preserving peace and order, or (*b*) to refuse admission or service because he or his white patrons are offended by Negroes.

Whatever the underlying explanation may be, three levels of response have been found in the present study. These are reactions to each of the three situations with which each manager was confronted. The letter, which may be described as a relatively impersonal contact, produced uniform results: no reply, or at most, one very belated reply. The phone call, which may be described as a partial personal contact, produced a variety of responses ranging from implied acceptance to attempts to rationalize or justify outright rejection of the requests with numerous intermediary responses ("call back," "come in and see us," "couldn't you go to another place?" etc.). The direct contact, which may be described as fully personal in nature, also produced uniform results: admission of the Negro and excellent service in each establishment.

Thus, in addition to the contradictory behaviors found by La-Piere, the managers in the present study exhibited relatively consistent techniques designed to dissuade or discourage our requests for reservations when such requests were made by phone.

Taking the three situations into consideration it would appear, at least for our sample, that the mode of dealing with a minority group member whose presence "violates" culturally established norms varies widely. Discriminatory treatment is minimized when challenged in a direct face-to-face situation but is maximized when proposals to "violate" group norms are *suggested*. Indirect evidences of discriminatory behavior (subterfuges of various sorts) appear when a direct non-face-to-face challenge is made. At least in the cultural climate of a suburban northeastern community, the hypothetical Negro is more easily discriminated against than is the Negro-on-the-spot. Certainly we do not expect identical results in different cultural climates (e.g., in the South or, to take a less extreme illustration, the East Side Restaurant Survey of New York City, which has shown that Negroes are accorded inferior treatment—poor service, undesirable seating locations, etc.—in many New York restaurants. It may, however, be presumed that the same or related dynamic factors are operating in all three instances.

REFERENCES

Chein, I.; Deutsch, M.; Hyman, H.; and Jahoda, Marie, eds. 1949. Consistency and inconsistency in intergroup relations. *Journal of Social Issues* 5, no. 3, entire number.
LaPiere, R. T. 1934. Attitudes vs. actions. *Social Forces* 13: 230–37.

◢◣ STATUS EFFECTS

Some experimental variables are easier to deal with than others in both field and laboratory situations. Status, race, sex, and linguistic grouping are examples of variables that are highly visible or salient to everyone so that experimenters can manipulate them with some precision. In both of the studies in this section perceived status was manipulated by changing those features of the experimenter's model that we associate with wealth or status.

The Lefkowitz, Blake, and Mouton study reports that higher status persons have greater influence in a norm or rule violation situation, while the Doob and Gross study demonstrates that persons are less likely to make their presence known to high status persons who block their paths. The Doob and Gross study also demonstrates that what people say they will do and what they actually do in specific circumstances may not be at all consistent. It should be noted, however, that the class survey study is not a nonfield experimental study. Laboratory-based experiments of status effects are quite consistent with the field results reported in these two experiments.

In this section we also introduce the notion of statistical treatment of research data. This is not a book on statistics, of course, but readers should have a firm idea of what researchers mean when they talk of statistical significance and parenthetically insert a few symbols. Statistical methods and principles are not easy to comprehend or to communicate, and many readers find that they are confused by the statistical aspects of research papers.

Briefly, in experimental research we typically compare the results (e.g., arithmetic means) of groups of subjects exposed to various levels or degrees of experimental manipulation. Sometimes the groups consist of the same people observed or tested over and over again, as were the students in the Sarbin and Allen experiment. Other times the groups consist of different people, as in the Doob and Gross experiment. The different levels of the manipulated experimental variable may include a no-treatment or control condition (e.g., the no-model-present condition in the Lefkowitz, Blake, and Mouton study) and various levels of treatment conditions, such as high status versus low status.

Researchers refer to their confidence that apparent differences between descriptive numbers, such as means and percentages, are repeatable or real by determining just how often such a difference could be expected by chance alone. Thus when Doob and Gross state that 47 percent of the subjects in the low status condition honked twice at the experimental car as compared to 19 percent of the subjects in the high status condition ($X^2 = 5.26, df = 1, p < .05$) they are stating that statistically the difference between 19 percent and 47 percent can occur less than 5 times out of 100 occasions by pure chance alone. A ($p < .01$) symbolization reads "probability less than one in a hundred that the differences reported could happen by chance."

For our purposes the first part of the symbolized statement can be ignored. The X^2 or F or t refers to the type of statistic used, and the df notation refers to restrictions on the test. The entire notation ($X^2 = 8.37, df = 1, p < .01$) rather than only the probability statement ($p < .01$) appears in the articles for the benefit of readers with statistical backgrounds.

It is important to understand that statistical significance is the least crucial aspect of any particular reported finding. We must also ask "does the result make sense?" or, more precisely, "is the researcher telling us that he believes the finding is repeatable (i.e., reliable) and not the result of error, poor experimental procedures, or chance?" And it is also important to distinguish between statistical significance and meaningfulness. Very small numerical differences can be statistically different but still totally trivial to our understanding of human behavior.

Researchers use many different types of statistical procedures. Since we are dealing here almost entirely with experimental data, the explanation above should allow an understanding of the statistical data treatment procedures.

6. Status of actors in pedestrian violation of traffic signals
Monroe Lefkowitz, Robert R. Blake, and Jane S. Mouton

Pedestrians violated the prohibition of an automatic traffic signal more often in the presence of an experimenter's model who violated the prohibition than when the model conformed or was absent. Significantly more violations occurred among pedestrians when the nonconforming model was dressed to represent high social status than when his attire suggested lower status.

An important aspect in determining whether a person will conform to or violate a prohibition or law is that person's knowledge of how the restriction has affected the behavior of others. In everyday life we find situations in which a greater number of people

Abstracted from: "Status of actors in pedestrian violation of traffic signals." *Journal of Abnormal and Social Psychology* 51 (1955): 704–6.

will conform to a prohibition when they see others conform, whereas knowing that other people are breaking a rule will increase the probability of rule infraction. This issue is important, especially for those in positions of authority, such as parents, school principals, or legislators who are involved with the formation of viable prohibitions and laws from curfews to pollution regulation.

Many studies, including the present one, have attempted to investigate this aspect of conformity behavior. An earlier experiment by Freed, Chandler, and Mouton (1955) examined reactions to signs forbidding entry into a building as a typical situation in which a person is faced with a prohibition. The study found that when subjects saw another person entering the building despite the sign they also violated it more frequently than when they saw a person comply with the sign message. The question then arises: Does it matter who the violator is, or will a person's readiness to violate a prohibition depend on who the others are?

In an attempt to answer this question, Blake and Mouton (1955) proposed that the perceived status of the person whose behavior serves as a model will be an important factor in determining whether other people will violate or conform to the law.

The present experiment is concerned with testing this proposal. The prediction is that when faced with a prohibition a naïve person will be more likely to violate or conform when a high status person serves as a model than when a low status person does so. The prohibition chosen for this experiment was the well-known pedestrian traffic signal that alternately flashes from *wait* to *walk* as the red, amber, and green signals regulate motor traffic flow. During every 55-second interval the *wait* signal flashed for 40 seconds and the *walk* signal for 15 seconds. The experimental observations were made during the *wait* signal, which forbade pedestrians to walk across the street.

Data were collected on 3 afternoons during the hours of 12 to 1, 2 to 3, and 4 to 5 by an observer stationed 100 feet from the street corner. The pedestrian signals were located on three street corners that were positioned at right angles to the main street of a large city. The 2,103 pedestrians who passed the 3 locations during the afternoon hours served as subjects. The experimenter's model was a 31-year-old male. To test the study's predictions, two aspects of social background were simultaneously varied. One was the behavior of the model, who either complied with or violated the pedestrian *wait* signal. The second variable was the perceived status of the model, which was manipulated simply by changing the model's attire. For half of his compliance and violation responses the experimenter's model dressed in clothing that typified a high-status person—neatly pressed suit, white shirt, tie, polished shoes, and a straw hat. In the remaining half the model wore an unpressed denim shirt, soiled trousers, and scuffed shoes to define himself as a low-status person. In a control or neutral situation the rate of pedestrian violation of the *wait* signal was measured when the model was absent from the street corners.

The typical experimental session proceeded as follows. At noon of one day the model, dressed in one status attire, complied with the *wait* signal and crossed the street when the *walk* signal flashed. This sequence was repeated for five trials, and the number of pedestrians who conformed with the *wait* signal and those who violated it were recorded. After these trials pedestrians were observed for five more trials in the control situation when the model was absent. The model then returned in the other status attire and violated the *wait* signal for the same number of trials by crossing the street at approximately the midpoint of every *wait* interval. The reverse order of conforming and violating was used the next day, and so on.

The experimenters constructed two criteria for determining whether the pedestrians actually were violating the *wait* signal: (1) only those subjects standing with the model at the street corner were included in the data; (2) pedestrians who reached or passed the center white line of the street when the signal still flashed *wait* were recorded as violators. Use of the center line as the criterion for violation made the recording observer's judgments much easier and therefore less subject to error.

The results shown in Figure 6.1 indicate that the presence of a model of either low or high perceived status who complied with the prohibition, the *wait* signal, did not increase the rate of pedestrian compliance above the rate in the control situations without the model present. Statistical tests verified this conclusion, and because

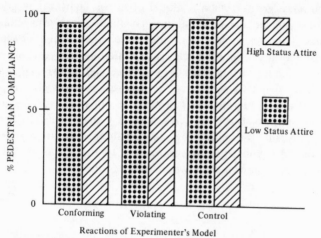

Figure 6.1

the rates of pedestrian conformity were so high (99 percent) the experimenters concluded that this study did not really test the proposition that seeing another person conform increased the rate of conformity.

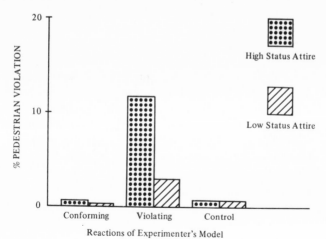

Figure 6.2

However, as shown in Figure 6.2, the rates of pedestrian violation were greater when a model of either high or low perceived status violated the prohibition. This finding was also statistically verified and resembles the results of the experiment with the violation of a sign prohibiting entry into a building (Freed et al., 1955). Figure 6.2 shows that when the perceived high status model violated the *wait* signal 14 percent of the pedestrians also violated the prohibition. The presence of a low status violator also increased the pedestrian violation rate. Thus, when a violating model's perceived status quality was either high or low the pedestrian violation rate increased significantly in comparison to the violation rate when the model conformed or was absent.

REFERENCES

Blake, R. R., and Mouton, Jane S. 1955. Present and future implications of social psychology for law and lawyers. *Symposium Issue, Emory University Journal of Public Law* 3: 352–69.
Freed, A. M.; Chandler, P. J.; and Mouton, Jane S. 1955. Stimulus and background factors in sign violation. *Journal of Personality* 23: 499.

(7) **Status of frustrator as an inhibitor of horn-honking responses** Anthony N. Doob and Alan E. Gross

An experimental confederate frustrated a driver by waiting at an intersection after a traffic light had turned green. For half the trials the confederate drove an old, low-status car; for the other half of the trials he drove a new, luxury model, high status car. Low status cars were honked at

Reprinted with permission of the authors and The Journal Press from *The Journal of Social Psychology* 76 (1968): 213–18.

more often and with shorter latency than were high status cars.

Modern automobile traffic frequently creates situations which closely resemble classical formulations of how frustration is instigated. One such instance occurs when one car blocks another at a signal-controlled intersection. Unlike many traffic frustrations, this situation provides a clearly identifiable frustrator and a fairly typical response for the blocked driver: sounding his horn. Horn honking may function instrumentally to remove the offending driver and emotionally to reduce tension. Both kinds of honks may be considered aggressive, especially if they are intended to make the frustrator uncomfortable by bombarding him with unpleasant stimuli.

One factor that is likely to affect aggressive responses is the status of the frustrator (Cohen, 1955; Hokanson and Burgess, 1962). The higher a person's status, the more likely it is he will have power to exercise sanctions, and although it is improbable that a high status driver would seek vengeance against a honker, fear of retaliation may generalize from other situations where aggression against superiors has been punished.

Aggression is not the only kind of social response that may be affected by status. High status may inhibit the initiation of any social response, even a simple informational signal. Although it is difficult in the present study to distinguish informational from aggressive motivation, it is hypothesized that a high status frustrator will generally inhibit horn honking.

Method

One of two automobiles, a new luxury model or an older car, was driven up to a signal-controlled intersection and stopped. The driver was instructed to remain stopped after the signal had changed to green until 15 seconds had elapsed, or until the driver of the car immediately behind honked his horn twice. Subjects were the 82 drivers, 26 women and 56 men, whose progress was blocked by the experimental car. The experiment was run from 10:30 a.m. to 5:30 p.m. on a Sunday, in order to avoid heavy weekday traffic.

A black 1966 Chrysler Crown Imperial hardtop which had been washed and polished was selected as the high status car. Two low status cars were used: a rusty 1954 Ford station wagon and an unobtrusive gray 1961 Rambler sedan. The Rambler was substituted at noon because it was felt that subjects might reasonably attribute the Ford's failure to move to mechanical breakdown. Responses to these two cars did not turn out to be different, and the data for the two low status cars were combined.

Six intersections in Palo Alto and Menlo Park, California, were selected according to these criteria: (a) a red light sufficiently long to ensure that a high proportion of potential subjects would come to a complete stop behind the experimental car before the signal changed to green; (b) relatively light traffic so that only one car, the subject's, was likely to pull up behind the experimental car; and (c) a narrow street so that it would be difficult for the subject to drive around the car blocking him. Approximately equal numbers of high and low status trials were run at each intersection.

PROCEDURE

By timing the signal cycle, the driver of the experimental car usually managed to arrive at the intersection just as the light facing him was turning red. If at least one other car had come to a complete stop behind the experimental car before the signal had turned green, a trial was counted, and when the light changed an observer started two stopwatches and a tape recorder. Observers were usually stationed in a car parked close to the intersection, but when this was not feasible they were concealed from view in the back seat of the experimental car. High and low status trials were run simultaneously at different intersections, and the two driver-observer teams switched cars periodically during the day. Drivers wore a plaid sport jacket and white shirt while driving the Chrysler, and an old khaki jacket while driving the older car.

At the end of each trial, the observer noted whether the subject had honked once, twice, or not at all. Latency of each honk and estimated length of each honk were recorded and later double-checked against tape recordings.

Immediately after each trial, the observer took down the year, make, and model of the subject's car. Sex and estimated age of driver, number of passengers, and number of cars behind the experimental car when the signal changed were also recorded.

Results and Discussion

Eight subjects, all men, were eliminated from the analysis for the following reasons: four cars in the low status condition and one in the high status condition went around the experimental car; on one trial the driver of the experimental car left the intersection early; and two cars in the low status condition, instead of honking, hit the back bumper of the experimental car, and the driver did not wish to wait for a honk. This left 38 subjects in the low status condition and 36 in the high status condition.

Although the drivers of the experimental cars usually waited for 15 seconds, 2 of the lights used in the experiment were green for only 12 seconds; therefore, 12 seconds was used as a cutoff for all data. There were no differences attributable to drivers or intersections.

The clearest way of looking at the results is in terms of the percentage in each condition that honked at least once in 12 seconds. In the low status condition 84 percent of the subjects honked at least once, whereas in the high status condition, only 50 percent of the subjects honked ($X^2 = 8.37$, $df = 1$, $p < .01$). Another way of looking at this finding is in terms of the latency of the first honk. When no honks are counted as a latency of 12 seconds, it can be seen in Table 7.1 that the average latency for the new car was longer for both sexes ($F = 10.71$, $p < .01$).

Thus, it is quite clear that status had an inhibitory effect on honking even once. It could be argued that status would have even greater inhibitory effects on more aggressive honking. Although one honk can be considered a polite way of calling attention to the green light, it is possible that subjects felt that a second honk would be interpreted as aggression.[1]

Forty-seven percent of the subjects in the low status condition honked twice at the experimental car, as compared to 19 percent

1. Series of honks separated by intervals of less than one second were counted as a single honk.

Table 7.1
Field Experiment (Mean Latency of First Honk in Seconds)

	SEX OF DRIVER	
FRUSTRATOR	MALE	FEMALE
Low status	6.8 (23)	7.6 (15)
High status	8.5 (25)	10.9 (11)

NOTE: Numbers in parentheses indicate the number of subjects.

of the subjects in the high status condition $(X^2 = 5.26, df = 1, p < .05)$. This difference should be interpreted cautiously because it is confounded with the main result that more people honk generally in the low status condition. Of those who overcame the inhibitions to honk at all, 56 percent in the low status condition and 39 percent in the high status condition honked a second time, a difference which was not significant. First-honk latencies for honkers were about equal for the two conditions. The overall findings are presented in Table 7.2.

Table 7.2
Number of Drivers Honking Zero, One, and Two Times

	HONKING IN 12 SECONDS		
FRUSTRATOR	NEVER	ONCE	TWICE
Low status	6	14	18
High status	18	11	7

Sex of driver was the only other measure that was a good predictor of honking behavior. In both conditions men tended to honk faster than women $(F = 4.49, p < .05)$. These data are consistent with laboratory findings (Buss, 1966) that men tend to aggress more than women.

Most experiments designed to study the effects of frustration have been carried out in the laboratory or the classroom, and many of these have employed written materials (Cohen, 1955; Pastore, 1952).

It is undoubtedly much easier to use questionnaires, and if they produce the same results as field experiments, then in the interest of economy, they would have great advantage over naturalistic experiments. However, over 30 years ago, LaPiere (1934, p. 236) warned that reactions to such instruments "may indicate what the responder would actually do when confronted with the situation symbolized in the question, but there is no assurance that it will."

In order to investigate this relationship between actual and predicted behavior, an attempt was made to replicate the present study as a questionnaire experiment. Obviously, the most appropriate sample to use would be one comprised of motorists sampled in the same way that the original drivers were sampled. Because this was not practicable, a questionnaire experiment was administered in a junior college classroom.

Subjects were 57 students in an introductory psychology class. Two forms of the critical item were included as the first of three traffic situations on a one-page questionnaire: "You are stopped at a traffic light behind a black 1966 Chrysler (gray 1961 Rambler). The light turns green and for no apparent reason the driver does not go on. Would you honk at him?" If subjects indicated that they would honk, they were then asked to indicate on a scale from 1 to 14 seconds how long they would wait before honking. Forms were alternated so that approximately equal numbers of subjects received the Chrysler and Rambler versions. Verbal instructions strongly emphasized that subjects were to answer according to what they actually thought they would do in such a situation. No personal information other than sex, age, and whether or not they were licensed to drive was required.

After the questionnaire had been collected, the class was informed that different kinds of cars had been used for the horn-honking item. The experimenter then asked subjects to raise their hands when they heard the name of the car that appeared in the first item of their questionnaire. All subjects were able to select the correct name from a list of four makes which was read.

One subject (a female in the high status condition) failed to mark the honk latency scale, and another subject in the same condition indicated that she would go around the blocking car. Both of these subjects were eliminated from the analysis, leaving 27 in the high status condition and 28 in the low status condition. The results were analyzed in the same manner as the latency data from the field experiment. Means for each condition broken down by sex are presented in Table 7.3. Males reported that they thought that they would honk considerably sooner at the Chrysler than at the Rambler, whereas this was slightly reversed for females (interaction of sex and status $F = 4.97$, $p < .05$). Eleven subjects, six males in the low status condition and five females in the high status condition, indicated that they would not honk within 12 seconds.

Table 7.3
Questionnaire Experiment (Mean Latency of Honking in Seconds)

	SEX OF SUBJECT	
FRUSTRATOR	MALE	FEMALE
Low status	9.1 (18)	8.2 (10)
High status	5.5 (13)	9.2 (14)

NOTE: Numbers in parentheses indicate the number of subjects.

It is clear that the behavior reported on the questionnaire is different from the behavior actually observed in the field. The age difference in the samples may account for this disparity. Median estimated age of subjects in the field was 38, compared to a median age of 22 in the classroom. In order to check the possibility that younger males would indeed honk faster at the high status car, the field data were reanalyzed by age. The results for younger males, estimated ages 16 to 30, fit the general pattern of the field results and differed from the results of the classroom experiment. In the field, young males honked sooner at the Rambler than at the Chrysler ($t = 2.74$, $df = 11$, $p < .02$).

Unfortunately, because these two studies differed in both sample and method, it is impossible to conclude that the differences are due to differences in the method of collecting data. However, it is clear that questionnaire data obtained from this often-used population of subjects do not always correspond to what goes on in the real world.

REFERENCES

Buss, A. H. 1966. Instrumentality of aggression, feedback, and frustration as determinants of physical aggression. *Journal of Personality and Social Psychology* 3: 153–62.

Cohen, A. R. 1955. Social norms, arbitrariness of frustration, and status of the agent in the frustration-aggression hypothesis. *Journal of Abnormal and Social Psychology* 51: 222–26.

Hokanson, J. E., and Burgess, M. 1962. The effects of status, type of frustration and aggression on vascular processes. *Journal of Abnormal and Social Psychology* 65: 232–37.

LaPiere, R. T. 1934. Attitudes vs. actions. *Social Forces* 13: 230–37.

Pastore, N. 1952. The role of arbitrariness in the frustration-aggression hypothesis. *Journal of Abnormal and Social Psychology* 47: 728–31.

5 HELPING AND HONESTY

Probably almost everyone recalls the New York City incident in which at least 38 witnesses watched an attacker chase and stab to death Kitty Genovese. The attack lasted for more than a half-hour, and not one of the 38 persons who watched the murder from the safety of their apartments did so much as telephone the police. In other reported cases people have watched attacks and crimes without intervening or aiding the victim even after the attackers were gone.

Although a lot of folk wisdom explanations are given for the lack of honesty and humanity we witness so frequently, the systematic examination of helping behavior in field situations is of relatively recent origin. Studies of dishonesty and deceit conducted primarily on university students have a fairly long history.

The articles in this section were selected to provide a broad sampling of the types of prosocial behaviors that are being systematically investigated. In addition, the articles point out several technical and methodological issues of importance. The Latané and Elman article includes what might technically be called a laboratory study, which is contrasted with a field replication. This laboratory experiment, the only one included in this book, also points out quite clearly the denial strategy that subjects frequently adopt in intervention situations: if a person can successfully act as though he is not witnessing a crisis or distress situation, then, of course, he cannot be expected to intervene.

The Feldman article describes a variety of intriguing experiments on various forms of prosocial behavior and provides interesting cross-cultural and status effects that influence the giving of assistance. Of particular methodological interest is the seemingly unobtrusive field interviewing technique used in Feldman's third experiment.

To end on an optimistic note, the experiment reported in the Isen and Levin article indicates that when people feel good they help. Relatively little research has been addressed to the relationship between positive affective states and helping behavior. Available data indicate that good feeling, generated in a variety of different ways, leads to enhanced helping behavior. As the authors state, however, *why* feeling good leads to helping remains to be answered.

8. The bystander and the thief   Bibb Latané and Donald Elman

In a laboratory and a field experiment subjects either waiting alone or in pairs witnessed a theft. In both situations, subjects were more likely to report the crime if they alone witnessed it than if someone else also saw it.

Reprinted from *The Unresponsive Bystander: Why Doesn't He Help?* by Bibb Latané and John M. Darley, pp. 69–77. Copyright © 1970. Reprinted by permission of Appleton-Century-Crofts, Educational Division, Meredith Corporation.

When a bystander is faced with the possibility of a fire or confronted with the victim of an apparently serious accident, he is more likely to interpret the situation as an emergency, and consequently to take action, if he is alone than if he is in the presence of other bystanders. Fires and accidents certainly are emergencies, but they differ from the emergencies typically encountered in "apathy" stories. They are caused by impersonal agents and do not involve a villain.

A villain represents a danger not only to the victim, but to anybody who is rash enough to interfere with him. A single individual may be reluctant to tangle with a villain. If it comes to physical violence, his odds are at best equal. At worst, the villain will be armed and vicious. Undeterred from crime, he may be undeterred from violence as well. Even if the individual bystander can avoid immediate physical contact by reporting the villain to the authorities, he still faces future dangers of retribution, either from the villain himself or from his friends. And he may well find himself subpoenaed to appear in court.

When several bystanders witness a crime, the dangers to any one for intervening are lessened. Together, they may be physically able to overpower the criminal. If one or more of them report the crime, they will be less identifiable than a single person, and thus less likely to suffer retribution. If several are witnesses, the chances of any one being called to testify may be lessened. Under these conditions, even if one person is reluctant to take action, the presence of other people as potential risk-sharing allies might embolden him to intervene. These considerations suggest reasons why groups might be more likely than single individuals to intervene in a crime. However, despite these considerations, social inhibitions provided by the presence of other people may still be sufficient to lead individuals to react more quickly to a crime when they are alone than when they are with others. In this chapter we report two experiments that explore this question.

Experiment I. The Hand in the Till

Male undergraduates witnessed a theft while waiting for an interview. In one condition, each subject was the sole witness; in another, two subjects were present. The dependent variable was whether the subjects reported the crime.

PROCEDURE

Columbia College freshmen signed up on a volunteer sheet posted in their dormitories to participate in a one-hour interview for a fee of two dollars. After being contacted by telephone to schedule a time, subjects came for their interviews. They were greeted by an attractive receptionist and led into the waiting room. The waiting room was equipped with a row of five chairs along one wall and a small desk and chair on the opposite wall.

Among the subjects who arrived was a short, clean-cut student wearing a conservative sport jacket with an open shirt. Although sounds of distant thunder did *not* appear on the sound track, this "subject" was soon to become a criminal. He was, of course, an accomplice of the experimenter.

When all the subjects had arrived, the receptionist, sitting at her desk, checked off their names on her schedule sheet and announced that they would be individually interviewed by a team of experts from the Institute for the Study of Human Problems on the reactions of college students to the urban environment of New York City. She apologized that the interviews were running a few minutes behind schedule, and, to save time, paid the subjects in advance. Picking up an envelope from her desk, she pulled out several large bills and some smaller ones to pay the subjects their two dollars. To emphasize the large amount of money in the envelope, she asked if anyone in the room had change for 20 dollars. After paying the subjects, she put the remainder of the money (between 30 and 50 dollars) back in the envelope, returned to her desk and sat down, putting the envelope on the top of the desk. Shortly afterward a buzzer sounded, and she left the room, ostensibly to answer the call.

The theft. Several seconds after the receptionist left the room, the Thief stood up, walked over to the desk, and fumbled with a magazine that had been lying on top of it. Then, clumsily but blatantly, seemingly trying to hide his actions but performing in full view of the other subject(s), he reached into the envelope, took out the cash, stuffed it into his jacket pocket, picked up the magazine, and returned to his seat. At no time did he say a word. If addressed, he either ignored the comment, continuing to leaf through his magazine, or answered with an innocent "I don't know what you are talking about."

About one minute after the theft, the receptionist returned. At this time, the subject(s) had an opportunity to report the crime if he was willing to confront the Thief to do so. After half a minute, the receptionist sent the Thief to his "interview." Now the subjects could report the theft without directly confronting the Thief. We were interested, of course, in what proportion of subjects would responsibly report the theft spontaneously to the receptionist.

If the subject did not report the theft, we were concerned to make sure that he had actually seen it, and followed an elaborate procedure to determine this. If the theft had not been reported within one minute after the Thief left for his interview, the receptionist opened her envelope, noticed that some money was missing, and attempted to elicit a report by questioning the subject(s) about the money. Then she sent the subject(s) to another room with a male interviewer, who began by asking some questions about the subject's background and mentioned that the topic for the interview would be "crime on the streets." Gradually during the course of the interview he raised the question of what had happened in the waiting room and asked the subjects to describe their reactions, again trying to find whether the subject had actually noticed the theft. Finally, he explained the deceptions and purposes of the experiment and used the incident as a starting point for a discussion of some of the conditions of life in modern American cities.

RESULTS

Despite the smallness of the room, the absence of things to look at, and the blatant clumsiness of the theft, many subjects steadfastly claimed throughout the entire interview that they had not noticed the crime. Table 8.10 presents the number of subjects or pairs who noticed, or professed not to have noticed, the theft.

Fifty-two percent of subjects in the Alone condition claimed not to have noticed the theft, while 25 percent of the Together pairs said they had not seen it. These apparently different noticing rates are really quite similar when we consider that the expected joint probability of two subjects failing to notice the theft if they do not

Table 8.10
Frequency of Noticing Theft

CONDITION	N	NOTICED	DID NOT NOTICE
Alone	25	12	13
Together	16 pairs	12 pairs	4 pairs

influence each other is the product of the individual probabilities, that is, 27 percent.

The high proportion of subjects in both conditions who professed not to have noticed the crime is surprising in light of the obviousness of the theft and the lack of other things to distract their attention. It is also surprising in the light of observers' reports. Observers, watching the scene through a one-way mirror, were convinced, by the direction of subjects' gazes, by their quickly suppressed startle reactions, and by their too carefully studied expressions of nonchalance, that the majority of subjects actually did see the theft.

We suspect that, in one sense, the claim of many subjects that they had not noticed the theft may be accurate. That is, it is possible that many subjects had not *completed* noticing the event. As we shall discuss more fully in the next chapter, noticing the theft would have put subjects in an avoidance-avoidance conflict such that they were torn between the negative alternatives of risking confrontation with the Thief by acting and risking guilt at not acting. A good way to avoid this conflict was not to see the theft at all. Many subjects may have noticed the beginnings of the theft, and without fully thinking about the implications of what they had seen, unconsciously turned their attention away from what was happening.

Other subjects may have noticed the theft, but, anxious to make their nonintervention consistent with their self or public images, may have clung to a story which, to themselves and to the interviewer, provided a perfect justification for not acting. Some of these subjects may have come to believe their story, while others, of course, may not.

Reporting the theft. The widespread failure to notice an obvious crime is an interesting phenomenon, but it also presents a problem for the interpretation of further results. Since it is difficult to determine which of the nonnoticers were genuine and which were fabricators, let us be conservative and look at the proportion of all subjects, noticers and nonnoticers, who reported the crime. In the Alone condition, 24 percent of all subjects spontaneously reported the theft to the receptionist. From this, we would expect that at least 42 percent of the pairs would include at least one person who would report the theft. Actually, in only 19 percent of the pairs did even one person report the crime ($p < .05$). Only 3 out of the 32 people who were tested in pairs told the receptionist that her money had been stolen.

If we consider only subjects who admitted noticing the theft, the results become even stronger. From the fact that 50 percent of Alone noticers reported, we would expect 75 percent of noticing pairs to include one reporter. Only 25 percent of these pairs did.

Subjects who noticed but did not report the theft often generated elaborate but somewhat implausible interpretations. "It looked like he was only making change," said several subjects. "I thought he took the money by accident," said one charitable soul. A number of subjects seemed to feel some conflict between their responsibilities to the receptionist and to law and order on the one hand and to the "obviously" poor (but well-dressed) college peer on the other. Some decided that not much money had been in the envelope after all. Each subject in the group condition, looking at the inactivity of the other bystander, seemed to be led to decide that the theft was not too serious and that squealing would be most inappropriate.

The results of this experiment, like those of the previous two, show that individuals may be less likely to take action in an emergency if others are present, even when the emergency involves a villain. However, the effect was not sufficiently strong to overcome the fact that with two people present, there are twice as many people free to act. The theft was reported slightly, but not significantly, less often when two witnessed it than when one did. The receptionist was actually only slightly better off when one person saw her money stolen than when two did. This may indicate that the presence of a villain led to a smaller social inhibition effect than would occur in other situations. It may also indicate that, given the relatively low rate of response caused by the failure to notice the theft, there was little room for a larger effect to occur.

Experiment II provides a new test of social influence effects in a field setting and introduces a new variable, the number of villains.

Experiment II. The Case of the Stolen Beer

There are several difficulties in laboratory experiments as contrasted to experiments carried out in the field. If the subject knows he is in an experiment, his experiences may have an "as if" quality about them, such that the subject feels he is only playacting. Many laboratory experiments subject people to strange situations and make strange requests of them. And subjects experience peculiar pressures stemming in part from the fact that they are known by name to the experimenter.

In designing the laboratory experiment we tried to avoid these problems as much as possible. We staged our scenes in a waiting room where the subject sat before taking part in an interview. We used all the theatrical talent at our command to make the emergencies as realistic and plausible as possible (although, being emergencies, they were of necessity somewhat unusual). But in each experiment we knew the name of the subject (although, by policy, we forgot them as soon as the subject was finished). The relationships shown in these experiments would probably not have been different had they been conducted in field settings. To make sure, however, we designed an experiment to be conducted in the field, where subjects would be, and know they were, completely anonymous. Since the results of the theft experiment were somewhat complicated by the large number of people who claimed to have missed the action, we decided to repeat that experiment in a new setting. And we decided to add a new variable.

If the hypothesis that people will be importantly deterred from reporting a crime by the possibility of retribution from the villain is correct, then they should be more concerned the more vicious and the more numerous the villains are. In the last experiment, the Thief seemed a relatively mild-mannered, nonviolent young man. It is possible that he tended to generate feelings of sympathy at his poverty, rather than fear at his audacity and evil intent. It is possible that two Robbers would be a greater deterrent to intervention than one Thief. To test these possibilities, two Columbia undergraduates, Paul Bonnarigo and Malcolm Ross, turned to a life of crime.

PROCEDURE

The Nu-Way Beverage Center in Suffern, New York, is a discount beer store. It sells beer and soda by the case, often to New Jerseyans who cross the state line to find both lowered prices and a lowered legal drinking age. During the spring of 1968 it was the scene of a minor crime wave—within a 2-week period, it was robbed 96 times.

The robbers, husky young men dressed in T-shirts and chinos, followed much the same modus operandi on each occasion. Singly or in a pair, they would enter the store and ask the cashier at the check-out counter, "What is the most expensive imported beer that you carry?" The cashier, in cahoots with the Robbers, would reply, "Löwenbräu. I'll go back and check how much we have." Leaving the Robbers in the front of the store, the cashier would disappear into the rear to look for the Löwenbräu.

After waiting for a minute, the Robbers would pick up a case of beer near the front of the store, remark to nobody in particular, "They'll never miss this," walk out of the front door, put the beer in their car, and drive off. On 48 occasions, 1 Robber carried off the theft; on 48 occasions, 2 Robbers were present.

The robberies were always staged when there were either one or two people in the store, and the timing was arranged so that one or both customers would be at the check-out counter at the time when the Robbers entered. On 48 occasions, 1 customer was at the check-out counter during the theft; on 48 occasions, 2 customers were present. Although occasionally the two customers had come in together, more usually they were strangers. Sixty-one percent of the customers were male, 39 percent female. Since the check-out counter was about 20 feet from the front door, since the theft itself took less than 1 minute, and since the Robbers were both husky young men, nobody tried directly to prevent the theft. There were, however, other courses of intervention available.

When the cashier returned from the rear of the store, he came back to the check-out counter and resumed waiting on the customers there. After a minute, if nobody had spontaneously mentioned the theft, he casually inquired, "Hey, what happened to that man (those men) who was (were) in here? Did you see him (them)

68 *Helping and Honesty*

leave?" At this point, the customer(s) could either report the theft, say merely that he had seen the man or men leave, or disclaim any knowledge of the event whatsoever. Overall, 20 percent of the subjects reported the theft spontaneously, and 51 percent of the remainder reported it upon prompting. Since the results from each criterion followed an identical pattern, we shall report only the total proportion of subjects in each condition who reported the theft, whether spontaneously or not.

RESULTS

Fear of future retaliation from the Robbers did not seem to be a major concern of the bystanders. Doubling the number of Robbers made little difference in reporting the theft. Customers were actually somewhat, but not significantly, more likely to report the theft if there were two Robbers (69 percent) than if there was only one (52 percent, $p < .20$). This slight difference may be due to the fact that two Robbers were more visible and harder to ignore than one.

Sex of the bystander also had no effect on reporting; females were as likely to report as males.

As in the previous study, the number of bystanders had an important effect on reporting the theft. Thirty-one of the 48 single customers, or 65 percent, reported the theft. From this, we would expect that 87 percent of the 2-person groups would include at least 1 reporter. In fact, in only 56 percent of the 2-person groups did even 1 person report the crime ($p < .01$). Social inhibition of reporting actually made the theft somewhat, though not significantly, less likely to be reported when two people saw it than when only one did.

Discussion

In both the experiments reported in this chapter, subjects were more likely to report a crime if they alone witnessed it than if someone else saw it also. The receptionist and the cashier were no better off if they had two people "minding the store" than if they had only one.

For the first time in our studies, the agent that caused the emergency was a person. He may not have been a particularly admirable one, but even a bad man deserves some consideration. This divided the loyalties of our subjects. Regardless of what is abstractly right, reporting this emergency meant putting another person in trouble. It meant squealing. It meant balancing the rights of an individual against those of an institution. Many subjects may have chosen to side with the villain rather than with his victim. Even so, group size still proved a major determinant of bystander action.

9. Response to compatriot and foreigner who seek assistance   Roy E. Feldman

Five experiments examined the differential treatment of foreign and compatriot strangers by Parisians, Athenians, and Bostonians in different social contexts. In each case Ss could have been helpful or antisocial toward the compatriot or foreign stranger. Generally, a social classification of the Ss was positively related to their helpfulness. The foreigner's use of the language of the city was positively related to the helpfulness received in Paris and Athens, but not in Boston. When differences occurred in the treatment of compatriots and foreigners, the compatriots were treated better in Paris and Boston, but the foreigners were treated better in Athens. Some results in Athens support ingroup–outgroup and role differential findings of Triandis, Vassiliou, and Nassiakou.

Reprinted from the *Journal of Personality and Social Psychology* 10 (1968): 202–14. Copyright 1968 by the American Psychological Association, and reproduced by permission. In 1965 the investigation was supported by a Ford Foundation Grant in International Studies under the auspices of the Department of Social Relations, Harvard University. In 1966 the research was supported, in part, by a grant from the Comparative International Studies Program of the Harvard Department of Social Relations and by a grant from the Milton Fund of Harvard University.

This is a report of five field experiments designed to explore the dimensions of cooperation toward foreigners and compatriots in three different sociocultural settings. The objectives of the experiments were, first, to discover the general nature of the response to foreigners and compatriots who asked for help in different sociocultural contexts. Triandis, Vassiliou, and Nassiakou (1967) have demonstrated the utility of the constructs ingroup and outgroup in interpreting cultural differences in the perception of a variety of Greek and American roles, among them the native–tourist role. They suggest that different cognitive definitions of the ingroup and the outgroup help account for differential behaviors toward members of respective ingroups and outgroups. The experiments described here add overt behavioral data to the empirical role differential method of Triandis et al. (1967). Inkeles and Levinson (1954) have noted that significant behavioral differences have not yet been established for large populations using relatively large samples. These experiments do this and take us beyond earlier conjectural approaches, permitting objective descriptions of some behavioral characteristics of Parisians, Athenians, and Bostonians along with social correlates of these behaviors. Since impressionistic observations are at least partially responsible for national stereotypes, the collection of data sheds some light on their validity.

The second objective was to examine the general concept of "cooperation" as a way of describing the interactions of foreigners with compatriots of different populations. The initial hypothesis was that "cooperation" could be operationally defined by a series of typical social encounters which would be intercorrelated. The third aim was to establish a logical base line for discussing the treatment of the foreigner in different sociocultural settings. This was done by examining the treatment of the compatriot under identical circumstances in each city. Since we only used three cities, it made more sense to emphasize the differential treatment of compatriots and foreigners *within* each city rather than across three cities. The fourth object was to determine the relationship between social class differences and the treatment of the foreigner within cities. The fifth aim was to determine the importance of situational factors such as whether the encounter was casual or structured, whether the foreigner spoke the language of the city or a foreign language, and how opportunity to cheat the foreigner influenced the encounter. Finally, the experiments permitted direct examination of the relevant behavior under standardized conditions to reduce the effects of personal bias and make measurement more precise. The basic paradigm consisted of controlled standardized observations of behavioral episodes that were initiated via the intervention of a member of the experimental team.

Research Design

In carrying out experimental research on population characteristics, it was not possible to work with all-embracing characterizations. The study focused upon specific themes which have general social significance and can be approached by experimental means. Five experiments were devised in which subjects could show cooperative or uncooperative behavior in natural ongoing field situations. Paris and Athens were selected as the sample populations because data on stereotypes regarding treatment of the foreigner were available and contrasting, and Boston was added as a third population because it provided a convenient testing ground for developing the research design.

In varying the social context for each of the experiments, four structural factors can be used to differentiate the experimental encounters: whether the encounter was (*a*) casual or (*b*) occupational, and (*c*) whether there was the opportunity to cheat the stranger or (*d*) whether the stranger asked for a nonmonetary favor.

Casual encounter. In the first three experiments subjects were stopped under a reasonable pretext and confronted by a person under apparently chance and casual circumstances. The subject's behavior was free from any formal supervision and he was free to respond without the possibility of reproach or reprimand from anyone outside of the encounter. Subjects remained anonymous and might have anticipated thanks from the stranger for any obvious assistance rendered, but were unlikely to foresee any difficulty following unfriendly behavior on their part.

Occupational encounter. In the final two experiments all subjects were approached while performing their occupational duties. Moreover, that commercial service was performed on the premises occupied by the subject. Some of the subjects in Experiment IV were under formal supervision and all were subject to obvious legal sanctions if it were proved that they had violated the law. Freedom to respond was constrained by the institutional structure of the encounters with subjects. The probability of the subject's affective evaluation of a stranger influencing the interaction seemed less likely as the amount of formal structure surrounding the encounter increased.

Sampling considerations were (a) assuring the absence of experimenter bias in the selection of subjects, and (b) obtaining a representative sample within the city. The first three experiments drew the sample from people walking in the main shopping district of the city, with a relatively high density of people on the street. This prevented outside interference with the experimental paradigm. Socioeconomic classification was used as an independent variable in these experiments in order to ascertain the differential behavior of these classes. In Experiments IV and V the sample was randomly selected from specific occupational groups.

Experiment I: Asking for Directions

The general objective was to find out how Parisians, Athenians, and Bostonians treated foreigners (compared with fellow citizens) who stopped them on the street and asked for information in both their native language and in the major language of the citizens being questioned.

Experimenters. A native and a foreign couple were employed as experimenters in each city. The American experimenter couple in Boston also acted as the foreign experimenter couple in both Paris and Athens. The foreigners in Boston were French.

Subjects. Excluded as subjects were all women, males judged to be under the age of 18 years, and foreign tourists who could be identified because they were carrying a camera or tourist guide book. All other people were permissible subjects.

Apparatus. The FI-Cord 101 pocket tape recorder was used to tape episodes in Experiment I.

Location. The three locations used in this study were Paris, Ath-

Table 9.1

Treatment of Subjects in Each City: Experiment I

	LANGUAGE USED	
COUPLE	Ss ASKED IN NATIVE LANGUAGE	Ss ASKED IN FOREIGN LANGUAGE
Native Es	½ N	0
Foreign Es	¼ N	¼ N

NOTE: For each location N = total sample of subjects.

ens, and Boston. In each city the location chosen was a main shopping district: Boulevard Haussmann in Paris, Venizelou Street and Stadiou Street in Athens, and Washington Street in Boston. The locations were matched in terms of the heavy crowd of shoppers that was found in all three places. The target location was chosen to be about one and a half miles from the original location. In all three cities it was possible to go from the original location to the target location via underground public transportation.

Procedure. A compatriot couple and a foreign couple operated at each location on different days. The primary objective of the subject selection procedure was to avoid letting the experimenters bias the outcome by selecting subjects on the basis of some systematic, idiosyncratic bias. Experimenters began each experimental "episode" by counting subjects coming toward them. Each subject about to walk past the experimenters was counted and the fourth one was the automatic and compulsory choice as the subject for the experiment. Because of both the density of people on the street and the fact that people walk at different speeds, it was not possible to determine who the fourth man would be before beginning the counting procedure. The fourth man was approached just as he was about to pass the experimenters, and the male experimenter asked: "Excuse me, sir, how do I get to Copley Square?" (In Paris the target location was La Place des Ternes; in Athens, Plateia Kyriakou). Before asking for directions, the male experimenter activated a concealed tape recorder which continued for the duration of the episode.

In order to see if the socioeconomic variable was an important factor relative to the dependent variable (but without the possibility of obtaining relevant information from the subjects) each subject was classified into one of three categories according to the clothes he wore at the time of the experimental episode. For each city a determination was made of what constituted well-dressed, upper socioeconomic status (Class 1), poorly dressed, "working clothes" (Class 3), or medium-dressed, between Class 1 and Class 3 (i.e., Class 2). For each city native social scientists helped in formulating the categories. Experimenters practiced classifying men on the street until there was almost no disagreement in classification. During the experimental episode, it was the female experimenter who was primarily responsible for this classification. When rare disagreements occurred, they were resolved by placing the subject into Class 2. Subjects who attempted to give directions by underground transportation were asked to give directions by foot. After the subject had finished directing the experimenters, a brief summary of the episode was dictated into the tape recorder. The summary included: (a) socioeconomic classification, (b) whether or not the subject gave directions, (c) whether or not directions, if given, were accurate, (d) any accent discernable to the native experimenters, (e) any other miscellaneous information of interest. After this was done, the subject-selection procedure began again.

Table 9.1 illustrates the treatment of subjects for each city.

Experiment II: Doing a Favor for a Stranger

At major underground Metro stops, under a plausible pretext, male subjects were stopped and asked to mail a letter for a stranger who said that he was "waiting there for a friend." Half of the letters were unstamped. The main measure was the proportion of people who agreed to do the favor. The letter was addressed to the experimenter's headquarters (cf., Milgram, Mann, & Harter, 1965).

Experimenters. Two male experimenters were used in each city —a compatriot and a foreigner.

Subjects. Criteria for subjects were the same as in Experiment I.

Location. The sites of the experiments were the Washington Street Metropolitan Transit Association station in Boston, Chausée

D'Antin and Hàvre Caumartin Metro stops in Paris, and the Omonia Square Metro stop in Athens.

Procedure. Subject selection was the same as in Experiment I. Each time the experiment was begun, the fourth man to approach the experimenter was the automatic and compulsory choice of the experimenter as the next subject. Only on rare occasions was a man who appeared as a subject not selected. These instances occurred when the man was a severe cripple, or when he was carrying so much "baggage" that it was clear that he could not possibly take the letter in hand. Compatriot and foreign experimenters both addressed the subjects in the native language of the city involved.

As in Experiment I, each subject was classified into one of three categories according to the clothes he wore at the time of the experimental episode. Experimenters operated at each location at matched times of the day. After subject selection the subject was stopped and the experimenter said, "Excuse me, sir. I'm waiting for someone here. Could you please mail this letter for me?" If subjects said, "What?" or "Huh?" the question was repeated, or it was further explained that the experimenter was waiting for a friend, and wanted the letter to be mailed as soon as possible as it was an important letter. If the subject said, "Why don't you mail it yourself?" the experimenter repeated that he was waiting for someone where he was standing, and that he could not leave as he might miss his rendezvous.

Each letter was coded and the letters were addressed to the experimenter's headquarters, so that the ultimate disposition of each letter by each subject could finally be ascertained. For the half of the letters which were stamped at the foreign air mail rate on air mail envelopes, this was the full procedure. For the other half of the envelopes which were unstamped, the procedure was modified slightly: (*a*) If the subject did not notice that there was no stamp on the envelope, nothing was said; (*b*) for half of the subjects given unstamped envelopes (one-fourth of the total N) the experimenter looked for a stamp if the subject pointed out that there was no stamp on the envelope. The experimenter "failed" to find a stamp, and offered the subject cash for the amount of postage; (*c*) for the other half of the subjects given unstamped envelopes (one-fourth of the total N), the experimenter never spontaneously offered the cash amount of the postage. Cash was only given if the subject himself asked for it or suggested that possibility.

Experiment III: Falsely Claiming Money

In the first experiment (Asking for Directions), cooperativeness was exhibited by accurately telling a stranger how to get to his destination. In Experiment I, behavior was labeled "antisocial" only when it seemed quite clear that the strangers were *mis*directed *with intent* (see Results). There was no material profit for the subject. We can only speculate as to the "satisfaction" attained by directing a strange compatriot or foreigner into a cul-de-sac. In Experiment III, the subject had the opportunity to materially profit by falsely claiming money from the stranger. The experimenter approached the subject and asked if he had just dropped a five franc note (or an appropriate Greek or United States currency). Actually, the subject had not dropped the money.

Experimenters. Two male experimenters were used in each city, a compatriot and a foreigner (see Table 9.2).

The compatriot and the foreigner both addressed the subjects in the native language of the city involved. As in Experiment II, the accent of the foreigners was extremely obvious and the citizens of each country had no difficulty in establishing that the foreigner was indeed foreign, although his true identity was not always accurately perceived. This was determined through a number of interviews with the subjects after the termination of the experiment.

Selection of subjects. Subject selection was the same as in Experiments I and II. The fourth man coming toward the experimenter *and passing him* was the automatic and compulsory choice of the experimenter as the next subject. When the experimenter completed the experimental procedure with the subject, he recorded the outcome on tape or on a data sheet and began the same procedure to select a new subject.

Location. The site of the experimental procedure was the same as in Experiment I.

Procedure. As in Experiments I and II, each subject was classified into one of three categories according to the clothes he wore at the time of the experimental episode.

Table 9.2
Experimenters Used in Each City—
Experiments II, III and IV

	Es	
CITY	COMPATRIOT	FOREIGNER
Paris	French	American
Athens	Greek	American
Boston	American	French

Two sets of experimenters operated at each location at matched times of the day. After subject selection, the experimenter came up from behind the subject and said, "Excuse me, sir. Did you just drop this dollar bill?" The subject's behavior and his positive or negative response were noted on the data sheet along with notation of his dress classification.

For half of the subjects in each city (total $N = 160$ in each city) the approximate equivalent at the current exchange rate of $1 was offered. For the other half of the subjects, the note of the next highest denomination existent was used (see Table 9.3).

A set of interviews was obtained with some "typical" subjects *following* the experimental procedure. No subjects knew that they were involved in an experimental episode, and none of the interviewed subjects knew that they had been interviewed. The interview procedure was conducted so as to obtain the subjects' perceptions of the experimental episode which had just transpired about a quarter minute before. The interviewer walked along the crowded street, and positioned himself to be walking beside the subject just as the experimental episode terminated. When a subject took the money from an experimenter and walked on, the interviewer, who was then walking next to the subject, turned to the subject and said, "Hey, is that guy giving money away?" Almost all subjects approached in this manner then proceeded to give their version of the experimental episode. The interviewer, after listening to the subject's story and asking a few probe questions, walked away and recorded the conversation to the best of his recollection.

Table 9.3
Amount of Money Used in Each City: Experiment III

	MONEY USED	
CITY	LOWER AMOUNT	HIGHER AMOUNT
Paris	5 F[a]	10 F
Athens	20 DR[b]	50 DR
Boston	$1	$5

[a]5 francs = $1 (1966).
[b]20 drachmas = $.66 (1966).

Experiment IV: Cashier Experiment

In making a variety of small purchases, a few "pennies" over the actual cost were added to the payment by the experimenter, who then slowly left the store. The amount of overpayment actually was from one-fourth to one-third of the total purchase. The behavior of the cashier in keeping or returning the overpayment to the experimenter was recorded. In Experiment III (Falsely Claiming Money) above, the subject had to overtly *take* the money which did not belong to him. In this situation, he only had to tacitly accept the overpayment.

Experimenters. Two male experimenters were used in each city, a compatriot and a foreigner. The compatriot and foreigner both addressed the sales person and cashier in the native language of the city involved.

Selection of shops and subjects. One necessity in this experiment was to make a relatively large number of purchases on a relatively small budget. Pastry shops were prevalent in large numbers in all three cities and in all sections of each city, and relatively good guides were available to compile complete lists of *all* of the pastry shops in each city from which random samples were drawn. Details of sampling are given in Feldman (1967). Thirty-nine percent of all shops were sampled in Paris, 31 percent in Athens, and 18 percent in Boston.

Procedure. The experimenter entered the shops selected in the random sample and requested an item or items which cost approximately 20 cents. Where the price was not known, an item (or items) was chosen which the experimenter estimated to cost about 20 cents. After being told the total cost of his purchase, the experimenter paid that amount *plus* about 25 percent above the total cost of the purchase. For the total cost of 20 cents, for example, the experimenter paid the cashier 5 nickles (25 cents). He then gave the cashier a chance to count the money and slowly began to walk out of the pastry shop. The behavior of the cashier was observed and recorded as soon as the experimenter had left the premises. The main measure was whether or not the cashier returned the overpayment.

Experiment V: Taxicab Charges

Some taxicab drivers have a reputation for taking passengers to the destination via indirect and longer routes, and for overcharging people who appear to be unfamiliar with the vicinity. This study investigated whether or not compatriots and foreigners were charged the same fare over identical routes.

Experimenters. Two male experimenters were used in each city, a compatriot and a foreigner (see Table 9.3).

Subjects. Cabs were "hailed" in different parts of the city. A number of identical cab drivers were used as subjects for both the compatriot and the foreigner. Sixty rides were taken in Paris, 42 in Athens, and 44 in Boston; half by compatriot and half by foreigner.

Location. Most of the taxi rides in each of the three cities were taken from one public place to another. Many locations were matched in each city—for example, railroad stations, the stock exchange, a post office, an observatory, a hospital, and a sports stadium. A few addresses of private residences were also used. A complete listing for each city is presented in Feldman (1967). The beginning points for each of the individual rides taken by compatriot and foreigner were always identical, but there were occasions when the foreigner was not taken to the destination requested.

Procedure. Compatriot and foreigner did the experiment at the same time of day, and within minutes of each other in each of the three cities. The compatriot addressed the taxicab driver in his native language. The foreigner did not *directly* ask for the location to which he was going. Rather, he handed the taxi driver a slip of paper with his destination written on it in script by a compatriot and read the destination location from the slip of paper. First, one of the two experimenters would hail a cab, and after he had left the starting location, the other experimenter would hail another cab to the same location. At times it was possible for the first of the experimenters to hail the cab which had just deposited the second experimenter. Thus it was possible for the compatriot experimenter to hear a taxicab driver's remarks about the foreign experimenter who was the previous rider in that taxi. The main dependent variable was the cost of the ride to the compatriot as compared to the foreigner.

Experimental Findings

RESULTS OF EXPERIMENT I: ASKING FOR DIRECTIONS

Behavior toward foreigners versus compatriots. Both the Parisian and Athenian samples gave help more often at the request of fellow citizens than at the request of foreigners. Use of native versus a foreign language was a contributing factor (see Table 9.4). In Boston there was no large difference between the treatment of the American compatriots and the French foreigners. Asking for directions in French made little difference in the way Bostonians treated Frenchmen.

Forty-five percent of the Parisian sample either did not give directions at the request of the foreigners, or directed them the wrong way if they did stop, compared with 24 percent who refused to stop at the request of fellow citizens. Thirty-six percent of the Athenian sample either did not give directions at the request of the foreigners, or gave them false directions, compared with 32 percent toward fellow citizens. Twenty percent of the Bostonian sample did not give directions at the request of the foreigners or sent them the wrong way. This was about the same as the treatment of the American compatriots (21 percent). The Bostonians were more helpful in terms of giving directions and accuracy toward foreigners (80 percent) than either the Athenian (64 percent; $p <$ .001) or the Parisian samples (55 percent; $p < .001$). The Parisian and Athenian samples differed by 9 percent ($.10 < p < .20$).

Table 9.4

Information Given to Foreigner in Each City

	INFORMATION GIVEN			
GROUP	DID NOT GIVE DIRECTIONS TO COMPATRIOTS	DID NOT GIVE DIRECTIONS TO FOREIGNERS	GAVE FALSE DIRECTIONS TO COMPATRIOTS	GAVE FALSE DIRECTIONS TO FOREIGNERS
Paris[a]	24	35	0	10
In French		31		
In English		40		
Athens[b]	26	33	6	3
In Greek		29		
In English		37		
Boston[c]	17	15	4	5
In English		13		
In French		17		

NOTE: The foreigners asked for directions in the language of the city and in a foreign language. Figures given are in percentages.
[a]$N = 401.$
[b]$N = 551.$
[c]$N = 422.$

Accuracy of directions. In Paris, the compatriots were never given inaccurate directions, but the foreigners were directed the wrong way 10 percent of the time ($p < .001$). The misunderstanding of the foreigner was ruled out for the case of the foreigner using the native language of the city because all responses were tape-recorded and the subjects clearly *repeated* the name of the target location. Bostonians gave equally accurate directions to compatriots versus foreigners (96 percent versus 95 percent). The Athenians gave more accurate directions to foreigners than compatriots, but the null hypothesis is not rejected ($.10 < p < .20$).

Socioeconomic classification. Giving help in the Parisian sample was positively related to higher socioeconomic classification ($p < .001$). This was also true for the Athenian sample ($p < .01$). The null hypothesis could not be rejected for the Boston sample ($.05 < p < .10$).

Observations. The experiment received considerably more attention in Athens than in either Paris or Boston. In Paris and Boston the experiment proceeded with relative anonymity. In Athens, sales personnel in the stores observed experimenters asking for directions, and on one occasion, a saleslady came out to the street and told a subject not to respond because the experimenters had already asked someone else. The subject responded, but the experimenters had to move from Stadiou Street to Venizelou Street. In all three cities, the foreigners were sometimes asked where they were from, but only in Athens was the compatriot asked this. One subject maintained that he was a countryman of the Greek compatriot experimenter (it was not true) and offered the experimenter five drachmas to go where he wanted by bus.

RESULTS OF EXPERIMENT II:
DOING A FAVOR FOR A STRANGER

The main measure here was whether or not people would take the letter from the foreigner or compatriot stranger. Except for the socioeconomic dress classification of the subjects, other measures did not prove especially interesting. Virtually all of the letters accepted by the men in the subway were mailed. In general, more people took the stamped envelopes than the envelopes without stamps. The only exception to this was the treatment of the foreigner in Athens where there was no difference (Table 9.5).

Base line: Treatment of the compatriot. The treatment of the compatriot in Boston and Paris did not differ significantly, varying between 32 and 35 percent, but the treatment of the compatriot for both cities differed significantly from the treatment in Athens ($p <$ .001), where 93 percent of the Athenian sample refused to mail a letter for a fellow-Greek.

Treatment of the foreigner. Although compatriots were treated about the same in Boston and Paris, this was clearly not so for the foreigners we have studied. The Parisians treated the American foreigner significantly better than the total sample of Bostonians treated the French foreigner, helping 69 percent versus 51 percent ($p < .01$). This is clearly at odds with part of the American stereotype of the Parisian's behavior toward the American. In fact, the American received exactly the same level of cooperation in Boston

Table 9.5
Percentage Refusing to Mail a Letter for a Compatriot versus a Foreigner

CITY	REFUSAL TO COMPATRIOT		REFUSALS TO FOREIGNER	
	WITH STAMPED LETTER	WITH UNSTAMPED LETTER	WITH STAMPED LETTER	WITH UNSTAMPED LETTER
Paris	32[a]	38[b]	12[a]	44[b]
	(73)	(81)	(57)	(89)
Athens	88[c]	97[d]	52[c]	51[d]
	(33)	(36)	(35)	(33)
Boston	15[e]	44[f]	25[e]	60[f]
	(59)	(90)	(55)	(125)

NOTE: Total $N = 765$ (ns in parentheses).
[a] $\chi^2 = 5.82$, $p < .05$. These cells differ from the findings in the other experiments.
[b] $\chi^2 = .33$, ns.
[c] $\chi^2 = 7.21$, $p < .01$.
[d] $\chi^2 = 14.30$, $p < .001$.
[e] $\chi^2 = .84$, ns.
[f] $\chi^2 = 4.84$, $p < .05$.

and in Paris. The Frenchman, on the other hand, was refused help by 36 percent of his compatriots, but by 49 percent of the Bostonians. Bostonians and Athenians did not treat the foreigner significantly differently, not helping him 49 percent and 52 percent of the time. The treatment of the foreigner in Paris was significantly better than the treatment of the foreigner in Athens ($p < .01$).

Paris. Summing across all 300 subjects studied in Paris during Experiment II, there was no significant difference in the treatment of compatriot and foreigner, but for subclasses of these subjects in Paris, and for subparts of the experiment, differences did appear. In the experimental paradigm in which Parisians were asked to mail a letter *which was stamped,* the American foreigner actually received better treatment than the French compatriot ($p < .05$; see Table 9.5). As the amount of cooperation requested was increased, however, from just mailing a letter to providing a stamp or buying one, the amount of cooperation exhibited toward the American decreased considerably, and at this level there was no significant difference between the treatment of the American foreigner and the French compatriot (see Table 9.5). The proportion of those who refused to help the American foreigner increased from 12 percent when aid was to mail a stamped letter to 44 percent when asked to mail an unstamped letter. This 44 percent refusal rate is exactly the same as the American is accorded under the same circumstances in Boston (see Table 9.5). Although no difference was reported between the treatment of the compatriot and the American foreigner who asked Parisians to mail letters without stamps, there was an important difference which suggests that the Frenchman was better received than the American when the demand of the stranger was increased. Only 12 percent (6/50) took money from their compatriot to mail the unstamped letter, but 44 percent (22/50) took money from the foreigner. In the condition in which the subject himself had to ask for money in order to receive it 36 percent of the Parisians (9/25) asked the American foreigner for the money, but none of the Parisians asked his compatriot for the money.

Socioeconomic classification. As in Experiment I, prosocial behavior declined with lower socioeconomic dress classification ($p < .01$; see Table 9.6). Parisians in the highest socioeconomic classification treated the American foreigner better than any other subsample in this entire experiment, with only 6 percent of these subjects refusing to help the foreigner when asked to mail a stamped letter. When we look at the lowest class, however, we find that the refusal rate has gone up to 50 percent. In the experiment without stamps the rate of refusal rose from 34 percent for Class 1 to 71 percent and 70 percent for Classes 2 and 3, respectively. These class differences relative to the treatment of the foreigner are not duplicated with regard to the treatment of the compatriot. Here the relationship appears more complex, particularly in the condition without stamps, where a curvilinear relationship appears. The middle-class subjects treat their compatriot considerably better than the upper or lower classification (see Table 9.6). The question of money rarely arose in the case of the French compatriot without stamped letters.

Athens. The compatriot is treated overwhelmingly worse in Ath-

Table 9.6
Treatment of Foreigner and Compatriot by Socioeconomic Dress Class of Subjects: Paris

GIVE HELP	CLASS		
	1	2	3
FOREIGNER WITH STAMPED LETTERS[a]			
Yes	94	88	50
FOREIGNER WITH UNSTAMPED LETTERS[b]			
Yes	66	29	30
COMPATRIOT WITH STAMPED LETTERS[c]			
Yes	76	61	65
COMPATRIOT WITH UNSTAMPED LETTERS[d]			
Yes	52	76	53

NOTE: In percentages.
[a]$n = 56$.
[b]$n = 89$.
[c]$n = 74$.
[d]$n = 81$.

ens than in either Paris or Boston. The foreigner, on the other hand, was treated about the same as the foreigner in Boston, but significantly worse than the foreigner in Paris. In spite of the fact that the foreigner is treated worse here than in Paris or Boston, the Athenians treated a foreigner better than a compatriot. Across all subjects in this experiment in Athens ($N = 137$), 52 percent of the Athenian subjects refused to help the foreigner, but 93 percent of the Athenian subjects refused to help a compatriot ($p < .001$). This finding remained in the paradigm with stamps ($p < .01$) and without stamps ($p < .001$; see Table 9.5). Since nearly all the Athenians refused to help their compatriot in this experiment, it is not possible to discriminate their behavior as a function of class. Table 9.7 suggests that under the condition of highest demand the lowest class may be the most helpful toward the foreigner, but the very small number of subjects who fell into cells of Class 1 and

Table 9.7
Treatment of Foreigner by Socioeconomic Dress Class of
Subjects: Athens

	CLASS		
GIVE HELP	1	2	3
WITH STAMPED LETTERS[a]			
Yes	40	57	25
WITH UNSTAMPED LETTERS[b]			
Yes	20	48	71

NOTE: In percentages.
[a]$n = 35$.
[b]$n = 33$.

Class 3 in this condition prevent us from meaningfully resorting to
tests of significance. In this condition, the Greek compatriot was
never able to get to the point of offering money to the subjects for
the unstamped letter. Refusals were quite blunt and adamant. Fifty-
six percent took money from the American foreigner when asked
to mail the letter.

Boston. As noted above, the Bostonians ($N = 328$) treated the
French foreigner significantly worse than the American compatriot
($p < .01$), helping 51 and 68 percent of the time, respectively.
This was true for the condition without stamps ($p < .05$; see Table
9.5). For the condition with stamps the foreigner is treated worse
by 10 percent of the Bostonians, but the difference was not statistically significant.

The association between behavior and dress classification of the
Bostonians was not statistically significant, but it is clear that the
Bostonians in the lowest class accorded the French foreigner the
worst treatment. In the paradigm with stamps, 18 percent of the
subjects in Class 1 refused to help. Twenty-two percent of the subjects in Class 2 refused, and 45 percent of the subjects in Class 3
refused. In the condition without stamps, 59 percent of the Class 1
subjects refused, 56 percent of the Class 2 subjects refused, and 70
percent of the Class 3 subjects refused. For all paradigms and five

of the six class comparisons the Bostonians treated the French foreigner worse than the American compatriot (see Table 9.8).

RESULTS OF EXPERIMENT III: FALSELY CLAIMING MONEY

The main dependent variable in Experiment III was whether the subject would falsely claim money from a stranger. Interviews following the experimental procedure indicated that the desired social context was established. This experiment did not establish differences between the treatment of the compatriot and foreigner within cities, but did show differences between cities and between socioeconomic classifications within cities. Since there were only 160 subjects in each city sample for this experiment, and since the actual number of subjects who falsely claimed money never exceeded 16 percent in any city, the actual number of subjects who falsely claimed money was quite low—too low to meaningfully compare the treatment of compatriot versus foreigner within cities.

Table 9.8
Treatment of Foreigner and Compatriot by Socioeconomic Dress Class of Subjects: Boston

	CLASS		
GIVE HELP	1	2	3
FOREIGNER WITH STAMPED LETTERS[a]			
Yes	82	78	55
FOREIGNER WITH UNSTAMPED LETTERS[b]			
Yes	41	44	30
COMPATRIOT WITH STAMPED LETTERS[c]			
Yes	60	56	52
COMPATRIOT WITH UNSTAMPED LETTERS[d]			
Yes	60	56	52

NOTE: In percentages.
[a] $n = 55$.
[b] $n = 125$.
[c] $n = 59$.
[d] $n = 90$.

The best treatment accorded a stranger was in Paris where 6 percent of the Parisians falsely took money from their compatriot or the American foreigner. The next best treatment accorded the stranger was in Athens where 13 percent took money falsely, and the worst treatment was shown the stranger in Boston, where 17 percent of the people kept the money. Such differences should not be expected to occur by chance ($p < .05$).

Over all subjects, conditions, and cities there was a trend for the proportion of takers to decrease as the amount of money increased. However, the trend is only large enough to amount to a suggestion that needs further testing (see Table 9.9). An alternative hypothesis still compatible with the data is that people are less likely to

Table 9.9
Proportion of People Falsely Claiming Money: Summary

E	LOWER AMOUNT[a]	HIGHER AMOUNT[b]
PARIS (6 PERCENT KEPT MONEY)		
American foreigner	5	0
	(40)	(40)
French compatriot	8	10
	(40)	(40)
ATHENS (13 PERCENT KEPT MONEY)		
American foreigner	15	12
	(40)	(40)
Greek patriot	12	10
	(40)	(39)
BOSTON (17 PERCENT KEPT MONEY)		
French foreigner	27	11
	(41)	(36)
American compatriot	10	18
	(40)	(40)

NOTE: The observed frequencies of people keeping the money in the three cities differed from the expected frequencies. $\chi^2 = 7.15$, $p < .05$ (n's in parentheses). Figures in percentages.

[a]Paris: 5 francs; Athens: 20 drachmas; Boston: 1 dollar.
[b]Paris: 10 francs; Athens: 50 drachmas; Boston: 5 dollars.

falsely claim larger amounts of money from foreigners than from compatriots. A larger quota of subjects who falsely claim the money must be obtained before this can be determined. A comparison of the lower of the two amounts of money offered to the men in each city is interesting. Five percent of the Parisian sample took five francs from the American foreigner. Fifteen percent of the Athenian sample took twenty drachmas from the American foreigner. Twenty-seven percent of the Bostonian sample took one dollar from the French foreigner.

As in Experiment II, the American stereotype of the Parisian treating the American foreigner unfairly was not confirmed in comparison with how the Bostonian treated a fellow citizen under the same circumstances (see Table 9.9). The Bostonians falsely took the money from 14 percent of their American compatriots, but the Parisians falsely took the money 2.5 percent of the time from the American foreigner. Although differences were not large, the Parisian population was the only one which treated the foreigner better than the compatriot.

Socioeconomic classification. The lower the class, the higher the proportion of "takers." For the treatment of foreigners in each city, in spite of the *very small* absolute number of takers in the experiment, this relationship is clear (see Table 9.10). This tendency of the lower-class people to take the money which did not belong to them also appeared in the treatment of the compatriot (see Table 9.10).

RESULTS OF EXPERIMENT IV: CASHIER STUDY

No differences were found between the treatment of compatriot and foreigner in Paris, Athens, or Boston. In Paris, 54 percent kept the money from both. In Athens, the overpayment was not returned to the compatriot 50 percent and the foreigner 51 percent of the time. In Boston, the money was kept 38 percent from the compatriot and 27 percent from the foreigner.

RESULTS OF EXPERIMENT V: TAXI CHARGES

In neither Boston nor Athens was the foreigner overcharged significantly more often than the compatriot, and the compatriot never believed that he was ever taken by any other than the most direct

Table 9.10

Percentage Falsely Claiming Money: Socioeconomic Dress Classification of Subjects

	CLASS		
CITY	1	2	3
FALSELY CLAIMING MONEY FROM FOREIGNERS			
Paris	2	0	14
	(44)	(29)	(7)
Athens	12	13	25
	(42)	(30)	(8)
Boston	7	21	50
	(29)	(38)	(10)
FALSELY CLAIMING MONEY FROM COMPATRIOTS			
Paris	3	10	20
	(36)	(29)	(15)
Athens	0	11	28
	(14)	(54)	(11)
Boston	13	16	12
	(23)	(31)	(26)

NOTE: n's in parentheses.

route known to the driver. In Paris, however, the American foreigner *was* overcharged significantly more often then the French compatriot, in a variety of ingenious ways ($p < .02$; see Table 9.11). The cases of equal fares were divided equally between "more" and "less" categories.

The compatriot in Paris was generally taken by the most direct route to his destination. The foreigners in both Athens and Boston believed that they were always taken by a direct route, and that the driver did not attempt to take advantage of them. This was confirmed by a number of discussions with the drivers. The taxi drivers in Paris had a wide variety of techniques for increasing the fare to the American foreigner. Some drivers gave the wrong change and suggested what amount the tip ought to be (eliminating the possibility that they were including the tip in the total fare). Some drivers began the ride with the meter reading continuing from their

Table 9.11
Taxi Charges Across Cities: Charges to the Foreigner
Compared with the Compatriot

	PAYMENT OF THE FOREIGNER		
CITY	MORE	EQUAL	LESS
Paris	18*	7	5
Athens	10	2	9
Boston	9	10	3

NOTE: No significant differences were found between the treatment of the compatriot and the foreigner in Boston or Athens.
*$p < .02$.

previous fare. Occasionally drivers hung a rag over the meter after the foreigner entered the taxi and said that the meter was not working. Some drivers misread meters which were outside of the cab out of the direct view of the passenger. One driver drove the foreigner kilometers out of the way and abandoned the passenger a number of kilometers away from the destination written on the slip of paper handed to him. The driver incorrectly insisted that this was the correct location, pointing to a nonexistent sign for confirmation.

A number of drivers in Boston expressed verbal hostility toward Frenchmen in conversation with the American compatriot; one even said that he would "take" (cheat) any Frenchmen riding in his cab. As a matter of fact, however, this Boston driver was entirely honest with the French rider, took him by the most direct route and charged him the correct fare.

Discussion and Conclusions

Data on over 3,000 subjects in the 5 field experiments revealed consistent differences in the treatment of compatriots and foreigners in different sociocultural environments. In general, when a difference was observed, the Athenians treated the foreigner better than the compatriot, but Parisians and Bostonians treated compatriots better than foreigners. We could, however, also differentiate socioeconomic correlates within the cities studied. This means that we can do considerably better than speak of Parisians, Athenians, and

Bostonians in sweeping terms. We can make meaningful statements about subgroups of these populations.

DIMENSIONS OF COOPERATION

We can also elaborate on the concept of cooperation, which the five experiments were intended to operationally define. It would appear that cooperation is a multidimensional concept. One dimension is related to the role of the subject from whom cooperative behavior is solicited. Is the subject approached in a casual situation or in an occupational context? The first three experiments were designed to measure cooperation in casual encounters and the last two to measure it in occupational encounters, where, presumably, modes of response were more narrowly circumscribed by role. A second dimension is related to the nature of the cooperative act required of the subject. Did the experimenter seek a favor from the subject or simply a discrimination between right and wrong? The first two experiments involved "doing a favor" for a stranger, while the last three involved a choice between honesty and "cheating." The first two were personal nonfinancial transactions, while the last three involved money and were, therefore, to some extent less personal.

Thus far, the nature of the cooperative act is a better indicator of the conditions under which populations discriminate between compatriot and foreigner than is the fact that the encounter is casual or occupational. Across the five experiments in each of the three cities, the casual encounter condition discriminated between compatriot and foreigner 33 percent of the time, and occupational encounter, 17 percent. The difference in discrimination related to whether the subject was asked to perform a personal favor or to choose between right and wrong was larger. The "doing a favor for a stranger" experiments discriminated 50 percent of the time, while the honesty experiments discriminated in only 11 percent of the cases. Subjects were more likely to treat compatriots different from foreigners when they were asked to provide a personal service than when they were required to enter into a monetary transaction.

INGROUP–OUTGROUP CONCEPTUALIZATION

We have indicated above that situational factors seem to affect the differential treatment of foreigners and compatriots in different sociocultural environments. Attitudinal factors prior to and operating within the experimental encounter also seem important. Our data provide some behavioral confirmation for the role differential method of Triandis et al. (1967) and an extension of their ingroup–outgroup conceptualization from role perception to overt social behavior.

Athens. Triandis et al. (1967) defined the ingroup in Greece to include: family, friends, friends of friends, and tourists, "who are treated as members of the ingroup because of an age-long hospitality norm which is an important aspect of the culture." Our data tend to substantiate this definition and to confirm a second hypothesis that members of the upper class have a more inclusive definition of the ingroup than members of the middle and lower social classes.

In our experiments, when Athenians discriminated between strange compatriot and foreigner, the Greek compatriot received worse treatment than the foreigner. Data on the role differential (Triandis et al., 1967) indicated that suspicion and hostility characterize behavior toward outgroup members, while cooperation and concern over welfare characterize behavior toward ingroup members. The hostility expressed by Athenians toward Greek compatriots thus suggests that native strangers were defined as outgroup members while foreign tourists, in line with the hypothesis of Triandis et al., were defined as (temporary) members of the ingroup.

Field reports provide supporting observations regarding outgroup discrimination in Greece. Lee (1953) noted that Greek cooperation is obtained by personal loyalty and that Greeks do not respond to an impersonal plea from another Greek. Sanders (1962) has asserted "that the Greeks cooperate only in a crisis." Among the historical events likely to leave behind suspicion and fratricidal hostility was the mass removal of over 23,000 Greek children from the country during the Greek Civil War of 1944–1949 (cf. Report of United Nations Balkan Commission, Dec., 1948, in O'Ballance, 1966). Arnhoff, Leon, and Lorge (1964) found that 78 percent of a Greek student sample believed that "old people are suspicious of others," but only 38 percent of United States college students believed this ($p < .01$). Triandis (1965) also found that Greeks claimed to trust Americans even more than Americans see themselves as being trusted by Greeks.

In Experiment I, upper-class Greeks were more often helpful to the foreigner than were lower-class Greeks. There was also a tendency in this direction in Experiment III. In Experiment II (mailing a letter for an American foreigner), however, there was a tendency for the lower-class subjects to give better treatment than the upper-class subjects. The strong rural tradition of hospitality to the foreigner may help explain this finding. If it is true that lower-class subjects in Experiment II were closer to rural origins than middle- or upper-class subjects, we might have a plausible explanation of the preferential treatment by the lower-class Athenian subjects. Subjects in this experiment were specifically asked to go out of their way to assist the foreigner. This was not true in Experiment I, where saying a few words accommodated the foreigner, and was not true of Experiments III, IV, or V, where the subjects were presented with the opportunity for material gain if they took advantage of the American foreigner.

Paris. Role differential data are not available for a Parisian sample. Pitts (1957) has suggested that the Frenchman is likely to snub an outgroup member whenever possible to demonstrate his superiority over that person, but Pitts' suggested definition of the ingroup is generally restricted to the family circle, and data reported here imply that there is a broader definition of the ingroup, at least for the Parisian upper class. The restricted definition of the ingroup may hold, however, for some subgroups of the Parisian population. Examples would include taxi drivers and lower-class men.

Antisocial behavior toward Americans is not an all-pervasive phenomenon in Paris. It is more manifest under some types of situations than others. In Experiments II (Doing a Favor for a Stranger) and III (Falsely Claiming Money) the Parisians treated the American foreigner better than the Americans in Boston treated a Frenchman. On the other hand, when Americans in Paris have occasion to ask for directions and to use taxis, they are likely to encounter uncooperative behavior and to be cheated by the taxi drivers of Paris. Although these two social contexts are typical of encounters which some American foreigners are likely to have with Frenchmen, interactions in other social contexts and comparisons with how the American is treated in Boston warn us against sweeping generalizations about "the Frenchman."

Boston. Defining the ingroup for Bostonians as "people like me" (Triandis et al., 1967) helps explain some of the discrimination against the French foreigner. The experimenters were upper middle class in appearance and were treated better by subjects in the upper class than in Class 2 or 3. Varying the appearance of the experimenters would help determine the effect of status disparity between the subjects and the stranger who approached them upon the treatment of the stranger. By doing this we could specify the range of the "people like me" category for different social classes, and determine how status disparity has contributed to our finding and the suggestion of Triandis et al. (1967) that upper classes in general have a more inclusive definition of the ingroup. The fact that a language other than English was the mother tongue of any Bostonians may have helped label the French-speaking foreigner as someone "like me." Throughout Experiment I it was observed that many of the Bostonians had foreign accents. This may account for the special consideration showed to the Frenchman who asked for directions in French.

OTHER CONSIDERATIONS

Although the correlation of the subjects' behavior with socioeconomic classification was an important finding in this series of experiments, the socioeconomic classification is still a mask for more specific antecedent variables. By identifying populations grossly by the city they live in and by socioeconomic classification or occupational group, we are delimiting some antecedent contingencies presumably encountered by our subjects earlier in their lives. In future research we wish to identify the occasions on which learning of ingroup–outgroup discriminations take place, and then to isolate specific learning patterns which are correlated with differential treatment of compatriot versus foreign strangers. One way to make this easier would be to observe the behavior of people who had a more homogeneous background than the subjects we observed.

REFERENCES

Arnhoff, F. N., Leon, H. F., and Lorge, I. 1964. Cross cultural acceptance of stereotypes toward the aging. *Journal of Social Psychology* 63: 41–58.

Feldman, R. E. 1967. The response to compatriot and foreigner who seek assistance: Field experiments in Paris, Athens, and Boston. Unpublished doctoral dissertation, Harvard University.

Inkeles, A., and Levinson, D. J. 1954. National character: The study of modal personality and sociocultural system. In *Handbook of social psychology,* ed. G. Lindzey, vol. 2. Cambridge: Addison-Wesley.

Lee, D. 1953. Greece. In *Cultural pattern and technical change,* ed. M. Mead. Paris: UNESCO. (Republished 1958. New York: New American Library.)

Milgram, S., Mann, L., and Harter, S. 1965. The lost letter technique: A tool of social research. *Public Opinion Quarterly* 29: 437–38.

O'Ballance, E. 1966. *The Greek civil war, 1944–1949.* New York: Praeger.

Pitts, J. R. 1957. The bourgeois family and French economic retardation. Unpublished doctoral dissertation, Harvard University.

Sanders, I .T. 1962. *Rainbow in the rock: The people of rural Greece.* Cambridge: Harvard University Press.

Triandis, H. C. 1965. An exploratory study of barriers to cooperation between persons belonging to different cultures. University of Illinois. Mimeographed.

Triandis, H. C.; Vassiliou, V.; and Nassiakou, M. 1967. Some cross-cultural studies of subjective culture Technical Report no. 45. Group Effectiveness Research Laboratory, University of Illinois Office of Naval Research.

10. Effect of feeling good on helping: Cookies and kindness   Alice M. Isen and Paula F. Levin

Two experiments with adult subjects investigated the effects of a person's positive affective state on his or her subsequent helpfulness to others. "Feeling good" was induced

Reprinted from the *Journal of Personality and Social Psychology* 21 (1972): 384–88. Copyright 1972 by the American Psychological Association, and reproduced by permission. This research was supported in part by a grant from the Grants Committee of Franklin and Marshall College to the senior author and, in part, by the Department of Psychology, Swarthmore College.

by having received cookies while studying in a library (Study I) and by having found a dime in the coin return of a public telephone while making a call (Study II). In Study I, where the dependent measure involved volunteering in reply to a student's request, a distinction was made between specific willingness to help and general willingness to engage in any subsequent activity. In Study II, the dependent measure was whether subjects spontaneously helped to pick up papers that were dropped in front of them. On the basis of previous research, it was predicted that subjects who were thus made to "feel good" would be more helpful than control subjects. Results support the predictions.

Recent investigations of determinants of helping have begun to focus on the role of mood state in producing differences in helpfulness. The first studies that indicated the relevance of a potential helper's internal affective state used reports of success and failure at a task as their independent variable. A study by Berkowitz and Connor (1966) indicated a relationship between success and helping, when the beneficiary was dependent on the subject. A later study (Isen, 1970) also indicated a link between success and helping, where there was no relationship between the people involved and where helping was a low-cost, naturalistic, behavioral measure. It was postulated that in just such a situation (i.e., nonsolicited, low-cost helping), an important determinant of helpfulness may be the potential helper's positive affective state or "warm glow of success" (Isen, 1970). In addition, even though their success/ failure manipulation was not aimed specifically at affecting internal mood state, Berkowitz and Connor (1966) also made reference to a "glow of goodwill" in their discussion. In both of these studies which suggested that "feeling good" may be a determinant of helping, positive affective state was induced via a report of success. However, report of success may not be an entirely satisfactory way of manipulating mood, since induced affective state may be confounded with estimates of competence.

Several recent studies have indicated that manipulation of affective state in ways other than via success/failure also results in differential helping, thus lending credibility to the hypothesis that a relationship between feeling good and helpfulness does exist. Two naturalistic experiments seem to indicate that good feeling aroused through positive verbal contact results in increased aid, both solicited (Berkowitz & Macaulay, as cited in Aderman, 1971) and non-solicited (Isen, Becker, & Fairchild).[1]

Studies by Aderman (1971) and Aderman and Berkowitz (1970), while conducted in an experimental setting, manipulated mood state in several novel ways. In the Aderman and Berkowitz study, the subject's mood state was varied by having him observe one of several interactions between two male college students, one who needed aid and one who was a potential helper. The experimental condition varied according to the person with whom the subject was instructed to empathize, the helping response of the second person (helped or did not help), and the reaction of the helped person (thanked the helper or did not). The subject then filled out a mood questionnaire and finally was given an opportunity to comply with the experimenter's request for help. The results of the experiment, though complex, tended to support the idea that feeling good can be related to increased helping under some circumstances (empathy with the thanked helper), while feeling bad can be associated with increased helping under other circumstances (empathy with the nonhelped person in need).

In the study by Aderman (1971), elation or depression was induced in subjects by having them read sets of mood statements. Aderman found that following the reading of the cards, subjects in the elation condition wrote more numbers for the experimenter, when this task was presented as a favor rather than a requirement of the experiment. In addition, elation subjects volunteered more often for a future experiment. Such findings do lend credence to the "glow" hypotheses, yet one complexity of the findings is that the "help" was solicited. *164031*

A further question remaining is whether success, or good mood, leads specifically to helping or, more generally, to increased activity and/or productivity. In other words, does the good feeling lead to

1. A. M. Isen, D. M. Becker, and P. Fairchild. Effects of nature of verbal contact on helping. Manuscript in preparation.

an increased desire to do something nice for someone else, or would subjects who have been made to feel good, as opposed to those who have not, engage in more or any subsequent activity?

Using a 2 × 2 design, we performed an experiment that attempted to answer the two questions posed above: First, whether feeling good leads to increased helping; second, whether, following the induction of good feeling, the response to an opportunity to help differs from the response to an opportunity to engage in some other activity. We predicted an interaction between the two independent variables such that those subjects who were feeling good would subsequently be more willing to help but less willing to hinder (distract) than those not made to feel good.

Study I

METHOD

Subjects. The study, which spanned five sessions, was conducted in the libraries of a university and two colleges in the Philadelphia area. Fifty-two male college students who were studying in individual carrels served as subjects.

Procedure. At the beginning of the session, a coordinator randomly assigned rows of carrels to the feeling good or to the neutral condition. The assignment to condition was based on rows, rather than on individuals, in order to insure that subjects would be unaware that two conditions existed.

To induce good mood, confederates distributed cookies along the rows that had been assigned to the feeling good condition, while they merely walked by the rows in the neutral condition. This task was performed by a male and female pair of confederates in two of the sessions and by a female confederate in the remaining three sessions.

The coordinator also randomly divided subjects in each condition into "help" or "hinder" groups. The experimenter was told this assignment of "help" and "distract" subjects, but was kept unaware of whether a particular row was "cookie" or "no cookie." Similarly, the coordinator was careful to withhold from the confederates information as to help or distract condition of the subjects.

A few minutes after the confederates returned following the distribution or nondistribution of cookies, the experimenter approached each subject individually and asked if, and for how many 20-minute sessions, the subject would serve as a confederate in a psychology experiment. In the help condition, the purpose of the experiment was given as an investigation of creativity in students at examination times, as opposed to other times during the year. The confederate was needed in this experiment to act as helper to subjects who would be attempting to conceive of novel uses for ordinary items. The confederate's aid, which involved holding and manipulating the items, was described as "something which the subjects usually found very helpful to them." In the distract condition, the job of the confederate was described as a distractor of a randomly chosen, unwitting student who happened to be studying in the library. As distracter, he would stand near the subject and drop books, make noises, rattle papers, all while the experimenter unobtrusively recorded the subject's reactions. The purpose of such an experiment was given as an investigation of distractibility of students at examination time as opposed to other times during the year. In addition, the experimenter cautioned each subject in the distract condition by saying, "I think it only fair to tell you before you decide to act as distracter, that the subjects find the distraction to be an unpleasant annoyance." Thus, in the help condition the role that the subject was invited to play was clearly that of a helper, one appreciated greatly by the creativity subjects; in contrast, the role that a confederate would play in the distract condition was clearly described as that of an annoying distracter of unsuspecting students studying in the library.

A debriefing and discussion period followed each subject's reply. Subjects' reports indicated that the independent and dependent manipulations were plausible, and that they had not been associated in the subjects' minds prior to the debriefing.

RESULTS

Since the five sessions yielded comparable results, the data were combined. Table 10.1 shows the proportion of subjects volunteering in each condition and the means and variances of number of minutes volunteered. A *t* test for proportions was performed on the number of subjects volunteering in each condition. This test re-

Table 10.1

Study I: Means and Variances of Amount of Time
(in Minutes) Volunteered and Proportion of Subjects
Volunteering in Each Condition

CONDITION	HELP	DISTRACT
COOKIE		
M	69.00	20.00
s^2	6923.08	1400.00
P	.69 (9/13)	.31 (4/13)
NO COOKIE		
M	16.70	78.60
s^2	563.64	11659.34
P	.50 (6/12)	.64 (9/14)

vealed the predicted interaction between receiving a cookie or not
and volunteering to help or to distract. That is, subjects receiving
cookies volunteered to help more, but to distract less, than those not
receiving cookies ($t = 1.96$, $p < .05$).

Analysis of variance of the number of minutes volunteered data
(square root transformation) indicated that the predicted interaction was significant ($F = 7.71$, df = 1, 51, $p < .01$). When subjects received cookies, they volunteered more time to help but less
to distract than did no cookie subjects.

DISCUSSION

The results of this experiment indicate that in terms of both number of subjects volunteering and amount of time volunteered, subjects who have unexpectedly received cookies help more, but distract less, than do those who have not received cookies. Thus,
feeling good, induced naturalistically and in a way other than via
report of success, seems to lead to increased helping, and to helping
specifically, rather than to general activity.

Although this finding provides evidence for the "warm glow"
hypothesis—people who feel good themselves are more likely to
help others—an alternative interpretation is possible. Following
from a modeling or a normative explanation, cookie subjects might
have been more helpful simply because they had just been exposed
to a helpful model (the person passing out the cookies) who may

have reminded them of norms of kindness to others. Furthermore, a few aspects of the dependent measure complicate the warm glow interpretation. Although the independent manipulation was more naturalistic than that found in many experiments, the dependent measure was one of *solicited* helpfulness. In addition, help was only volunteered, rather than actually performed.

Thus, a second study was conducted to determine whether non-solicited, low-cost helpfulness increases following the induction of good feeling, without the good mood being directly brought about by another person. The question was, Does feeling good lead to increased helping, even if there is no helpful model? In the "dime" study, which is directed at this question and which is presented below, good feeling was induced in a subject by the discovery of an unexpected dime in the coin return slot of a pay telephone. The dependent measure was that of helping a young woman pick up papers which she had just dropped.

Study II

METHOD

Subjects. Subjects were 24 female and 17 male adults who made calls from designated public telephones located in enclosed shopping malls in suburban San Francisco and Philadelphia. Excluded from the subject pool were those shoppers who were not alone and those who were carrying packages.

Procedure. Telephone booths were "set up" in the following manner. The experimenter made an incomplete call, ostensibly took her dime from the return slot, and left the booth. In actuality, the dime was left in the coin return slot for a randomly selected half of these trials. Thus, subjects using such telephones received an unexpected 10 cents when they checked the coin return before, during, or upon completion of their calls; these subjects constituted the experimental group. The control group was made up of individuals who used a telephone that had not been "stocked" with a dime and who therefore did not receive unexpected money.

The experimenter set up the experimental and control telephones without informing the confederate as to condition. This was done in order to eliminate any possible systematic bias in the confederate's performance of the paper dropping. The experimenter also checked to make sure that all subjects did look in the coin return slot. Only a few subjects failed to meet this requirement, and these were not included in the data analysis. This was done in order to avoid ultimately obtaining a sample of subjects which was inadvertently selected for attention. For this reason, no subject who was at an "experimental" condition telephone and simply failed to see his dime was included in the control group.

During the call, the confederate was able to observe the outline of the subject unobtrusively by pretending to "window shop," while actually watching the subject's reflection in one of the store windows. The aim of this surveillance was simply to know when the subject was leaving the telephone. When the subject did leave, the confederate started in the same direction as the subject and, while walking slightly ahead and to the side of him or her, dropped a manila folder full of papers in the subject's path. The dependent measure was whether the subject helped the female confederate pick up the papers.

RESULTS

Table 10.2 shows the number of males and females helping in each condition. A Fisher exact test on the data of the females indicated a significant relationship between getting a dime and helping ($p <$ .005). A similar finding ($p = .025$) was obtained for the males.

DISCUSSION

These results indicate that differential unsolicited helping occurs even when good mood is induced in an impersonal manner. The

Table 10.2
Study II: Number of People Helping in Each Condition

	FEMALES		MALES	
CONDITION	HELPED	DID NOT HELP	HELPED	DID NOT HELP
Dime	8	0	6	2
No dime	0	16	1	8

finding appears to be less pronounced for males than for females, but the smaller number of male subjects may be responsible in part for this apparent difference. Because our society has specific norms applying to this particular helping situation for males, one might have expected the behavior of the males, more than that of females, to reflect not only the independent manipulation but also these norms for courtesy. The data show that while no females in the control condition helped, one male in the same condition did help. However, it must also be noted that two males in the experimental condition failed to help, while no female experimental subjects failed to help. Thus, while it is true that the behavior of the males may be more complex than that of the females, the simple courtesy expectation is not supported.

The results of the two studies taken together provide support for the notion that feeling good leads to helping. Because feeling good has been generated in a variety of ways and settings, and since the type of helping measure and the source of the subject populations have also varied, this relationship seems to have some empirical generality. We recognize, however, that the question of why feeling good leads to helping, or more properly, what mediates the relationship between the two, remains to be answered. Moreover, such an answer may provide some insights into the more general and important issue of how the observed determinants of helping, such as success, feeling good, feeling bad in some circumstances, guilt, verbal contact, and the presence or absence of other people, relate to one another. That is, while these states or events may seem unrelated as determinants of helping, they may have some common aspects in that capacity. If so, then the determination of helping may be more parsimoniously understood in terms of broader concepts, such as maintenance of positive affective state, perception of costs and rewards, or both, and this possibility is now under investigation.

References

Aderman, D. 1971. Effect of prior mood on helping behavior. Unpublished doctoral dissertation, University of Wisconsin.

Aderman, D., and Berkowitz, L. 1970. Observational set, empathy, and helping. *Journal of Personality and Social Psychology* 14: 141–48.

Berkowitz, L., and Connor, W. H. 1966. Success, failure, and social responsibility. *Journal of Personality and Social Psychology* 4: 664–69.

Berkowitz, L., and Macaulay, J. 1971. Ideals, ideas and feelings in help-giving. Unpublished manuscript, University of Wisconsin. Cited by D. Aderman. Effect of prior mood on helping behavior. Unpublished doctoral dissertation, University of Wisconsin.

Isen, A. M. 1970. Success, failure, attention, and reaction to others: The warm glow of success. *Journal of Personality and Social Psychology* 15: 294–301.

6 DECISIONS AND DISSONANCE

We cannot see (i.e., directly observe) a person's confidence, likes, beliefs, preferences, or attitudes; he must tell us in some way. A variety of devices, such as questionnaires, interviews, and choice situations, may be used to determine subject's cognitive behavior, but the usual problem is that he knows he is giving such information. If the subject realizes that he is in some sort of evaluative situation, such as a survey or an experiment, his answers may be very biased. People do not want to reveal personal beliefs and feelings that they feel might make them appear unintelligent, foolish, or bigoted. To overcome such biases experimenters frequently concentrate on designing situations to keep subjects unaware of the exact nature of the information being sought. Sometimes, for example, experimenters are interested in only a few answers, but they bury the questions in long questionnaires. Sometimes information is sought under false pretenses.

The procedure in determining the effects of an independent variable manipulation—say a persuasive communication—on attitude change would be one of measuring a subject's attitudes both before and after the communication (the before-after-within design). The problem, of course, is that persons may be influenced or sensitized by the first measurement, which could contaminate the post-treatment measurement. However, this straightforward method would seem to be the best way to find out whether a person was or was not influenced in that any changes in his stated attitudes are visible. The studies of Walster and Swingle in this section used the before-after-within design.

An alternate design is the before-after-between design used in the Knox and Inkster experiments. This design involves measurement of one group before introduction of the independent variable, followed by measurement of the dependent variable on a second group. Experimental measurement procedures include many such variations designed to control and sometimes to assess subject bias.

It is important to note the different assumptions that underlie each of the designs. In the before-after-within design, for example, it is assumed that the before measurement procedure itself does not influence the after measurement. The before-after-between design involves a different assumption—namely, that the people in each group have been randomly assigned. In effect, therefore, any single subject has an equal chance of being part of either the before or the after group. If the assumption of random assignment is satisfied we usually may assume that differences between the groups will average out.

A design related to the before-after-between is the after-only design. This procedure assumes that people have been randomly assigned to both the treatment and any control conditions such that their before scores on the average would be the same.

The following table lists three of the more common simple designs and one total design. Typically the simple designs include a control group to determine if any change would occur had nothing been done to the subject. For example, the before-after-within (group A) might combine with a group F control.

Consider the comparisons possible in using the total design shown in the table. By comparing the difference between group I^3 and group F^1 with the difference between

Experimental Designs

TIME 1 PRETEST	TIME 2 EXPERIMENTAL TREATMENT	TIME 3 POSTTEST	TYPE
Group A[1]	T	Group A[3]*	Before-after-within
	T	Group B[3] Group C[3]	After only
Group D[1]	T	Group E[3]	Before-after-between
Group F[1] Group G[1] Group H[1]	T T	Group G[3] Group H[3] Group I[3] Group J[3]	Total design

*The superscript denotes testing time. Group A[1], for example, means that group A is tested at time period 1. The T indicates exposure of the group to a treatment condition.

group G[3] and group G[1], we can obtain an estimate of the effects of the pretest on the aftertest. Any differences between groups F[1], G[1], and H[1] would indicate nonrandom assignment, leading us to question the group I results. If group F[1] differs from group J[3] but not from groups H[1] or H[3], we might consider the possibility that time itself makes a difference in the subjects' scores but that this difference is masked by subjects' reactions to pretesting.

Many such comparisons are possible even in this most simple of situations in which only one treatment condition is included. Given, however, that one might want to explore different types or magnitudes of the treatment condition or include more than a single presentation of that treatment with the attendant multiple measurements, the experiment can become too complex to manage as well as wasteful of time and effort. Experimenters normally never use a total design but usually rely instead on the simple designs with a well-planned control condition to check on possible contaminations.

Dissonance Theory

Throughout early childhood training we are taught that our attitudes, behaviors, and opinions must be consistent. That is, things we do must make sense and must not appear to be irrational or erratic. We expect our friends not to do things that are unpleasant for us, and we are suspicious if a person we dislike does something nice for us. We do not expect people who do not believe in God to go to church without a good reason, such as wanting to appear reputable in the community, wanting to sell insurance, or wanting to enjoy the music (but falling asleep during the sermon).

Numerous theories have attempted to formalize these notions of consistency. All of the theories start with the assumption that we have cognitions about our behavior, attitudes, opinions, and beliefs. That is, we have a certain perception of our behavior that includes our intentions or purpose for the behavior and how we think it looks to others. Behaviors and attitudes must be seen by ourselves and by others in our environment as being consistent. We do not cause physical discomfort to friends unless we are fooling around and expect the same treatment in return. We do not lie unless we are being well paid or expect favorable returns from being dishonest, and we do not publicly express inconsistent attitudes, such as believing that free speech is a good thing but speeches that attack or protest government policy should be prohibited.

Cognitive dissonance theory (Festinger, 1957) assumes within the person a basic tendency to maintain consistency in his cognitions about his behaviors, opinions, or beliefs, and cognitions about his environment. When cognitions that are part of the same grouping—that is, related to one another—follow logically from one another, the person is in the equilibrium state of consonance. Dissonance results whenever a person becomes aware that two or more of his cognitions are in conflict. According to the formal theory, dissonance exists any time one cognition in a system logically follows from the obverse of some other cognition in the same system.

Dissonance results when a person is made aware of the logical inconsistency among his cognitions about his behavior, attitudes, and beliefs. A person who must choose between two objects, as in purchasing an automobile, finds that the chosen object increases in attractiveness, whereas the unchosen object is perceived as less attractive. When the choice is between two equally attractive objects, the positive qualities of the unchosen object are dissonant with not choosing the item.

If one can be induced to read persuasive propaganda for a trivial payoff, one is more likely to be persuaded by the propaganda. Objects obtained with effort are perceived as more attractive than objects obtained without effort. Similarly, whenever membership becomes costly in terms of severe initiation rites or high membership fees, the organization tends to be perceived as more attractive than less costly organizations. Then the costliness or effort associated with attaining membership would lead to dissonance if the organization was of only moderate attractiveness. To restore consonance, the organization's attractiveness is enhanced, thereby justifying the cost or effort expended to attain membership status.

The first two articles in this section demonstrate how, once a person is committed to a choice, the chosen alternatives increase in attractiveness. Walster's study also demonstrates the "period of regret" phenomenon in which, after making an irrevocable choice, a person goes through a period of second thoughts about the wisdom of his choice as evidenced by decreased attractiveness of the selected alternative. The third article demonstrates the contrast phenomenon, which can give rise to dissonance-like effects: if a person is exposed to an unpleasant situation, events that follow may seem more pleasant, or objects reassessed after a noxious event may seem more attractive. Since in many dissonance experiments subjects are exposed to unpleasant situations before being asked to rate the attractiveness of objects, events, and the like, some differences attributed to dissonance effects may, in fact, simply result from emotional contrast.

REFERENCE

Festinger, L. 1957. *A theory of cognitive dissonance*. Stanford,
Calif.: Stanford University Press.

11. Postdecision dissonance at post time   Robert E. Knox and James A. Inkster

Two experiments were conducted to investigate postdecisional dissonance reduction processes following a commitment to bet on a horse in the natural and uncontrived setting of a racetrack. In the first study, 69 $2 Win bettors
rated the chance that the horse they had selected would win
the forthcoming race, and 72 other bettors provided ratings
immediately after making a $2 Win bet. On the 7-point
rating scale employed, prebet subjects gave a median rating
of 3.48, which corresponded to a "fair chance of winning";
postbet subjects gave a median rating of 4.81, which corresponded to a "good chance of winning." The general
findings were replicated in a second study in which harness-
race patrons rated how confident they felt about their
selected horse either just before or just after betting. Results
from both studies provide support for Festinger's theory
in a real life setting and indicate that dissonance-reducing
processes may occur very rapidly following commitment
to a decision.

Reprinted from the *Journal of Personality and Social Psychology* 8 (1968):
319–23. Copyright 1968 by the American Psychological Association, and
reproduced by permission. This study was supported by a grant from the
Faculty of Graduate Studies, University of British Columbia.

In the last decade there have been numerous laboratory experiments conducted to test various implications of Festinger's (1957) theory of cognitive dissonance. In spite of sometimes serious methodological faults (cf. Chapanis & Chapanis, 1964), the laboratory evidence as a whole has tended to support Festinger's notions. Confidence in the theory, as Brehm and Cohen (1962) have previously suggested, can now be further strengthened by extending empirical tests from lifelike to real life situations. The present study investigates the effects of postdecision dissonance on bettors in their natural habitat, the racetrack.

Festinger (1957) had originally contended that due to the lingering cognitions about the favorable characteristics of the rejected alternative(s), dissonance was an inevitable consequence of a decision. Subsequently, however, Festinger (1964) accepted the qualification that in order for dissonance to occur, the decision must also have the effect of committing the person. A favorite technique for reducing postdecisional dissonance, according to the theory, is to change cognitions in such a manner as to increase the attractiveness of the chosen alternative relative to the unchosen alternative(s). At the racetrack a bettor becomes financially committed to his decision when he purchases a parimutuel ticket on a particular horse. Once this occurs, postdecisional processes should operate to reduce dissonance by increasing the attractiveness of the chosen horse relative to the unchosen horses in the race. These processes would be reflected by the bettor's expression of greater confidence in his having picked a winner after his bet had been made than before.

In order to test this notion, one need only go to a racetrack, acquire a prebet and postbet sample, and ask members of each how confident they are that they have selected the winning horse in the forthcoming race. The two samples should be independent since the same subjects in a before–after design could contravene the observed effects of dissonance reduction by carrying over consistent responses in the brief interval between pre- and postmeasurements. In essence, this was the approach employed in the two experiments reported here. More formally, the experimental hypothesis in both experiments was that bettors would be more confident of their selected horse just after betting $2 than just before betting.

Experiment I

SUBJECTS

Subjects were 141 bettors at the Exhibition Park Race Track in Vancouver, British Columbia. Sixty-nine of these subjects, the prebet group, were interviewed less than 30 seconds *before* making a $2 Win bet. Seventy-two subjects, the postbet group, were interviewed a few seconds after making a $2 Win bet. Fifty-one subjects, interviewed before the fourth and fifth races, were obtained in the exclusive Clubhouse section. Data from the remaining 90 bettors were collected prior to the second, third, sixth, and seventh races at various betting locations in the General Admission or grandstand area.

No formal rituals were performed to guarantee random sampling, but instead, every person approaching or leaving a $2 Win window at a time when the experimenters were not already engaged in an interview was contacted. Of those contacted, approximately 15 percent refused to cooperate further because they could not speak English, refused to talk to "race touts," never discussed their racing information with strangers, or because of some unexpressed other reason. The final sample consisted of white, Negro, and Oriental men and women ranging in estimated age from the early twenties to late sixties and ranging in style from ladies in fur to shabby old men. The final sample was felt to be reasonably representative of the Vancouver racetrack crowd.

PROCEDURE

The two experimenters were stationed in the immediate vicinity of the "Sellers" window during the 25-minute betting interval between races. For any given race, one experimenter intercepted bettors as they approached a $2 Win window and the other experimenter intercepted different bettors as they left these windows. Prebet and postbet interview roles were alternated with each race between the two experimenters.

The introductory appeal to subjects and instructions for their ratings were as follows:

> I beg your pardon. I am a member of a University of British Columbia research team studying risk-taking behavior. Are you about to

place a $2 Win bet? [Have you just made a $2 Win bet?] Have we already talked to you today? I wonder if you would mind looking at this card and telling me what chance you think the horse you are going to bet on [have just bet on] has of winning this race. The scale goes from 1, a slight chance, to 7, an excellent chance. Just tell me the number from 1 to 7 that best describes the chance that you think your horse has of winning. Never mind now what the tote board or professional handicappers say; what chance do *you* think your horse has?

It was, of course, sometimes necessary to give some of the subjects further explanation of the task or to elaborate further on the cover story for the study.

The scale, reproduced here in Figure 11.1, was prepared on 8½ × 11-inch posterboard. The subjects responded verbally with a number or, in some cases, with the corresponding descriptive word from the scale.

After each prebet rating the experimenter visually confirmed that this subject proceeded directly to a $2 Win window. In the few instances that subjects did wander elsewhere, their data were discarded. No effort was made to collect data in the three frantic minutes of betting just prior to post time.

RESULTS

The median for the 69 subjects in the prebet group was 3.48. In qualitative terms they gave their horse little better than a "fair" chance of winning its race. The median for the 72 subjects in the

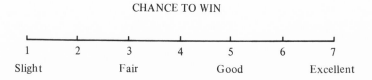

CHANCE TO WIN

| 1 | 2 | 3 | 4 | 5 | 6 | 7 |
| Slight | | Fair | | Good | | Excellent |

Figure 11.1.
The rating scale shown to subjects in the study

postbet group, on the other hand, was 4.81. They gave their horse close to a "good" chance in the race. The median test for the data summarized in Table 11.1 produced a χ^2 of 8.70 ($df = 1$), significant beyond the .01 level.

Table 11.1.

Division of Subjects with Respect to the Overall Median for the Prebet and Postbet Groups: Experiment I

	PREBET GROUP	POSTBET GROUP
Above the *Mdn*	25	45
Below the *Mdn*	44	27

These results, in accord with our predictions from dissonance theory, might also have arisen, however, had a substantial number of bettors simply made last-minute switches from relative long shots to favorites in these races. Although this possibility was not pursued with the above sample of subjects, two follow-up inquiries on another day at the same racetrack indicated that the "switch to favorites" explanation was unlikely. The first of these inquiries involved 38 $2 bettors who were contacted prior to the first race and merely asked if they ever changed their mind about which horse to bet on in the last minute or so before actually reaching a Sellers window. Nine of the 38 indicated that they sometimes changed, but among the 9 occasional changers a clear tendency to switch to long shots rather than to favorites was reported. Additional evidence against a "switch to favorites" explanation was obtained from a sample of 46 bettors for whom the prebet procedure of Experiment I was repeated. Each of these bettors was then contacted by a second interviewer just as he was leaving the $2 Win window and asked if he had changed to a different horse since talking to the first interviewer. All 46 responded that they had not changed horses in midinterviews.

In order to investigate the robustness of the findings in Experiment I a second study was undertaken which was like the first study in its essentials but employed different experimenters, a different response scale, and a different population of subjects. It also provided for a test of the "switch to favorites" explanation among subjects in a postbet group.

Experiment II

Subjects and Procedure

Ninety-four subjects were interviewed at the Patterson Park Harness Raceway in Ladner, British Columbia. Forty-eight of these subjects, the prebet group, were interviewed prior to the first six races as they approached one of the track's four $2 Win windows. This contact was usually completed just a few seconds before the subject actually reached the window to make his bet, but occasionally, when the betting lines were long, up to three-fourths of a minute elapsed between interview and bet. Forty-six subjects, the postbet group, were interviewed a few seconds after leaving one of the $2 Win windows. As in Experiment I, all persons approaching or leaving a $2 Win window at a time when the experimenters were not already engaged were contacted. Of those contacted, fewer than 10 percent refused to cooperate, thus producing a heterogeneous and, presumably, representative sample of $2 Win bettors.

The overall design was the same as in the first study. Two experimenters, different from those who interviewed bettors in Experiment I, were located in the immediate area of the Sellers windows. One of these experimenters would intercept bettors as they approached a $2 Win window and the other intercepted different bettors as they left a $2 Win window. The prebet and postbet interview roles were alternated between the two experimenters as in the first study.

After a brief introductory preamble, the experimenter established whether a bettor was about to make a $2 Win bet (or had just made such a bet) and whether he had been previously interviewed. The experimenters proceeded only with those $2 bettors who had not already provided data. These subjects were then asked to indicate on a 23-centimeter scale how confident they felt that they had picked the winning horse. The mimeographed response scales were labeled with the words "No confidence" at the extreme left and "Complete confidence" at the extreme right. Although no other labels were printed on the scale, the experimenters made explicit that mild confidence would fall in the middle of the scale and ". . . the more confident that a person felt, the further along he should put his mark on the scale." When subjects indicated understanding, they were handed a pencil and a mimeographed scale and directed to ". . . just draw a line across the point in the scale that best corresponds to your own confidence." All bettors in the postbet sample were also asked if they changed their mind about which horse to bet on while waiting in line or while on the way to the window.

Within the limits permitted by extremely crowded conditions, the prebet experimenter visually confirmed that subjects in his sample proceeded to a $2 Win window. Data collection was supended during the last minute before post time.

Confidence scores for each subject were determined by laying a ruler along the 23-centimeter scale and measuring his response to the nearest millimeter.

Table 11.2

Division of Subjects with Respect to the Overall Median for the Prebet and Postbet Groups: Experiment II

	PREBET GROUP	POSTBET GROUP
Above the *Mdn*	19	28
Below the *Mdn*	29	18

RESULTS

The median rating for the 48 subjects in the prebet group was 14.60, and for the postbet group it was 19.30. The median test for these data, summarized in Table 11.2, produced a χ^2 of 4.26 ($df = 1$), significant at less than the .05 level.

Since data in Experiment II might reasonably be assumed to satisfy interval scale assumptions, a *t* test between pre- and postbet means was also performed. The difference between the prebet mean of 14.73 and the postbet mean of 17.47 was also significant ($t = 2.31$, $p < .05$).

No subject in the postbet sample indicated that he had changed horses while waiting in line or, if there was no line, just before reaching the window.

Discussion

These studies have examined the effects of real life postdecisional dissonance in the uncontrived setting of a racetrack. The data furnished by two relatively heterogeneous samples of bettors strongly support our hypothesis derived from Festinger's theory. The reaction of one bettor in Experiment I well illustrates the overall effect observed in the data. This particular bettor had been a subject in the prebet sample and had then proceeded to the pari-mutuel window to place his bet. Following that transaction, he approached the postbet experimenter and volunteered the following:

> Are you working with that other fellow there? [indicating the prebet experimenter who was by then engaged in another interview] Well, I just told him that my horse had a fair chance of winning. Will you have him change that to a good chance? No, by God, make that an excellent chance.

It might reasonably be conjectured that, at least until the finish of the race, this bettor felt more comfortable about his decision to wager on a horse with an excellent chance than he could have felt about a decision to wager on a horse with only a fair chance. In the human race, dissonance had won again.

The results also bear upon the issue of rapidity of onset of dissonance-reducing processes discussed by Festinger (1964). On the basis of an experiment by Davidson described in that work, Festinger argued that predecisional cognitive familiarity with the characteristics of alternatives facilitated the onset of dissonance reduction. It is reasonable to assume that most bettors in the present studies were informed, to some extent, about the virtues and liabilities of all the horses in a race before making a $2 commitment on one. Since never more than 30 seconds elapsed between the time of commitment at the window and confrontation with the rating task, the present results are consistent with the notion that the effects of dissonance reduction can, indeed, be observed very soon after a commitment is made to one alternative, providing that some information about the unchosen alternatives is already possessed. Furthermore, the exceedingly short time span here suggests that the cognitive reevaluation process could hardly have been very explicit or as deliberate as conscious rationalization.

Finally, these studies, like the earlier Ehrlich, Guttman, Schonbach, and Mills (1957) study, which showed that recent new car buyers preferred to read automobile advertisements that were consonant with their purchase, demonstrate that meaningful tests of dissonance theory can be made in the context of real life situations. Insofar as real life studies are unaffected by contrived circumstances, improbable events, and credibility gaps, they may offer stronger and less contentious support for dissonance theory than their laboratory counterparts. It is also clear that such studies will help to define the range of applicability of the theory in natural settings.

REFERENCES

Brehm, J. W., and Cohen, A. R. 1962. *Explorations in cognitive dissonance.* New York: Wiley.

Chapanis, N. P., and Chapanis, A. 1964. Cognitive dissonance: Five years later. *Psychological Bulletin* 61: 1–22.

Ehrlich, D.; Guttman, I.; Schonbach, P.; and Mills, J. 1957. Postdecision exposure to relevant information. *Journal of Abnormal and Social Psychology* 54: 98–102.

Festinger, L. 1957. *A theory of cognitive dissonance.* Evanston, Ill.: Row, Peterson.

Festinger, L. 1964. *Conflict, decision, and dissonance.* Stanford, Calif.: Stanford University Press.

Siegel, S. 1956. *Nonparametric statistics for the behavioral sciences.* New York: McGraw-Hill.

12. The temporal sequence of post-decision processes
Elaine Walster

Army draftees, led to believe that they were choosing occupational specialties to which they wanted to be assigned for their two-year service, were offered a choice between two approximately equally attractive jobs. Reratings of job attractiveness indicated that shortly after a decision had been made the unchosen alternative was seen as more attractive than the chosen job. Following the period of regret, the draftees restored cognitive harmony by depreciating the attractiveness of the unchosen alternative—the traditional dissonance reduction effect.

This experiment was performed in order to obtain evidence bearing directly on the hypothesis that immediately following a decision there is a temporary period in which the person experiences regret. The clearest and most direct way in which this hypothesis can be examined is to have subjects make a decision and then to remeasure the attractiveness of the alternatives at varying intervals of time following the decision. If the regret phenomenon occurs, one should find that in a period soon after the decision the chosen alternative becomes *less* attractive and the rejected alternative *more* attractive than they had been before the decision. After this, of course, if the theory is correct, one would obtain the usual evidence of dissonance reduction.

The consideration of such a design, however, brings us face to face with a difficult problem. There have been many studies concerned with post-decision dissonance reduction, all of which have remeasured the attractiveness of the alternatives very soon after

Reprinted from "Experiment: The Temporal Sequence of Post-Decision Processes," by Elaine Walster from *Conflict, Decision, and Dissonance* by Leon Festinger and others with the permission of the publishers, Stanford University Press. © 1964 by the Board of Trustees of the Leland Stanford Junior University.

the decision. They have all yielded evidence that dissonance reduction occurs. Clearly, if we are to maintain the hypothesis about the regret period in the face of the evidence from these experiments, we are forced to contend that, at least in those experiments, the regret period was very fleeting indeed. The question of design then becomes: How can we construct a decision situation in which the regret phase in the post-decision process is relatively long-lasting?

The attempt was made, consequently, to find a situation in which subjects could be offered a decision between alternatives that had both positive and negative aspects, that would be reasonably important to the subject, and in which the decision would have lasting consequences. Furthermore, one would want to be able to employ this decision situation in a well-controlled context. It would be necessary to measure the attractiveness of the alternatives before the decision and, assigning subjects to conditions at random, remeasure the attractiveness at different lengths of time after the decision. One would also want to control the activity of the subject and his interactions with others during the entire period between initial measurement and final measurement.

Fortunately, we were able to obtain the cooperation of the Sixth Army District Reception Center at Fort Ord, California. Arrangements were made to use as subjects in the experiment men who were drafted into the Army. They were each to be given a choice of which of two occupational specialties they wanted to be assigned to for their two years in the service. Certainly, such a decision, affecting two years of their lives, is reasonably important; the descriptions of the occupational specialties could be written so as to emphasize both positive and negative aspects of each alternative; and dissonance reduction in this situation should not be a particularly easy affair. In short, this seemed a reasonable situation for testing the validity of the hypothesis about post-decision regret. The details of, and the reasons for, the experimental procedure are given below.

Procedure

Two hundred and seventy-seven draftees who reported for processing at the Fort Ord Reception Center were used as subjects. Each subject was run in the experiment within a day or two of his arrival at the Reception Center—before he had gone far enough in his initial processing to have any information about his probable job assignment in the Army. Men who had enlisted, or who for any other reason had something to say about their job assignment, were excluded from the sample. Men were made available for the experiment on weekends and on days when there were so many arrivals at the Reception Center that not all of them could be processed. In this way, the study did not interfere with the normal processing activity at the Reception Center, nor did it prolong the time any man spent there.

The Army personnel were asked to select men to assign to the study who had had at least some high school education but who had not completed college. It was felt that the job selections to be offered would be most appropriate for men with intermediate education. Frequently, however, information on educational level was not available to the Army personnel at the time they assigned men to the study and so this selection on educational criteria was not rigorous. In our total sample, 6 subjects had had no high school education at all and 15 had completed college.

Early in the course of running the experiment it was realized that most of the alien draftees and many of the Spanish-speaking men had difficulty understanding the instructions and had trouble in making the ratings required of them. Consequently, we requested the Army personnel to exclude such subjects in the future. Nineteen Spanish-speaking and four alien draftees who had already been run in the experiment were discarded from the sample.

Five subjects at a time were run through the experiment. A uniformed driver met the five men at the Reception Center and drove them to the experimental building, about 10 minutes away. During the drive he told them that they had been randomly selected for a special job placement program that the Army was conducting and that they would receive a definite job assignment some time during the day. The driver also commented that although the jobs the special placement program had to offer were, perhaps, not as good as those they might have in civilian life, they were better than those the men could hope to get under the regular job placement program. These comments were intended to make the men believe that, whatever job they were assigned that day, it was definite and as good as or better than anything else they could get.

As soon as the driver arrived at the experimental building, he assembled the men and introduced them to the two experimenters standing in the doorway.

Experimenter 1 then explained to the men:

> As he has probably told you, we're working for the Army on a special experimental program of job placement. You were more or less randomly selected from men in your educational category. Today, I'm going to interview each one of you. I can only see one of you at a time, so while you're waiting for your interview, Miss Turner (Experimenter 2) will be getting some other necessary information from you. She'll ask you to fill out some questionnaires concerning the kind of jobs you've held, the things you like and dislike in a job, and so forth.
>
> O.K. [*Pointing to the closest man*] I'll be seeing you first. Miss Turner will tell the rest of you what to do.

The first subject was then led into the large room where Experimenter 1 conducted all the interviewing. Experimenter 2 took each of the other four men to separate small cubicles in the experimental bulding. When all four men had been seated, Experimenter 2 distributed Questionnaire 1 which asked the men about their previous job and educational experience.

At the same time, in the main experimental room, Experimenter 1 asked the first subject to be seated. On the table in front of the subject's chair was a large chart titled "How Much Would You Like to Work at This Job in the Army for the Next Two Years?" Underneath the title was a 31-point scale. The highest point on the scale (Point 1) was labeled "Would like extremely much." Point 31 was labeled "Would dislike extremely much."

Experimenter 1 then explained to the subject:

> Today we're interested in getting a fairly precise idea of how attractive a number of jobs that the Army is especially interested in seem to you. So, I'll tell you a little bit more about 10 different jobs. I'd like you to think about these jobs and decide how much you'd like to work at each one during your next two years in the Army. Do take into account all those personal things and preferences that make you want one job more than another. You will be assigned to one of these jobs, and I'll be able to tell you which one you got before you leave today.

To help you to give us a pretty clear idea of how you feel about each of these jobs, we've made up this scale.

The scale on the chart was then explained to the subject; some civilian job titles, printed on arrow-shaped cards, were placed at various points on the scale by the experimenter to demonstrate further how the scale was to be used. At this point, the subject was encouraged to ask questions.

Experimenter 1 then picked up a packet of 10 arrow-shaped cards, each having an Army job title and job description printed on it. She told the subject:

> Now whichever of these jobs you're assigned to, you will have to go to school for from six to eight weeks to learn how to do that job in the Army manner.
>
> Now I'll read the job description that's printed on each arrow along with you. Then take your time and decide how much you like each job, and then put the arrow at the right spot. If you should change your mind as we go along, and feel that some job should be rated higher or lower, naturally, it's all right to change that job's position. However, it's probably a good idea to reread the description of the job you're thinking of changing, because sometimes the reason you think you've made a mistake is that you've forgotten some of the things that are involved in the job.
>
> Take as much time as you want. We're anxious to get a really accurate idea both of how much you like each job relative to the others, and how much you like each job absolutely; that is, exactly at which of the points on the scale you think it belongs.

Experimenter 1 then read the 10 job titles and descriptions to the subject, pausing after each description so the subject could place a titled arrow at the appropriate point on the scale.

These job descriptions were written so that each job appeared to have a few really desirable and a few really undesirable features. It was hoped that this obvious mixture of good and bad elements in each job would increase the amount of dissonance subjects experienced and make dissonance reduction more difficult.

When the subject had finished placing all 10 job arrows, the experimenter suggested:

> Now that you've seen all the jobs, it's probably a good idea to reread the job descriptions and make sure you get everything just where you

want it. Sometimes we just can't give you the jobs you like most, and so we'd like to know how you feel about every one of the jobs.

When this subject had finished his final ratings of the jobs, Experimenter 1 took him to a separate cubicle and then returned to the large experimental room to record where on the 31-point scale he had rated each of the 10 jobs. This initial interview usually took 12 to 15 minutes.

Experimenter 1 then called in the second subject from his cubicle to the large experimental room and followed a procedure identical to that followed for the first subject. At the same time, Experimenter 2 asked Subject 1 to fill out Questionnaire 1, which the other subjects had completed earlier, and asked Subjects 3 through 5 to fill out Questionnaire 2.

Approximately every 15 minutes another subject was interviewed by Experimenter 1, and the remaining subjects were given the next in a series of 4 questionnaires to fill out. The purpose of these questionnaires was primarily to keep the subject occupied while Experimenter 1 was interviewing the other men. Also, the questionnaires, taken from material contained in the subtests of the Strong Vocational Interest Inventory, helped make the later job selection seem more plausible.

Subjects filled out questionnaires and were interviewed according to the following sequence.

TIME SCHEDULE	SUBJECT 1	SUBJECT 2	SUBJECT 3	SUBJECT 4	SUBJECT 5
1st 15 min.	Interview	Ques. 1	Ques. 1	Ques. 1	Ques. 1
2nd 15 min.	Ques. 1	Interview	Ques. 2	Ques. 2	Ques. 2
3rd 15 min.	Ques. 2	Ques. 2	Interview	Ques. 3	Ques. 3
4th 15 min.	Ques. 3	Ques. 3	Ques. 3	Interview	Ques. 4
5th 15 min.	Ques. 4	Ques. 4	Ques. 4	Ques. 4	Interview

The purpose of the initial interview was to obtain a measure of how each subject evaluated each job before he was faced with a decision. The next step was to select two jobs and to offer the subject a choice between them. Ideally, it would have been desirable to offer each subject a choice between jobs that he had rated near the middle of the scale, with the initial ratings separated by a constant amount and identical for all subjects. To approach this as closely as possible without discarding too many subjects, Experimenter 2 examined the initial ratings of each subject and selected the two jobs he should be offered according to the following criteria.

1. The job the subject liked best was never used as one of the alternatives for choice. Similarly, none of the three least attractive jobs was used. When possible, the next to the most attractive job was also avoided.

2. No job rated above 6 on the attractiveness scale ("Would like very much") or below 18 (between "Would like and dislike equally" and "Would dislike fairly much") was ever offered as one of the two choice alternatives.

3. Within the above restrictions, two jobs were selected to offer the subject that were rated approximately five units apart on the 31-point scale. If there were no two jobs rated five units apart that satisfied the other criteria, jobs rated six units apart were used. If this too were not possible, jobs rated four units apart, seven units apart, or three units apart were used.

If none of these conditions could be met, the subject was not used in the experiment. Ten subjects were discarded because no pair of jobs could be offered them under the above set of restrictions.

After Experimenter 2 had made the selection of which jobs should be offered to each subject, Experimenter 1 called the first subject back into the experimental room.

She stated:

> Well, by now we can give you some definite information about your Army assignment for the next two years. We've examined all the preferences you expressed to me, the scores on the tests you took for Miss Turner, and considered your background information and job experience.
>
> You understand that in the Army, job assignment is in large part determined by what jobs the Army has to fill at any given time. In this experimental job placement program, we are trying to work out a really good compromise between what you can do, what you want

to do, and what jobs we have to fill. The very best we can do for you, considering your test scores and the Army's needs, is to offer you a choice between these two jobs.

Experimenter 1 then handed the subject the arrows (containing job titles and job descriptions) for the two jobs between which he was to decide and reread the descriptions to him.

Experimenter 1 then concluded: "As soon as you decide which of the two jobs you want, tell me. I can definitely assign you to whichever one you choose for your time in the Army."

If the subject asked why he had not been offered the job he ranked first in the initial interview, Experimenter 1 told him that the main determinant could have been his test scores, the Army's current needs, or the qualifications of the other draftees. For specific information he was told that he would have to see Miss Turner. It was stressed, however, that these were the only jobs available to him.

Subjects were randomly assigned to one of four experimental conditions, the only difference between the conditions being the interval of time allowed to elapse between the decision and the remeasurement of the attractiveness of the jobs. One-fourth of the subjects rerated the jobs immediately after the decision. The others rerated the jobs after an interval of 4 minutes, 15 minutes, or 90 minutes.

If the subject was assigned to the "Immediate Condition," the experimenter continued:

O.K. There are a couple of other things I'd like you to do. The next thing I'd like you to do will in no way affect your Army assignment, but it will help us in developing and improving our job placement program.

By now you've had quite a bit of time to think about these jobs [*pointing to the 10 jobs*], and jobs in general, and you've probably thought of a lot of things that make a job good or bad that just didn't occur to you before. What we'd like you to do is to rerate all these jobs now that you've had a reasonable length of time to think about them.

The subject was then handed a 10-page questionnaire, each page exactly like the chart on which he had rated the jobs during his first interview.

Experimenter 1 continued:

The scale they've provided is just like the one you used earlier, only there's a separate rating page for each job. If you'd write the job number up at the top of each page, we'd know which one you are talking about. Then just draw an arrow at that place which most accurately represents how you feel about each job, *right at this moment.*

If the subject had been assigned to the 4-minute, 15-minute, or 90-minute condition, then, after saying "O.K. There are a couple of other things I'd like you to do," Experimenter 1 added, "but there's some work I have to do first. If you'd just wait 'right here' (4-minute condition), or 'across the hall in your room' (15-minute and 90-minute conditions), I'll get back to you just as soon as I can. Sometimes it takes quite a while. Don't worry, I haven't forgotten you." The experimenter then left the subject alone with nothing to do for the appropriate number of minutes.

When Experimenter 1 returned (after 4 minutes, 15 minutes, or 90 minutes), she followed the same procedure described for the immediate condition.

Results

If the phenomenon of post-decision regret is a real one, and if evidence of it exists in this experiment, it should be reflected in a drawing together of the two alternatives soon after the decision is made. That is, sometime in the immediate post-decision period the chosen alternative should *decrease* in attractiveness and the rejected alternative *increase* in attractiveness. This, of course, should be followed by the usual spreading apart of the alternatives that is the normal evidence of dissonance reduction.

The experiment was designed in ignorance, of course, of the time interval at which post-decision regret would be at its maximum. That is, it was theoretically conceivable that regret would be seen as soon as the decision was made. It was also theoretically conceivable that it could take a little time before the regret would develop to measurable quantities. For this reason we included an immediate condition, a 4-minute-delay condition, and a 15-minute-delay condition. Conceivably, it could take as long as 15 minutes, or even longer, for regret to develop. We simply did not know ahead of time. The 90-minute condition was included to make sure that we had at least one interval long enough for recovery from regret to occur and for the effects of dissonance reduction to be evident. The interval of 90 minutes was chosen as the longest time that it seemed at all feasible to keep a person sitting alone in a small room with nothing to do but wait.

Before we look at the data, there is one decision that must be made about the analysis. Of the 244 subjects from whom usable data were obtained, 51 (21 percent), when asked to make a choice, chose the job that they had originally rated as the *less* attractive of the two they were offered. This is, of course, a rather high percentage of such inversions. In any experiment of this type a certain number of inversions will occur because new considerations of a major character occur to the subject between the time of making the rating and the time of making the decision. There are also, usually, some subjects who make the ratings on a rather abstract basis, but who, when faced with the decision, suddenly consider the alternatives in a new light of reality. In addition to this, in the current experiment there were undoubtedly many subjects who simply did not understand the rating scale fully, some who did not listen to or did not adequately comprehend the job descriptions, and some who were simply not interested. It must be remembered that the subjects comprised a very heterogeneous population, many of them being run through the experiment on the very first day that they reported to the Army Reception Center.

Whatever the reasons for the inversions, they represent a difficulty for analysis. It represents something of a distortion to disregard them or simply to throw them together for analysis with data from other subjects. Since there are so many subjects who show inversions, their data will be presented separately. Since these subjects come about equally from all conditions, this does not interfere with any comparison among the four conditions and, by presenting their data separately, we can determine whether they show the same trends as the other subjects. The data for the 193 subjects who chose the alternative they had rated as *more* attractive will be presented first, and then the other data will be examined for comparison.

Table 12.1

Mean Ratings of Chosen and Rejected Alternatives for Subjects Who Chose the More Attractive Job

EXPERIMENTAL CONDITION	PRE-DECISION RATINGS		CHANGE FROM PRE-DECISION TO POST-DECISION RATINGS		CHANGE IN DISCREPANCY
	CHOSEN	REJECTED	CHOSEN	REJECTED	
Immediate (N = 48)	9.80	15.09	.70	.00	.71
Four Minutes (N = 48)	9.79	15.02	−.37	−.97	−1.34
Fifteen Minutes (N = 48)	10.04	14.98	1.56	.58	2.14
Ninty Minutes (N = 49)	9.91	14.84	.67	−.36	.31

NOTE: Change scores are indicated as positive if they are in the direction of dissonance reduction and as negative if they are in the opposite direction. Thus, changes toward greater attractiveness of the chosen alternative and toward less attractiveness of the rejected alternative are scored as positive changes.

Table 12.1 presents the data on ratings of the chosen and rejected alternatives for the major portion of the sample, namely, those who chose the job they had originally rated as more desirable. The first two columns of figures show the pre-decision ratings of the two alternatives. It is, of course, no surprise that these figures are so similar from condition to condition, since there were rather narrow limits within which the two jobs offered could have been rated and, in addition, subjects were assigned to conditions at random. The third and fourth columns of figures show the changes from the pre-decision to the post-decision ratings of each alternative. The last column shows the total amount of dissonance reduction that occurred.

A glance at the figures in this last column of Table 12.1 shows that there is, indeed, a period of post-decision regret followed by appreciable dissonance reduction. In the condition in which the alternatives were rerated immediately after the decision, there is a relatively small change of .71 in the direction of dissonance reduction, a change that is not significantly different from zero ($t = 1.38$). Those subjects who rerated the jobs after a four-minute delay period show the opposite of dissonance reduction, namely, regret. In this condition the chosen alternative decreases somewhat in attractiveness while the rejected alternative increases in attractiveness. The total change of -1.34 is significantly different from zero at the 7 percent level ($t = 1.80$) and significantly different from the change obtained in the immediate condition at the 2 percent level ($t = 2.26$).

It does, then, seem that in this experiment evidence of post-decision regret exists and that it takes a little time for this regret phenomenon to show itself. If one examines the data for those subjects who rerated the jobs after a delay of 15 minutes, one observes, furthermore, that the period of post-decision regret is, indeed, a temporary one. After 15 post-decision minutes have elapsed there is no more evidence of regret but rather clear evidence of the usual dissonance reduction. By this time the chosen alternative is rated as more attractive and the rejected alternative as less attractive than they were initially. The total change of 2.14 is significantly different from zero ($t = 2.90$) and from the 4-minute condition ($t = 3.32$). It is clear that we did, indeed, obtain post-decision regret followed by dissonance reduction. The various experimental conditions are significantly different from one another in a clear and unequivocal manner.

The data for the 90-minute-delay condition, however, provide a rather surprising result. Instead of continuing to obtain dissonance reduction equal to or greater than than obtained in the 15-minute-delay condition, one finds that after 90 minutes have elapsed there is no evidence of any dissonance reduction at all. The change of .31 is not significantly different from zero and, because of increased variability in this condition, is not clearly different from either the 15-minute condition ($t = 1.69$) or the 4-minute condition ($t = 1.52$). It is difficult to understand this result, although there are some good hunches that can be offered. We will, however, postpone our discussion of the perplexing 90-minute condition temporarily.

Let us first turn our attention to the data obtained from those subjects who chose the job they had initially rated as the less at-

Table 12.2

Mean Ratings of Chosen and Rejected Alternatives for Subjects Who Chose the Less Attractive Job

EXPERIMENTAL CONDITION	PRE-DECISION RATINGS		CHANGE FROM PRE-DECISION TO POST-DECISION RATINGS		CHANGE IN DISCREPANCY
	CHOSEN	REJECTED	CHOSEN	REJECTED	
Immediate (N = 12)	14.78	10.18	4.70	2.03	6.73
Four Minutes (N = 13)	14.93	10.62	1.58	3.53	5.11
Fifteen Minutes (N = 13)	14.46	10.03	3.50	3.62	7.12
Ninety Minutes (N = 13)	15.04	10.56	2.99	2.44	5.43

tractive of the two they were offered. These data are presented in Table 12.2. It is clear from a glance at the last column in the table, which presents the total change in discrepancy between the two alternatives, that the absolute magnitude of these changes is very large. Undoubtedly, this is simply a reflection of the fact that for these subjects the initial rating is relatively meaningless. For these data one must simply ignore the absolute magnitude of the results and look just at the comparison among conditions. It may be seen that the results go in exactly the same direction as the previous results we discussed. From the immediate condition to the 4-minute condition the change in discrepancy decreases, from 4 minutes to 15 minutes it increases, and by 90 minutes it has decreased again. The numbers of cases are rather small, and the variability for these subjects is quite large. None of these differences is statistically significant. The only point to be made is that these subjects show largely the same pattern of results as the others, even duplicating the perplexing problem of the 90-minute condition.

What are some of the possible reasons for the results from the 90-minute condition? The first inclination, on obtaining a result that is so surprising from a theoretical point of view, is to suspect some purely technical methodological inadequacy. In this particular experiment there is a natural inclination to suspect that in the 90-minute condition, the very long period of sitting alone in a small room with nothing to do may have introduced boredom, anger, resentment, or any of a number of other factors that might have contributed to the obtained result. This may or may not be true, but the best judgment we can make is that it is not true. Let us look closely at some aspects of the "boredom" explanation to see why this judgment seems reasonable.

It is conceivable that after 90 minutes of sitting alone in a small room, these subjects felt angry with the Army. This experience may have confirmed all their worst expectations, with the result that they may have felt that everything in the Army is terrible, including the possible jobs. If this explanation had any validity at all, we would expect that the average post-decision rating of the jobs not involved in the choice would be considerably lower for subjects in the 90-minute-delay condition than for subjects in the other conditions. This, however, is not the case. The average post-decision ratings of the jobs not involved in the choice were 15.89, 15.35, 15.51, and 15.51 for the 4 conditions—differences which are certainly indistinguishable from one another.

Another possible aspect of the "boredom" explanation is that being bored and having lost interest in the whole proceedings, the subjects in the 90-minute-delay condition stop discriminating among jobs on the post-decision ratings. That is, out of boredom or, perhaps, anger, they make their second ratings in a perfunctory manner, essentially saying that everything is the same. To check on this possibility we computed the standard deviation of each subject's post-decision ratings of the jobs. If they stopped cooperating and stopped discriminating among jobs, we would expect this to be reflected in a small dispersion of the individual's ratings. This again is not true. The four conditions are almost identical.

Nowhere could any evidence be found to support a contention of methodological inadequacy in the 90-minute condition. Consequently, we have come to the conclusion that it is probably a real effect. But if it is a real effect, what does it mean? Is dissonance reduction just a temporary matter? This seems unlikely. Although there has been little done concerning long-range effects of dissonance reduction, what we do know would certainly argue against the disappearance of all effects within 90 minutes. Ninety minutes may be a long time to sit doing nothing in a room but, after all, it is a short amount of time in which to expect a rather pervasive process to be completely nullified.

This still, however, leaves us with no answer to the perplexing result of the 90-minute condition. And we can give no good answer —not in the sense of an answer that can be supported with data. We can, however, offer what seems to us to be a good hunch. We think the answer lies in the great difficulty of reducing dissonance in this experimental siutation. Let us look at this more carefully. In choosing this particular context for doing this experiment, we were motivated primarily by our intuitive notions concerning the conditions under which regret would be rather pronounced and would last for a sufficiently long time so that we could measure it. Intuitively, it seemed to us that this would happen if the decision were important, the alternatives possessed a mixture of good and bad characteristics, and dissonance reduction was very difficult. The idea was that under such circumstances the post-decision dissonance would be large and, if dissonance reduction were difficult and took time, that focusing on the dissonance in order to reduce it would produce the regret phase. If dissonance reduction were too easy, the regret phase might be very fleeting.

We were probably very successful in creating a situation in which dissonance reduction was, indeed, difficult. At least we know that we did obtain a period in which post-decision regret appeared. We probably created a situation in which only a limited amount of dissonance could be reduced by most subjects. Under most ordinary "real-life" circumstances, the person would go talk to others about it, seek new information, and generally try to get informational and social support for the process of further reducing dissonance. In our experiment this was impossible. The person was left entirely on his own resources. There was no new information obtainable and there was no one else he could even talk to about it. It is possible that after some dissonance had been reduced, the continued focusing on the remaining dissonance without further successful dissonance reduction could produce the effect obtained in the 90-minute condition.

If this is the correct explanation, there are certain implications. If one were to set up a situation in which dissonance reduction was even more difficult, almost impossible, the effect of focusing on and unsuccessfully trying to reduce the dissonance might result in a steady increase in the importance of the dissonance and a steady narrowing of the discrepancy between the alternatives. If in our experimental situation the subjects had been provided with more leeway, people to talk to, things to read about the Army and its jobs—anything that would have aided dissonance reduction— the results of the 90-minute condition might have been different.

13. **It feels good when it stops** Paul G. Swingle

Is the bus ride *from* more pleasant than the ride *to* the dentist's office? Could the neutral event of the bus ride after the unpleasant event make the neutral event seem more attractive?

Frequently subjects are placed in trying or emotionally taxing situations and then asked to assess the attractiveness of stimuli or events that follow termination of the somewhat negative situations. Being induced to lie or to expose oneself to boring or embarrassing procedures may be presumed to be unpleasant for most subjects. Similarly, recent evidence has indicated that choices between mutually exclusive, equally attractive or unattractive satisfactions can induce severe anxiety in animals. Monkeys given an exclusive choice between equally attractive amounts of different foods begin to develop such neurotic behaviors as tics and stupors (Masserman, 1967). And it has been known for some time that decision making is stressful for humans, particularly if the choice is difficult either because of the costliness of error or similarity of the alternatives.

Subjects in dissonance experiments often are forced to make such difficult choices between equally attractive alternatives. In other dissonance experiments subjects have been induced to lie, perform boring tasks, submit to embarrassment tests, eat grasshoppers, endure electric shocks, and deprive themselves of food or water. It is not unreasonable to suppose that such situations could be unpleasant for participants. The present experiment was designed to demonstrate that the attractiveness of a stimulus can be influenced when a distinctly separate and unrelated noxious event precedes such an evaluation.

A table with a large sign that read "Student Art Survey" was placed at the entrance to the laboratory wing of a psychology building. All female students entering or leaving the lab wing had to pass the table because it stood at the only portal. The female assistant (DA) to the director of the university's art gallery, seated at the table, asked each student who passed to rate four 8 × 10 inch black and white photographs of Rajput miniature paintings, two of which are shown in Figures 13.1 and 13.2.

The student received a sheet containing 4 sets of 3 scales, 1 set for each picture. The scales consisted of bipolar adjectives (good –bad, pleasant–unpleasant, meaningful–meaningless), each separated by a 100 mm. line. The student was asked simply to mark the line to indicate her rating. The closer the mark was placed to the positive adjective, the more positive the rating.

After the rating was completed, DA asked the student whether she expected to pass by the table again "within the next hour or so." After each said yes (it was the only way out of the building) the DA asked if she would mind stopping by again to give a second rating since "we are also interested in everyone's second impression."

In addition to students who normally pass through that section of the building, 50 female students were called and scheduled to appear for specific experimental conditions. When they arrived at the specified room they were greeted by a male experimenter who, on a random basis, sent each girl to one of three rooms. In the first room the girls were asked to read a short, mildly amusing *Reader's Digest* article, "The day grandfather tickled a tiger." After completion they were asked if they thought the material was enjoyable, if they had read the story at their normal reading speed, and how long they thought they had taken to read the story.

In the second room the girls received several 8½ × 11 inch sheets of ¼ inch graph paper and were requested to place an X

Figure 13.1

Figure 13.2

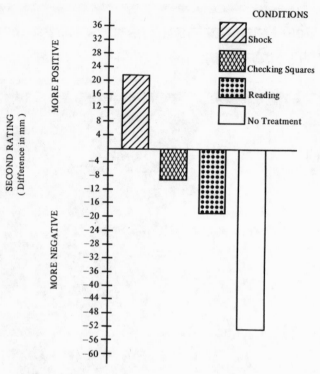

Figure 13.3
Change in Rated Attractiveness of Pictures

in as many of the squares as possible, completing one line at a time. After five minutes the experimenter stopped the subject, looked at the paper for a few moments, and then thanked and dismissed the girl.

In the third room each girl was seated in a chair facing an enormous quantity of electrical gadgetry that had many flashing lights, made a lot of clicking noises, and belched out copious amounts of paper containing lines and numbers. Shock electrodes were placed on the middle and index fingers of the left hand.

In addition to the shock electrodes several other contacts were taped to the girl's hand and wrist. Although these contacts led into the electrical gadgetry, they were in actuality not connected to anything. Each girl was told that she was involved in an experiment concerned with basal galvanic responses, and that it would be necessary at some time during the next five minutes to deliver at least one very painful but completely harmless electric shock through the electrodes on her fingers. Each girl was asked if she agreed to continue; one refused. After approximately three minutes of random noises generated from the machinery around the girl, she received a very uncomfortable inductorium shock that lasted for three-fourths of a second. After a total of five minutes the girl was thanked and dismissed.

All of the scheduled experimental procedures lasted approximately six minutes in total. As the girls were leaving the building the DA behind the "art survey table" again asked them to complete an evaluation of the pictures.

The rated attractiveness of the pictures was obtained by measuring the distance in millimeters from the negative adjective on the scale (e.g., unpleasant) to the point on the line where the student placed her mark. The sum of the differences between the first and the second ratings, therefore, was a measure of the change in the rater's evaluation of the picture. The results from the female students who filled out both ratings but did not participate in the scheduled experimental sessions are included in Figure. 13.3. However, because their activities during the time between ratings are not known, that group cannot be considered as a no-treatment control condition.

The results of this experiment indicate that the evaluation of objects can be influenced by preceding events. The present data demonstrate only the contrast effect of a noxious event. Could it be that neutral events seem more negative when they follow the end of a good time?

REFERENCE

Masserman, J. H. 1967. The neurotic cat. *Psychology Today* 1: 36.

■ INTERPERSONAL INFLUENCE

An obvious area for studies of interpersonal influence is buyer–seller interaction, because people constantly attempt to influence others in marketing situations in order to obtain the best price. Several experimental attempts have been made to determine the best approaches buyers or sellers can use to increase both sales and profits from sales. Salesmen usually attempt to increase their skills on a more or less trial-and-error basis by using various approaches to potential customers, and many salesmen attribute their successes to particular sales techniques they have developed.

Jung (1959) compared hard versus soft approaches to automobile purchases. Shoppers representing themselves as either naïve about car buying and anxious to purchase a car or as well-versed shoppers who would seek competitive bids obtained price quotations from Ford and Chevrolet dealers. Hard approach buyers received prices only slightly lower than those soft approach buyers obtained (i.e., a 1 percent difference in prices, which was not statistically reliable).

Dorris reports that the effectiveness of the soft approach can be enhanced by making a moral appeal. In his study when a totally naïve seller made reference to fear of exploitation, the need for cash, and the buyer's other customers, he received higher bids as compared to those received when no such statements were made.

Brock reports that salesmen can influence purchases by leading the buyer to believe that the two have a similar relationship to the product. Thus buyers were influenced to buy more or less expensive paint when the salesman claimed to have used the recommended paint. The extent of the compliance with the influence attempt was found to be greatest when the salesman claimed to have used a similar quantity of paint for a purpose similar to that of the buyer.

Several methodological features of the two readings included in this section are of particular interest. The problem of matching samples appears in both studies. In the Dorris experiment buyers were matched in terms of shop size, estimated in several different ways, whereas Brock's experimenters had to select male buyers whose purchases were made under reasonably comparable circumstances. Bias again is a serious problem whenever subject selection depends on on-the-spot application of several criteria.

Control of experimenter bias or error introduced by the experimenter's agents (i.e., the experimenter himself, confederates, observers, coders) is a most difficult problem in field studies. As mentioned earlier, one method for dealing with experimenter bias is the multiple agent technique. In both experiments reported in this section two agents were used equally often in each condition. In the Brock experiment judges evaluated the agents' "performances" before the actual experiment to determine if any important differences were noticeable. Important differences between agents might be eliminated by further rehearsal or by replacing one of the agents.

The data associated with each agent during the experiment are analyzed separately to determine if different results are obtained. Should differences emerge, then one must assume that the results may reflect agent differences rather than effects attributable to the independent variable manipulation. In both of the experiments in this section

the authors state that the data associated with each agent
were similar and therefore could be combined for analyti-
cal purposes.

REFERENCE

Jung, A. F. 1959. Price variations among automobile dealers
in Chicago, Illinois. *The Journal of Business* 32: 315–26.

14.   Communicator-recipient similarity and decision change   Timothy C. Brock

A field experiment in the paint department of a large retail store supported the hypothesis: a recipient's behavior
with respect to an object is modifiable by the communicator's appeal to the extent that the recipient perceives that
he and the communicator have a similar relationship to the
object. A salesman, who reported his own magnitude of
paint consumption as similar or dissimilar to the purchaser's, attempted to induce the purchaser ($N = 88$) to
switch to a different price level. The findings were ordered
to theories of identification (Stotland) and social comparison (Festinger).

The recipient's perception of his similarity to a communicator or
model has been hypothesized to account for change toward the
communicator (Back, 1951; Leventhal & Perloe, 1962), attraction

Reprinted from the *Journal of Personality and Social Psychology* 1
(1965): 650–54. Copyright 1965 by the American Psychological Association,
and reproduced by permission.

to the communicator (Byrne, 1961; Byrne & Wong, 1962; Gerard & Greenbaum, 1962) for adoption of the model's preferences (Stotland, Zander, & Natsoulas, 1961), ability level (Burnstein, Stotland, & Zander, 1961; Stotland & Dunn, 1962; Stotland & Hillmer, 1962), and "anxiety" (Stotland & Dunn, 1963). These studies, which can be fitted within the framework of Stotland's cognitive theory of identification or Festinger's (1954) theory of social comparison processes, do not yet sum to a set of principles shown to yield clear predictions of behavioral change in real-life situations. This shortcoming was noticed when an attempt was made, with the management of a department store, to learn more about the effects of interpersonal influence on consumer behavior.

Management assigned special value to informal, word-of-mouth endorsement (Katz & Lazarsfeld, 1955) of a product and sought means of improving interpersonal, rather than media, promotion. It was proposed that a communicator who is perceived to be thoroughly experienced with a product, will be more likely to influence the recipient than a less experienced communicator. Perceived expertise of the communicator was considered crucial in face-to-face contexts. To illustrate, management believed that a person about to buy a Chevrolet would be less influenced by a neighbor's approbation of his car (a Ford, say) than an equally enthusiastic endorsement by the owner of a fleet of Fords. The first hypothesis was: the more experience a communicator is perceived to have had with an object, the more likely it is that the recipient's behavior with respect to the object will be modified by the communicator's influence attempts.

The second hypothesis followed the aforementioned research on communicator-recipient similarity: to the extent that the recipient perceives that he and the communicator share an attribute, that is, have a similar relationship to an object, to that extent is the recipient's behavior with respect to the object likely to be modified by the communicator's influence attempts. The two forces, perceived communicator expertise and perceived communicator similarity, were pitted against one another by conducting a field experiment in which the communicator, for half the recipients, was perceived as similar but inexperienced while for the other half, he was perceived as dissimilar but experienced.

Method

In the paint department of a large retail store,[1] salesmen attempted to induce paint purchasers to change to a different price level. There were two independent variables: the similarity of the salesman and customer with respect to the salesman's prior magnitude of paint consumption; the direction of the advocated change in price level, upward or downward. The dependent variable was whether or not the paint purchaser changed his decision concerning the price level after an influence attempt by the salesman.

PROCEDURE

The role of experimenter-communicator was taken by two part-time salesmen. The experimenter selected customers or subject-recipients for inclusion in the experiment, attempted to modify the subject's price decision, and recorded whether or not the influence attempt was successful. Selected subjects were randomly assigned to a similar or dissimilar condition and to a higher or lower condition, resulting in a 2 × 2 design. Influence attempts were restricted to paint purchases, particularly the kinds and prices given in Table 14.1. In the higher condition, the experimenter advocated buying paint at prices in Column 3 rather than Column 2 in Table 14.1. In the lower condition, the experimenter advocated purchases at prices in Column 1 if the subject had chosen a price in Column 2, or in Column 2 if the subject selected a price in Column 3. In the similar condition, the experimenter emphasized that the magnitude of his own consumption was the same as the amount being purchased by the subject; in the dissimilar condition the experimenter reported his own magnitude of consumption to be 20 times that of the subject's prospective purchase.[2]

1. The experiment was conducted during a five-month period in the paint department of a retail store in an Eastern city. The store is a unit in an international chain with annual sales volume greater than one billion dollars. A *sine qua non* for conducting the experiment was preservation of anonymity for the store and its permanent staff in any public report.
2. The multiple of 20 was chosen because the experimenters' experience in the paint department led them to believe such a magnitude would be perceived by the typical paint purchaser as plausible but at the same time very different from his own acquisition of a gallon or two.

The treatments were administered after the subject indicated he wished to purchase X units at a given price and had proceeded with the experimenter to the cash register to "ring up" the sale. At this point, the experimenter delivered himself of the following well-practiced appeal. Alternative terms for the dissimilar and higher conditions appeared in brackets.

Listen, I just thought, I wonder if I can give you some advice. I'm going to college right now and working here part-time as a salesman to meet my expenses. Two weeks ago I bought X [20 X] gallons of a to help my dad on some work like your b that we were doing. It costs a little less [more] and [but] it turned out beautifully. I also got a little of the c you want to buy, and, honestly, it didn't work out as well at all. There just was no comparison. Those X [20 X] gallons at a have proved out terrifically for us in every way. [Pause] On the basis of my experience with X [20 X] gallons of a, I can really recommend your changing to the a if you want to. I certainly would if I were you.

The italicized a above refers to the type of paint at the advocated price; b refers to details of the experimenter's "job," described so as to seem akin to the subject's and, in the dissimilar condition, to require the use of much paint; and c refers to the subject's initial selection of paint and price level. In an actual appeal to a subject who decided to buy floor paint at $6.98 per gallon, the variations were: a, "the 4.98 paint" or simply "4.98"; b, "porches and basement too [in some duplexes]"; c, "6.98." The material in brackets would have been omitted in the similar condition.

In addition to noting whether or not the influence attempt was successful, the experimenter recorded the original price, the ad-

Table 14.1
Paints and Price per Gallon in Dollars

TYPE OF PAINT	1	2	3
Latex	2.97	5.59	6.90
House (outside)		5.89	6.98
Floor		4.98	6.69
Semigloss	3.98	6.59	7.98

vocated price, whether the sale was cash or charge, estimated the subject's age, and noted any contaminating factors.

The experimenters appeared before the writer's students (class $Ns = 25$ and 18) who rated their appeals using Likert scales with anchors labeled "none at all" and "to a very high degree." The experimenters were rated for warmth, expertness, believableness, speaking effectiveness, and the likelihood that "this salesman would make me change my mind." In addition, the raters were asked to reproduce the appeals in writing. The raters were told that the experimenters were sales trainees and the ratings would not affect the trainee's position and salary but would be important in deciding what kind of sales job he was given. The experimenters spoke in a balanced order before the two classes. The rating forms asked the raters to imagine they had just bought "some paint" at a specified price level: in this fashion half of each class was given a higher and half a lower treatment. The dissimilar experimenter reported his prior consumption as 20 gallons; the similar experimenter, as 1 gallon. Detailed description of the communicator's "job" and devaluation of the recipient's price were omitted. There were only three statistically reliable ($p < .05$, 2-tailed) outcomes: one of the experimenters was rated higher than the other in "warmth"; the dissimilar communicator was rated higher in expertness, defined for the rater as "knows what he is talking about"; and female raters gave higher ratings.

Both experimenters knew the hypotheses but their preferences, prior to the experiment, did not agree. The experimenters returned data cards to the writer biweekly, and they were not informed about the results during the course of the data collection. Since they were employed in the paint department anyway, the experimenters felt they might enliven a humdrum selling task by sometimes making it a meaningful scientific activity. The experimenters received no additional remuneration or inducements of any kind. One of the experimenters had taken advanced psychology courses; the other, a chemistry major, had taken only an introductory psychology course. The experimenters did not collect data at the same time.

A small proportion of the purchasers entering the paint department during the period of the experiment was selected as subjects. No attempt was made to collect data when: neither experimenter was on duty; the paint department or store was very crowded; there was a sale in the store, in the paint department, or in adjacent departments; remodeling was being done in the paint or adjacent departments; the sales help in the paint department was below full strength. A purchaser was excluded as a subject if: the purchaser was female or was accompanied by other persons; the purchaser was completing a project and returning for more supplies; the purchaser was not exclusively interested in the products listed in Table 14.1; the desired color was not available at the price level to be advocated by the experimenter; special color mixing was necessary; the purchaser did not appear to make a choice or decision concerning price but seemed to the experimenter to have had a definite price in mind before entering the paint department. The purchaser was excluded if he forced the experimenter to give information that was favorable or unfavorable to a certain price level prior to the influence attempt or in addition to the influence attempt. For example, if a purchaser wanted to know why the $6.90 Latex cost more than the $5.59 Latex the experimenter would first say "probably different chemicals in them." In many instances this ambiguous reply was insufficient and the experimenter had to endorse or evaluate the paints. A purchaser was excluded if his price decision did not permit the experimenter to apply the higher (or lower) treatment which had been randomly determined beforehand. When the experimenter was interrupted and not allowed to complete his influence attempt, the purchaser's data were omitted. Finally, the experimenters excluded purchasers who seemed disturbed (as reported by the experimenters) by words on the paint can label, such as "enamel." In sum, the subject obviously made a price decision, the surround was normal and tranquil, only the products in Table 14.1 were involved, and the experimenter was able to apply the treatments in standardized fashion. Data collection was terminated when the experimenters completed their period of employment at the store. At this time 88 subjects had been run, 22 in each of the 4 conditions, higher or lower, similar or dissimilar.

Results and Discussion

Before evaluating the hypotheses it was necessary to ascertain whether bias was introduced by excluding purchasers who did not make a decision about price, forced the experimenter to enlarge on the content of his influence attempt, elicited supplemental evaluation from the experimenter, or interrupted and prevented the experimenter from completing his appeal. If purchasers in these categories were disproportionately represented in the four cells of the design, the test of the hypotheses could be impugned. Appropriate analysis of the data revealed no relationship between the independent classifications (higher versus lower, similar versus dissimilar) and the frequency of subjects who made no real price decisions, who forced enlargement or endorsement, or who interrupted the experimenter. All exact test and chi-square p values were greater than .25.

The same pattern of outcomes was obtained for both experimenters, for cash and charge purchases, and for purchasers estimated to be over and under 40 years of age. The combined results, shown in Table 14.2, favored the second hypothesis. The dissimilar communicator, although presumably perceived as more knowledgeable, was less effective than the communicator whose paint consumption was the same as the purchaser's ($p < .05$). There was an expected tendency for downward influence attempts to encounter less resistance than upward advocacy.

Table 14.2
Number of Paint Purchasers Who Changed Decision in Relation to Direction of Influence Attempt and Similarity of Communicator's Consumption

DIRECTION OF INFLUENCE ATTEMPT	SIMILAR	DISSIMILAR	TOTAL
To a lower price level	16 (73%)	10 (45%)	26 (59%)
To a higher price level	12 (55%)	7 (32%)	19 (43%)
	28 (64%)[a]	17 (39%)[a]	

NOTE: Cell $N = 22$ purchasers.
[a]Chi-square, $p < .05$.

Note that half of the 88 subjects changed in response to the influence attempt. No base line was available for evaluating this overall frequency of change; it could be attributed to an inherent instability of price decisions or to the elaborate screening of subjects.

The findings add clarity to the literature in that previous attempts to demonstrate before–after change, as a function of identification with a model, yielded ambiguous results (Burnstein et al., 1961; Leventhal & Perloe, 1962). The present test of the perceived similarity hypothesis was considered stringent because the expertise effect, to the extent that it was operative, worked against confirmation of the hypothesis. Also opposing confirmation was the presumed reluctance of purchasers in the higher condition to spend more money than they had initially decided upon. The present results increased understanding of why a face-to-face encounter may be more effective in modifying a recipient than the importunities of mass-media communicators (Katz & Lazarsfeld, 1955); the recipient changes toward the position of a communicator to the extent he perceives that he shares with the communicator an attribute pertinent to the dimension along which change is advocated. An interesting problem for subsequent research is whether real-life behavior can be modified as readily when the similarity attribute is *irrelevant* to the change dimension.

Subsequent research must also deal with a possible alternative explanation for the present findings. Perhaps the decisive factor in producing the observed differences was not the similarity of the "X gallon" communicator but the dissimilarity of the "20 X gallon" communicator. The subject may have rejected the dissimilar communicator because his experience seemed irrelevant; or the subject may have resented the experimenter's "showing off" how much paint he used or disbelieved the experimenter's figure and regarded it simply as a sales ploy. If these processes were operative, it would affect the interpretation that similarity is a sufficiently powerful factor to overcome the effects of expertness. Although pretesting of the communicators showed no differences in their believableness, and the dissimilar communicator was rated higher in expertness, future replications should include a control group in which the appeal to change is unaccompanied by inductions of either similarity or expertness.

The cognitive theory of identification (Stotland et al., 1961) fits the present results, but it does not specify the likely motivational factors as well as the more dynamical theory of social comparison processes (Festinger, 1954). In terms of Festinger's theory, the purchaser wanted to evaluate the correctness of his price decision and, in the absence of nonsocial means of evaluation, would be sensitive to the judgment of other persons. The salesman, of course, provided the wanted standard, but when he was perceived as non-comparable on the relevant issue of paint consumption, the purchaser was neither attracted to him nor motivated to reduce discrepancy between the chosen and advocated price levels.

Kelman's (1962) presentation of hypotheses dealing with action and attitude change provided a third theoretical view. Kelman reasoned that gradients of approach or avoidance based on "identification" are steeper than those based on "internalization." Hence, when the purchaser's approach toward another price level was based on identification with the communicator, this sufficed to overcome avoidance based on internalized values such as "spend no more than necessary" and/or "take no advice from inexperienced persons." The relationship between communicator–recipient similarity and modification of the recipient requires further research in which an attempt is made to sort out *contrasting* predictions from theoretical formulations such as the three here examined.

Finally, the present study showed that contemporary theories in social psychology are not necessarily inadequate to "study the powerful forces which affect people in the real social world [Katz & Stotland, 1959, p. 467]." With some noteworthy exceptions (Hovland, 1961; Schachter, Willerman, Festinger, & Hyman, 1961), the problem may lie rather in the understandable reluctance of experimenters to forego the comfort, convenience, and methodological refinement of the laboratory.

REFERENCES

Back, K. 1951. The exertion of influence through social communication. *Journal of Abnormal and Social Psychology* 46: 9–24.

Burnstein, E.; Stotland, E.; and Zander, A. 1961. Similarity to a model and self-evaluation. *Journal of Abnormal and Social Psychology* 62: 257–64.

Byrne, D. 1961. Interpersonal attraction and attitude similarity. *Journal of Abnormal and Social Psychology* 62: 713–15.

Byrne, D., and Wong, T. J. 1962. Racial prejudice, interpersonal attraction, and assumed dissimilarity of attitudes. *Journal of Abnormal and Social Psychology* 65: 246–53.

Festinger, L. 1954. A theory of social comparison processes. *Human Relations* 7: 117–40.

Gerard, H. B., and Greenbaum, C. W. 1962. Attitudes toward an agent of uncertainty reduction. *Journal of Personality* 30, 485–95.

Hovland, C. I. 1961. Two new social science research units in industrial settings. *American Psychologist* 16: 87–91.

Katz, D., and Stotland, E. 1959. A preliminary statement to a theory of attitude structure and change. In *Psychology: A study of a science,* vol. 3, *Formulations of the person and the social context,* ed. S. Koch, pp. 423–75. New York: McGraw-Hill.

Katz, E., and Lazarsfeld, P. F. 1955. *Personal influence.* Glencoe, Ill.: Free Press.

Kelman, H. C. 1962. The induction of action and attitude change. In *Proceedings of the XIVth International Congress of Applied Psychology,* vol. 2, *Personality research,* ed. G. Nielson, pp. 81–110. Copenhagen: Munksgaard.

Leventhal, H., and Perloe, S. I. 1962. A relationship between self-esteem and persuasibility. *Journal of Abnormal and Social Psychology* 64: 385–88.

Schachter, S.; Willerman, B.; Festinger, L.; and Hyman, R. 1961. Emotional disruption and industrial productivity. *Journal of Applied Psychology* 45: 201–13.

Stotland, E., and Dunn, R. E. 1962. Identification, "oppositeness," authoritarianism, self-esteem, and birth order. *Psychological Monographs* 76(9), whole no. 528.

Stotland, E., and Dunn, R. E. 1963. Empathy, self-esteem, and birth order. *Journal of Abnormal and Social Psychology* 66: 532–40.

Stotland, E., and Hillmer, M. L., Jr. 1962. Identification, authoritarian defensiveness, and self-esteem. *Journal of Abnormal and Social Psychology* 64: 334–42.

Stotland, E., Zander, A., and Natsoulas, T. 1961. Generalization of interpersonal similarity. *Journal of Abnormal and Social Psychology* 62, 250–56.

15. Reactions to unconditional cooperation: A field study emphasizing variables neglected in laboratory research   J. William Dorris

Coin dealers were given the opportunity to buy coins from a naïve and totally trusting seller. Dealers offered higher prices for the coins when the seller presented himself as a person who needed money rather than as a person who simply wanted to dispose of the coins.

In everyday life situations, whenever we want to make a major purchase such as an automobile or household appliance, we tend to shop around to get the best price. Since we do not know precisely how much profit the seller may make, we obtain several prices to establish a criterion for evaluating a dealer's offer. We may then agree to pay a little more, say, for an automobile to obtain better service, to buy from an acquaintance, to receive the product more rapidly, and so on. Many consumers also believe that if they do not compare-shop, dealers will attempt to maximize their profits by not offering a fair trade-in allowance or by charging more than the market value for a product.

If you have no idea of the fair market value of something you want to sell, will you receive a higher price from a dealer by letting him know that you need money for a good reason? In the present experiment coin dealers were offered an opportunity to purchase coins with a retail value of $45. Some dealers were led to believe that the seller needed the money for books, whereas others were told that the seller was disposing of the coins because he had no

Abridged from the *Journal of Personality and Social Psychology* 22 (1972): 387–397. Copyright 1972 by the American Psychological Association, and reproduced by permission. Portions of the article comparing laboratory and field research settings have been omitted.

interest in coin collecting. In addition, half of the dealers were led to believe that the sellers had recently sold a coin to an exploitative coin dealer, whereas the others were led to believe that the previous dealer had been fair. In all cases the seller was portrayed as being totally naïve about the value of the coins.

Method

SUBJECT AND TASK

Approximately 150 shops that buy and sell rare coins were located by means of the Yellow Pages of the telephone directories for several metropolitan areas. Of these shops, 4 were used as sources of information and coins, 18 were used in the pilot study, 31 were closed or had disconnected telephones, and 71 were used in the study. The remaining shops were not used in any way. Of the 71 subjects, 6 were eliminated from our data analysis for such reasons as one dealer's being given the experimental treatment while another man in the same store eventually gave the price offer for the coins. These six subjects were almost equally distributed across conditions.

Assignment of subjects of experimental conditions was done on the basis of several theoretical and practical guidelines. Because the coin market is known to fluctuate, it was decided to attempt to run one subject in each of the four major conditions (Type of appeal × Prior dealer's behavior) of the study each day that data were collected. This distribution rule also served to minimize any effects that might have resulted from shop location. Thus, for instance, differences between two experimental conditions could not have resulted because the subjects in one condition were located in a wealthy business district while those in the second condition came from a modest one. The order in which dealers were used on a given day was determined by convenience, considering their various locations and business hours. Finally, because of the nature of the moral appeal, a shop had to do business in both coins and stamps to qualify for this condition.

The subject's task was one that regularly occurs in the course of his daily business. He was offered the opportunity to buy a small collection of coins from either the author or his assistant, who enacted the role of a male college student wanting to sell the coins. Eight coins were offered for sale. These coins were kept in separate clear plastic envelopes, each with a stapled-on label indicating the type of coin and an abbreviation of its condition. All of the coins were Lincoln pennies with a total retail selling price of about $45.

An empty envelope was used to vary the factor of prior dealer's behavior. Since all nine envelopes were given to the dealer in a Sucrets box, he was forced to notice the empty one first as it was always on top. The coin seller then explained that he had sold the missing coin to another dealer, and by reading the label on the empty envelope the subject learned that the prior dealer had been either fair or exploitative (see "Design" below).

Comments the coin seller made before giving the coins to the dealer determined whether the subject received a moral or neutral appeal. Since the coin seller made it quite clear that he had no idea of the worth of the coins, the dealer was led to believe that he had the opportunity to buy the coins as cheaply as he wanted. The coins, of course, were never sold to the dealer.

DESIGN

Four independent variables, each with two levels, were included in the experimental design. Two of these variables—type of appeal and prior dealer's behavior—were of theoretical interest. The other two variables—experimenter and shop size—were considered to be of possible importance and therefore were included in the design so that their effects would be equally distributed across the two main variables.

Type of appeal. The coin seller gave one of two explanations of why he was selling the coins. In the moral appeal the seller explained that he needed the money to help pay for some schoolbooks, and that he was offering them to this dealer on the basis of a recommendation by another customer, an acquaintance of the seller. In the neutral appeal the seller explained that he simply had some coins he wanted to sell because he was not interested in becoming a collector. In both appeals the seller's ignorance of the coin's value and his desire to sell them to this dealer were clearly indicated.

In the moral appeal the coin seller made the following comments:

Hi, do you buy coins? . . . My name's Jim Dorris/Gentry, and I have some coins that I need to sell. [If the dealer interrupts here or later, seller replies: "If it's OK, I'd like to take a minute to explain why I am selling the coins."] The coins belonged to my grandfather and I inherited them. Since I don't know anything about these coins . . . or coin collecting at all for that matter . . . I've been afraid that I might be exploited in selling the coins.

Because of this I showed the coins to a stamp collector who lives in my apartment house. [If the dealer asks for a name, seller knows only the first name.] He didn't know what the coins were worth, but he said he's done quite a bit of business with you and that I could trust you to give me a fair price for them.

Normally I wouldn't sell the coins, but I'm in kind of a jam. I need to buy some textbooks for my summer school classes to get ready for exams, and for some reason my check got held up at work. Since I need the books right now, I'm really in a bind. So whatever you can give me for the coins would really help.

[Seller takes Sucrets box from his shirt pocket and hands it to dealer.] Here are the coins. [When the dealer notices that the coin is missing from the top plastic envelope, which is labeled either 1909S XF, or 1914D XF, the seller comments] Oh, yeah! I was going to sell the coins to another dealer yesterday . . . but I got interrupted while I was putting the coins in the box. After I got off the phone, I just picked up the Sucrets box and went down to this other dealer's shop. I told him the same thing I told you about getting the coins from my grandfather, that I didn't know anything about them and why I was selling them. When we opened the box I discovered I had forgotten all of the coins except that one [seller points to empty envelope]. Anyhow he looked at that coin and immediately offered me 15 dollars for it. So I sold him that one for 15 dollars.

After I left the shop I started wondering about being exploited since I didn't know anything about the coins. That's when I decided to talk to the stamp collector, and he recommended that I sell the rest of the coins to you.

[After dealer makes initial price offer] _____ dollars. Gee, I was hoping they would be worth more, since those textbooks are expensive.

[After dealer responds to seller's comment] _____ dollars would help pay some of the expense, but it's still not enough. . . . I think I'll wait one more day to see if my check comes in the mail. If it does I'll be all set; if not I'll come by tomorrow.

The coin seller's comments in the neutral appeal were as follows:

Hi, do you buy coins? . . . I have some coins that I want to sell. They belonged to my grandfather and I inherited them. . . . I don't know anything about these coins, or coin collecting at all for that matter, and I don't really want to become a collector. So I want to sell the coins.

I don't want to take time to get a lot of appraisals from different people. So I thought I would sell them to you today for whatever you can give me for them. Here they are [hands dealer Sucrets box].

[When dealer discovers missing coin, seller's comments are the same as in the moral appeal, except for omission of the last paragraph about the possibility of being exploited and talking to the stamp collector.]

[After initial offer] _____ dollars. Gee, I was hoping they would be worth more.

[After response to this comment] _____ dollars is really not that much. I think I'll just hold onto them for a while and see if the price goes up. Thanks anyhow.

Prior dealer's behavior. In all cases the dealer "discovered" the empty envelope and then learned that the missing coin had been sold to another dealer the previous day for $15. When the prior dealer was fair the envelope was labeled 1909S XF, indicating a Lincoln penny with a listed retail price of $30 (*Coin World* newspaper, 7/8/70). When the prior dealer was exploitative our empty envelope was labeled 1914D XF, indicating another Lincoln penny listed at a retail value of $140. In either case the missing coin was reportedly sold for $15, and the seller made it obvious that he had no idea of whether or not this was a fair price. The dealer, being well aware of the values of the 1909S and the 1914D pennies in XF condition, knew immediately that the seller had received a fair price for the 1909S and had been exploited in selling the 1914D.

Experimenter. The author (B) and his assistant (G) each served as the coin seller for an equal number of times in each experimental condition. Two experimenters were used in order to minimize the possibility of experimenter effects (Rosenthal, 1966). Experimenters were alternated between the coin seller and data collector roles (described below) and made independent estimates of all observations.

Shop size. Pre-experimental discussions with both coin dealers and collectors suggested that large shops might be able to pay more money for the coins since they have more capital to invest and a greater volume of business than do the small shops. These discussions also suggested that a small shop might be less likely to exploit a naïve seller. To check such possibilities and to control their influence on the theoretical variables, the shops were divided into two categories, large and small, on the basis of their advertisements in the Yellow Pages of the telephone book. Ad sizes were rated from 1 (1–3 lines) to 9 (one-eighth of a page). All 1 and 2 shops were classified as small, and anything over 5 was large. Sizes 3 and 4 were classified either large or small depending on a number of other factors, such as physical size, presence of large safes and teletype machines, volume of coins on display, location, and decor.

The accuracy of the size of advertisement as an index of shop size is attested to by two independent checks. First, of the 31 shops that were closed or had disconnected telephones, 23 had ads of size 1, 3 were size 2, while only 1 shop had an ad of size 5 or greater. Second, shops that we had classified as large on the basis of the telephone ads had significantly more employees (average = 2.2) than did the small shops (average = 1.5; $p < .007$).

PROCEDURE

The two experimenters always entered the coin shop together. Both were dressed similarly in levis and short-sleeved sport shirts with tails hanging out (to conceal the tape recorder in the coin seller's back pocket). The experimenter posing as the coin seller waited until the dealer was not engaged with another customer (never more than a few minutes). He then approached the dealer with the opening question: "Hi, do you buy coins?" On receiving an affirmative answer or being directed to the person who bought coins, the experimenter explained why he wanted to sell the coins, gave the coins to the dealer, and then explained what had happened to the missing coin. During this period the coin seller was responsible for recording the conversation, timing interruptions due to such irrelevant events as speaking with other customers, and responding to the dealer in ways that were consistent with his initial story (such as being ignorant of the coins' value or having chosen this dealer on the basis of a customer's recommendation). The coin seller also noted any sources, such as the *Red Book* or *Coin World* newspaper, that the dealer might check in making his appraisal of the coins' value.

While the seller was engaged with the dealer, the second experimenter was busy collecting information about the coin shop. Unobtrusively, under the guise of casually browsing around the shop, the second experimenter measured the dimensions of the shop and the counter and bid board displays of both coins and stamps. These measurements were made by covertly pacing off the area accessible to customers while ostensibly looking at the display cases. The sizes of the bid boards and display cases were obtained simultaneously. The second experimenter also noted the number of customers and employees in the shop, the relative volume of coins and stamps on display, the percentage of coins priced at $10 or more, and the existence of expensive furnishings, safes, or teletype machines.

By the time the dealer was ready to make his initial price offer, the second experimenter usually had returned to the vicinity of the seller and the dealer. Thus both experimenters frequently were able to estimate the distance between the dealer and seller, as well as eye contact, at the time of the initial price offer.

After the dealer's final offer was declined, the seller thanked the dealer for his time and information (if any), and both experimenters left the shop together. They immediately returned to their car, where the information not on the tape recorder was entered on a record sheet for that particular dealer.

Results

CHECKS ON EXPERIMENTAL MANIPULATIONS

When tape recordings of the interactions were transcribed, a check was made to see if the dealer indicated his awareness of the appeal. Every dealer made at least one comment in response to our appeal, which indicated that he had heard it. Twelve of the dealers made statements or asked questions that suggested that they had not understood our story. Typical among these was the question of why we did not sell all of the coins to the dealer who bought the most valuable one. Whenever such a question was raised, the seller always reiterated that portion of the appeal that was not clear until the dealer indicated that he understood. Dealers who heard the moral appeal made more moral self-references (mean = 1.4) than did those who heard the neutral appeal (0.6; $F = 6.7$, $df = 1$, 47, $p < .01$). Finally, it should be noted that every dealer was willing to listen to our entire appeal; none gave any evidence of doubting its veracity, and several indicated that other people had sold them coins for similar reasons (inherited them and did not want to start collecting, or wanted to obtain money for some other purpose).

EFFECTS OF TYPE OF APPEAL

Price offers. When the prices the dealers offered to pay for the coins were compared, the moral appeal was found to elicit higher bids than did the neutral one (average = $13.63 for moral, $8.72 for neutral; $F = 20.6$, df = 1, 49, $p < .0001$). This difference involved only the initial bid. When the seller indicated disappointment with the bid, 10 of the 65 subjects changed their bids at least once. Four of these dealers were in the moral appeal condition, and six were in the neutral condition. The neutral appeal dealers were higher than the moral appeal dealers on the average number of price changes (2 to 1), the average amount of price increase ($2 to 40 cents), and the average percentage of increase from the initial offer (45 percent to 5 percent).

When the final offer for each dealer is considered, a significant difference still exists between the moral appeal and neutral appeal dealers, even though the neutral appeal dealers made greater increases in their price offers than did the moral appeal dealers.

Nonverbal measures. Eye contact was rated on a three-point scale, with 1 signifying that the dealer looked into the seller's eyes when he made his initial offer, 2 that he was looking in the seller's direction (but not in his eyes) and established eye contact during the comments he made immediately after the bid, and 3 that the dealer did not establish eye contact with the seller either during or immediately after the initial price offer. Eye contact at the time of the first bid was greater with the moral appeal (average = 1.2) than with the neutral appeal (1.8; $F = 13.9$, $df = 1$, 49, $p < .0005$).

Since the seller maintained a stable position at the counter while the dealer was appraising his coins, whatever distance there was between them at the time of the initial price offer was determined by the dealer's movement. The seller estimated this distance in terms of half feet. The results indicate that the dealer was closer to the seller when he made his initial offer after a moral appeal (average = 2.5 feet) than he was after a neutral appeal (3.1 feet; $F = 5.7$, $df = 1, 49$, $p < .02$).

Interaction measures. The tape recordings of the interactions were used to obtain two time measures and six ratings of the contents of the dealer's comments. The time lapse from the point when the dealer was given the coins until he made his first price offer (bid time) was longer after the moral appeal (average = 392 seconds) than after the neutral appeal (average = 238 seconds; $F = 6.1$, $df = 1, 47$, $p < .02$). This difference was even greater when the entire time of the interaction, including the dealer's comments after his initial offer, is considered (moral = 489 seconds; neutral = 310; $F = 8.1$, $df = 1, 47$, $p < .006$).

In four of the six content categories rated, moral appeal dealers were significantly more talkative than neutral appeal dealers. The moral appeal dealers made more moral self-references than did the neutral appeal dealers ($p < .01$). Moral appeal dealers also made more comments giving information about the coin sold to the prior dealer (average = 2.5 comments) than did the neutral appeal dealers (average = 0.9; $F = 20.5$, $df = 1, 47$, $p < .0001$). A similar difference was found in the amount of information given about the coins being offered for sale. The moral appeal dealers made a greater number of informative comments (average = 5.0) than did the neutral appeal dealers (average = 1.4; $F = 10.6$, $df = 1, 47$, $p < .002$).

The fourth category, which yielded an effect for type of appeal, involved statements suggesting profitable alternatives to accepting the dealer's highest price offer. The moral appeal dealers suggested more profitable alternatives (average = 1.6) than did the neutral appeal dealers (average = 0.9; $F = 6.1$, $df = 1, 47$, $p < .02$).

The two content categories, which did not yield significant effects for type of appeal, involved dealer statements that either substantiated or degraded the value of the coins being offered for sale.

EFFECTS OF PRIOR DEALER'S BEHAVIOR

Following prior dealer exploitation, the dealers gave more information about the coin that had been sold (average = 2.5 comments) than they did if the seller had obtained a fair deal (average = 0.9, $F = 20.5$, $df = 1$, 47, $p < .001$). This effect was strongest when the dealer was giving information to an exploited seller who made a moral appeal. When talking to a seller who had been exploited, dealers made fewer comments that degraded the value of his remaining coins (average = 3.4) than they did to sellers who had previously received a fair price for the sold coin (average = 5.5; $F = 3.7$, $df = 1$, 47, $p < .06$). Dealers who made offers to previously exploited sellers also maintained greater eye contact (mean = 1.48, see previous description of eye contact scale), than did dealers making an offer to sellers who had been treated fairly by preivous dealers (mean = 1.59) ($F = 4.8$, $df = 1$, 49, $p < .03$).

EXPERIMENTER EFFECTS

All of the dependent variables were analyzed to check for differences between the two experimenters—the author (B) and his assistant (G)—who enacted the coin seller role. Only one effect was found. Although the two experimenters served as sellers for equal numbers of small and large coin shops, G's shops had more employees (average 2.2) than did B's (average = 1.5; $F = 11.1$, $df = 1$, 48, $p < .002$).

SHOP SIZE

Considered as a group, the results attributable to differences in shop size suggest that small-shop dealers were more responsive to our experimental manipulations than were large-shop dealers. Small-shop dealers took a longer time to evaluate the coins and make comments before making their first bids (373 seconds) than did the large-shop dealers (258 seconds; $F = 3.4$, $df = 1$, 47, $p < .07$). Following the moral appeal, by far the greatest number of moral self-references were made by small-shop dealers. Although large-shop dealers were known to have more money available to buy coins, their average offer ($10.84) was not significantly different from that of the small-shop dealers ($11.51). In fact, after a moral appeal the small-shop dealers offered an average of nearly a dollar more than did the large-shop dealers. Again this difference is not significant, but given our knowledge that the large-shop dealers could pay more, these two results suggest that the small-shop dealers were most responsive to the moral appeal.

Discussion

When confronted with a naïve, readily exploitable, and totally co-operative seller, the dealers offered significantly more money with a moral appeal ($13.63) than without one ($8.72). A consideration of the other findings involving appeal type suggests that the moral appeal elicited a concerned effort to help the seller, while the neutral appeal resulted in a combination of businesslike responses and exploitative attempts.

The analyses of the verbal interactions provide the strongest set of data to support this explanation for the difference in the price offers of the moral and neutral appeal dealers. These analyses showed that after hearing the moral appeal, dealers took time to give the coin seller more information about his coins and the coin market, which would be helpful to him in obtaining the highest possible price for the coins. In a similar vein, the moral appeal dealers made more specific suggestions about ways in which the seller might compare prices and elicit higher offers.

Our nonverbal measures indicated that while making their initial offer moral appeal dealers stood closer to and had more eye contact with the seller than did the neutral appeal dealers. Mehrabian's (1968) discussion of research relating nonverbal behavior to inter-personal feelings indicates that both (1) a smaller distance between communicants and (2) more eye contact between them communicate a positive attitude. Particularly relevant is Machotka's (1965) finding (cited in Mehrabian, 1968) that the communicator's maintenance of eye contact indicates *concern* for the addressee. Applied to our results this earlier finding suggests a greater concern for the seller on the part of our moral appeal dealers.

Dealers in this study offered between $2.50 and $20 for the coins. Discussions with various informants indicated that offers of $12 and greater should be considered fair, and that a dealer might legitimately offer considerably less if he had no particular need for the coins or honestly felt they were overgraded. While such factors no doubt operated in some instances, they do account for the distribution of our lowest price offers. There were 14 final price offers of less than $8, and 12 of these came from neutral appeal dealers. Of these 14 low-offer dealers, 8 gave virtually no explanation for their low offers, while the others made considerable reference to legitimate factors such as those considered above. All 8 dealers who did not explain their offers had received the neutral appeal. Thus, while we have no conclusive evidence of attempted exploitation our data strongly suggest such efforts by at least 8 out of a total of 32 neutral appeal dealers.

Finally, a consideration of the 10 dealers who increased their initial price offers is equally consistent with the explanation that the neutral appeal dealers were acting as good businessmen while the moral appeal dealers were more concerned with helping the seller. About equal numbers of neutral appeal and moral appeal dealers increased their initial price offers. However, the neutral appeal dealers tended to start with lower initial offers, which allowed them to make larger bid increases ($2 to 40 cents for moral appeal subjects) and still end up with lower final offers than those of the moral appeal dealers.

In attempting to understand why the moral appeal elicited helping behavior, it is important to remember that the appeal was made on several bases. In the moral appeal condition the coin seller presented himself as a person who needed money for an admirable purpose (to buy textbooks to study for exams) and was in a financial bind through no fault of his own. Further, he was ignorant of the coins' value and had been sent to this dealer specifically by another customer who attested to the dealer's honesty and trustworthiness. Thus, in the moral appeal condition, external circumstances that he could not control made the coin seller dependent on coin dealers for help, and he chose to depend on a particular dealer on the basis of his ethical reputation.

This situation is similar to that involved in laboratory research of helping behavior in that the coin seller clearly evoked a norm of social responsibility in appealing to the dealer for help. As initially formulated by Berkowitz and Daniels (1963), the norm of social responsibility prescribes that a person help those in need of help. Further research relevant to the present study indicates that a powerful person's efforts to help a dependent person are greater when (1) the costs of helping are low (Schopler & Bateson, 1965) and (2) the dependence is perceived to be caused by external (environmental) rather than internal (personal) factors (Schopler & Matthews, 1965).

Both of these factors appear to have worked to the coin seller's advantage in our study. The financial costs of helping the dependent seller probably were low relative to the psychological rewards inherent in helping him or to the psychological costs of exploiting him. The cost of a few dollars risked in a high price offer was probably minimized by the satisfaction of helping an unfortunate victim of circumstances who recognized the dealer's magnanimity. To exploit the helpless seller would require violation of both the dictates of the social responsibility norm and the trust of a regular customer. These psychological costs were undoubtedly high relative to the potential monetary reward for exploitation.

In the second finding, involving the perceived cause of the dependence, our coin seller was clearly portrayed as being made dependent by external factors. Thus we may apply the conclusion of the Schopler and Matthews study (1965) to the relationship that existed between our coin seller and the moral appeal dealer: "If the partner [coin seller] is seen as a victim of circumstances he will be helped more than if he is seen as being dependent of his own volition [because] voluntary dependence lessens the salience of the social responsibility norm [pp. 611–12]."

In addition to evoking social responsibility pressures, our moral appeal also emphasized the relevance of moral standards of fairness or honesty to the evaluation of the dealer's behavior, a factor found to lessen exploitation in at least one laboratory study (Meeker & Shure, 1969). Although we cannot isolate the effects of the second component from those of the social responsibility norm in our moral appeal, the data from the prior dealer's behavior variable strongly suggest that social responsibility pressures were responsible for the helping behavior.

The few results attributable to prior dealer's behavior consistently suggest that when the earlier dealer purchased the valuable penny ($140) for only $15 he was rejected as a behavioral model, and his behavior made moral issues salient without the seller's ever making an independent moral appeal. The reactions of the dealers as they gave information about the valuable coin strongly suggest that this was the case. "My God! That's terrible!" and other similar exclamations, followed by a hurried leafing through a coin price guide and additional informative comments about how much they would have paid and how to get the coin back, clearly indicated that they rejected his behavior as unethical and dissociated themselves from it. The findings of greater eye contact (by small-shop dealers especially) and less degrading of the coins' value after prior dealer exploitation could also be viewed within this context as attempts to further dissociate oneself from the exploitative prior dealer by showing some concern for the seller.

Assuming that the exploitativeness of a prior dealer aroused the subject's awareness of the ethical issues involved in his transaction with the coin seller, it is interesting to note that prior dealer behavior had no effect on price offers. This finding suggests that the variations in price offers due to the type of appeal variable resulted from the dealer's response to the seller's need of financial help (and the social responsibility norm thereby elicited) rather than from his efforts to emphasize norms of honesty and trustworthiness.

Finally, it should be noted that in presenting himself as being ignorant of the coin's value our seller made it clear that only the dealer would know if he offered a fair price. This situation is quite different from the pacifist appeal cited above (Meeker & Shure, 1969), in which both the potential exploiter and the pacifist are able to evaluate the fairness of the behavior.

A conceivable alternative interpretation of our findings might be that the dealers who heard the moral appeal became concerned about maintenance of their reputations with the stamp collector who recommended them. Thus, to enhance their reputations the moral appeal dealers were helpful to the seller. Although this explanation cannot be entirely ruled out, it is belied by several factors, one of which is the spontaneity of the dealers' responses. They did not appear to take time to consider their responses before giving them. Only six of the dealers asked about the stamp collector, and the average price offer of these dealers ($12.67) was, in fact, less than the overall moral appeal offer ($13.63). Even if the dealers actually were concerned about maintaining their reputations, they would not have had to offer more than the neutral appeal dealers since the naïve seller would have had no way of judging the fairness of their offers. They could easily have convinced him of their fairness while making a lower offer.

REFERENCES

Berkowitz, L., and Daniels, L. R. 1963. Responsibility and dependency. *Journal of Abnormal and Social Psychology* 66: 429–36.

Meeker, R. J., and Shure, G. H. 1969. Pacifist bargaining tactics: Some "outsider" influences. *Journal of Conflict Resolution* 13: 487–93.

Mehrabian, A. 1968. Inference of attitudes from the posture, orientation, and distance of a communicator. *Journal of Consulting and Clinical Psychology* 32: 296–308.

Rosenthal, R. 1966. *Experimenter effects in behavioral research.* New York: Appleton-Century-Crofts.

Schopler, J., and Bateson, N. 1965. The power of dependence. *Journal of Personality and Social Psychology* 2: 247–54.

Schopler, J., and Matthews, M. 1965. The influence of perceived causal locus of partner's dependence on the use of interpersonal power. *Journal of Personality and Social Psychology* 2: 609–12.

8 GROUP INFLUENCE

Little available literature on the experimental analysis of group influence is concerned with long-term changes in behavior, attitudes, or beliefs. People display quite marked behavioral and attitudinal changes when their positions within groups are altered or when they perceive that the group's position or standing relative to other groups has changed. People do not care to be associated with poorly regarded groups, and they avoid being poorly regarded within their own groups. Members' positions and roles also change within groups when the group as a whole is experiencing periods of crisis, victory, low esteem, and the like.

The readings in this section concentrate on changes in members' behavior and attitudes as they occur over time. All experimental research in field situations is difficult to set up and control, but long-term studies are particularly troublesome. The first study is an excellent example of a controlled experimental culture, designed and manipulated to explore specific hypotheses. The Menzel and Lieberman studies both make use of naturally occurring variations of the independent variable.

Two of the articles in this section deviate from the general criteria for inclusion of readings. The Sherifs' study was conducted on children and is a perfect example of the type of important theoretical questions one can explore by using children as subjects. The Menzel study is the only selection that is not, in the strict sense, experimental. Menzel made use of a naturally occurring event, the introduction of a new drug, to determine the discrepancy between what a person said he did versus what he actually did. The important theoretical question Menzel considered is that of the effects of a person's status position within a group on that person's stated versus actual compliance with the group's norms or shared values. An experimental study addressed to this same question would require that the status position of the subject be manipulated—a task not at all easy to accomplish. The Lieberman study does demonstrate a role change experiment in which a person's actual position in the group was altered over time. A similar design concentrating on status changes within a natural group might well be possible.

In the Lieberman study matched control groups were used to provide baseline attitude change data on employees whose roles remained unchanged. The matched control problem in such natural field studies can be extraordinarily difficult to handle. For example, if one wanted to look at changes in a football player's attitudes toward aggression as he advanced from amateur to professional status one would not go to the geriatric ward of a hospital to obtain control subjects. But where should one go or, rather, whom should one select as a comparison group? Amateur ball players who remain amateurs might be chosen. Perhaps such players do not attain professional status because they have poorer motor coordination. Those who have superior coordination are more likely to make the professional teams and develop more aggressive attitudes. Perhaps, though, those amateurs who develop greater aggressive dispositions or attitudes make professional teams.

Usually in matched control group studies the experimenter decides what personal characteristics of the subjects are likely to be important. The researcher then selects control subjects whose characteristics match those of the experimental subjects on a subject-to-subject basis.

A more important demonstration of the causal relationship between the independent and dependent variable (besides indicating that the control group was properly matched) is to reverse the independent variable manipulation. If changes in the dependent variable follow the introduction as well as the removal of the independent variable condition, the experimenter can be far more confident that a causal relationship holds. Lieberman was able to collect some data on persons who returned to previous role positions, and he offers an example of an off-on-off type of independent variable manipulation.

16. Ingroup and intergroup relations: Experimental analysis   Musafer Sherif and Carolyn W. Sherif

The development and effects of ingroup and outgroup delineation in a situation that fostered rivalry were examined in an experimental study of boys in a summer camp setting. By structuring the boys' activities the experimenters were able to observe the effects of intergroup competitive tournaments and frustrating events on intergroup hostility. Hostile clashes were observed, but despite the high level of intergroup aggression, procedures were found that had the effect of reducing the level of conflict.

When individuals who have no established relationships are brought together to interact in group activities with common goals, they produce a group structure that contains hierarchical statuses and roles.

Abstracted from: *Social Psychology,* chap. 11 (New York: Harper & Row, 1969).

If two ingroups thus formed are brought into functional relationship in conditions of competition and group frustration, attitudes and appropriate hostile actions in relation to the outgroup and its members will arise and will be standardized and shared in varying degrees by group members.

To test these notions three separate experiments were conducted in the natural setting of a boys' summer camp. The subjects were 11- to 12-year-old boys who had similar family backgrounds but had no previous acquaintance with the other boys in the camp.

The specific hypotheses tested during the three-week camp sessions in the three experiments were as follows.

Group Formation

Hypothesis 1. When individuals participate in group formation, their initially formed friendship choices will be switched to favor members of their new group.

Hypothesis 2. When a collectivity of individuals, unknown to one another, interact together in activities that have a common goal and appeal and require their concerted effort, over time a group will form and will be evidenced by (1) differential roles and statuses and (2) norms regulating group behavior.

Intergroup Conflict

Hypothesis 3. When two established groups participate in competitive activities that only one may win, over time friendly competition will turn into intergroup hostility.

Hypothesis 4. During competitive activities unfavorable attitudes and conceptions (stereotypes) of the outgroup will form, resulting in lack of communication or contact between the groups.

Hypothesis 5. Conflict between the groups serves to increase ingroup unity.

Hypothesis 6. Ingroup unity and pride is shown by the members' overestimation of the ingroup's achievement and lower estimates of outgroup performance.

Hypothesis 7. Interaction between groups (i.e., conflict) will produce changes in the ingroup's organization and practices.

Conflict Reduction

Hypothesis 8. Activities that both groups' members participate in as individuals and that require no interdependency do not reduce intergroup conflict.

Hypothesis 9. When groups must work together toward a goal that is highly appealing to each group but cannot be attained by one group alone, they will cooperate.

Hypothesis 10. Cooperation between the groups toward a series of superordinate goals serves to reduce the social distance and negative impressions of the outgroup and thus reduces intergroup conflict.

In all three experiments the data were collected by trained observers who acted in roles of camp leaders and made daily ratings on the developing relationships among the boys in terms of the amount of effective initiative each boy showed (a measure of status). Informal interview notes also determined whom the boys considered to be their current best friends (sociometric measure). The camp leaders did not initiate or guide camp activities, and gave advice only when directly asked by the boys. Every effort was made to keep the boys naïve about the experimental nature of the camp.

At the beginning of camp the boys were free to choose companions in the camp activities. Following the formation of these small friendship circles, the boys in the first two experiments (1949 and 1953) were split into two groups in such a way that in each group two-thirds of the best friends were in different groups. In the 1954 study this stage of group formation began when Ss were divided into two groups according to the matched size and skills of the individual boys. During the week the groups in all three experiments had little contact with each other and separately engaged in appealing and cooperative activities (i.e., cooking, transporting canoes). At the end of the week (1949 and 1953 experiments) the boys were asked who their best friends were. As shown in Figure 16.1, Hypothesis 1 was confirmed—the boys switched their friendship choices to group members.

Gradually, as expected in Hypothesis 2, the experiments' two groups formed into a definite group organization involving differ-

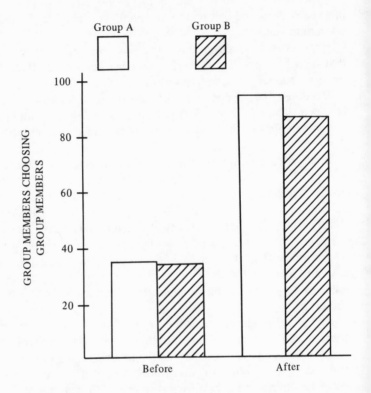

Figure 16.1.
Friendship Choices Before and After Group Formation.

entiated roles according to the boys' individual talents and status positions. The highest status boy showed effective initiative in many activities and assumed a leadership position. Also, as predicted, each group developed norms peculiar to the group. For example, in the 1954 study one group developed a norm of toughness to such an extent that members refused to report any injury to camp leaders. The other group, however, created a norm that emphasized the importance of being good (no swearing, praying before meals). Gradually, as the groups formed, nicknames were given to individual members, and each group developed a little culture consisting of secrets, private jokes and vocabulary, and secret hiding places. Further, each group developed ways of punishing those members who violated group norms. The groups then named themselves in order to be distinguished from the other groups—the Red Devils and the Bull Dogs (1949), Panthers and Pythons (1953), and Rattlers and Eagles (1954). Thus the criteria for group formation as described in Hypothesis 2 seem to be satisfied.

In order to begin to examine *inter*group relations in the three experiments, it was arranged for the two groups to compete in a tournament of games. Prizes were to be given to the victorious group and individual prizes to the winning group's members. The tournament in each experiment began with a spirit of friendly competition. However, as the games progressed, the sense of good sportsmanship vanished. For example, after the Red Devils (1949) had experienced a losing streak they began accusing the proud Bull Dogs of playing dirty.

After the tournament the camp leaders planned a purposely frustrating situation that appeared to have been devised by one group. A party was held for both groups in order to bury the hatchet. Through the camp leaders' careful timing (not suspected by the boys), the Red Devils arrived at the party before the Bull Dogs and were thus able to enjoy the best of the assorted refreshments. On arrival the Bull Dogs realized that they had been left the less delectable food and immediately started to insult and taunt the Red Devils.

A series of hostile clashes followed, including food wars, sneak raids on each other's cabins and hate posters displayed around camp. Gradually the hostility on both sides took on quite a premeditated and scheming character (i.e., collecting and hiding caches of green apples for ammunition). Thus, as predicted (Hypotheses 3 and 4), out of the competitive nature of the tournament rose intergroup hostility. Further, as evidenced by the posters and name calling, derogatory images and stereotypes of the outgroup (the beginning of prejudice) were formed and led to great social distance

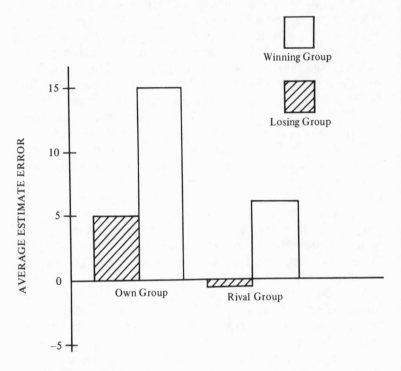

Figure 16.2.
Average Errors in Estimating Performance for Ingroup and Outgroup.

between groups. Also, boys described ingroup members in favorable terms (brave and tough) but rated outgroup members unfavorably (sneaky, smart alecks).

In order to test the predictions about a group's achievement estimation, a game of bean toss was arranged and a prize was offered to the group that not only collected the most beans but also judged the game's outcome most accurately. Figure 16.2 indicates judgment errors in the boys' estimates of the amount collected by ingroup and outgroup members. As expected (Hypothesis 6), the members of one group tended to overestimate their group's achievement and underestimate the performance of the other group. Winners tended to make larger errors.

Sociometric measures taken after the tournament further supported Hypothesis 5. The conflict between the groups tended to increase group unity, and friendship choices were made almost exclusively within the ingroup. The hostility also served to produce the expected organizational changes within the groups (Hypothesis

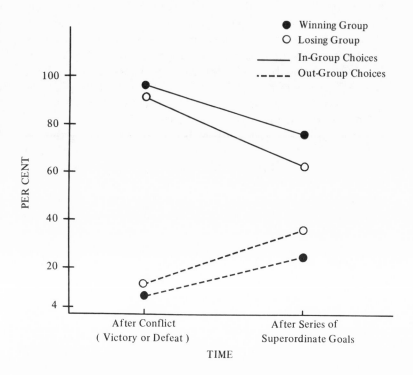

Figure 16.3.
Friendship Choices Before and After Series of Superordinate Goals. Figure 11.21b (p. 263) in *Social Psychology* by Muzafer Sherif and Carolyn W. Sherif (Harper & Row, 1969).

7). In the Eagles the leader role changed hands from peacetime (group formation) to this period of conflict. In another group a low status bully found himself in the leadership role when the intergroup conflict began. To an outside observer these intelligent, well adjusted, middle class boys would probably be described as violent, disturbed, or delinquent.

Now, to the constructive phase of these experiments. How can we reduce the intergroup conflict? As expected (Hypothesis 8), activities such as moviegoing or shooting firecrackers that had appeal but no need for cooperation between groups did not reduce hostility. Therefore, superordinate goals were created (i.e., goals that are important to both groups but cannot be attained by only one group), such as finding a fault in a water supply line and pooling money to see a desired movie. After a series of these cooperative activities, the amount of intergroup conflict was reduced (Hypothesis 10) and members began to act friendlier. Interviews reflected this change in attitudes. Many friendship choices were now made from the outgroup, and negative ideas about outgroup members rapidly dissipated (Figure 16.3).

Can we dismiss these findings as being true only among children and not applicable in the sphere of adults? Current research (Blake, Shepard & Mouton, 1964) suggests that we most definitely can not. Adults in human relations workshops were divided into two groups, given problems, and asked to find better solutions than the other group could devise. The events that occurred faithfully replicated the Sherifs' findings. The competitive activities engendered hostility between groups, but cooperative activities dissipated the hostility. Perhaps nations can coexist peacefully if they develop goals that are mutually meaningful and beneficial and can be realized only if the nations jointly cooperate.

REFERENCE

Blake, R. R.; Shepard, H. A.; and Mouton, Jane S. 1964. *Managing intergroup conflict in industry*. Houston, Texas: Gulf Publishing.

17. Public and private conformity under different conditions of acceptance in the group Herbert Menzel

Physicians were asked to state the date on which they prescribed a new drug. Actual dates of new drug introduction
were estimated by examining the local pharmacies' records
of prescriptions written by these same doctors over a 15-
month period. The physicians' status within the local medical community was determined sociometrically by asking
the doctors to specify three other physicians from whom
they would seek advice. The data indicated that low status
physicians reported that they used the drug earlier than the
prescription records indicated, whereas higher status
physicians seldom did so. The results suggest that low
status doctors conform more to the norm in order to be
up-to-date as compared with higher status doctors.

Dittes and Kelley (1956) reported an experiment on conformity
to group norms which showed, among other things, that the subject's experimentally induced feeling of acceptance within the group
had a rather different effect on his private and public expressions
of conformity to the group's previously established judgment. It
was found, in brief, that individuals whose feeling of being accepted
in the group was high felt the greatest freedom to express any
disagreement with the group's judgment publicly. Individuals whose
feeling of acceptance was low exhibited high public conformity but
showed little conformity in their private expressions. Individuals
who were made to feel an "average" level of acceptance exhibited
a "high degree of genuine adherence to the norms . . . extending

Reprinted from the *Journal of Abnormal Social Psychology* 55 (1957):
398–402. Copyright 1957 by the American Psychological Association, and
reproduced by permission. A fuller account of the research is contained in
James Coleman, Elihu Katz, and Herbert Menzel, *Medical Innovation—A
Diffusion Study* (Indianapolis: Bobbs-Merrill, 1966).

even to conditions of privacy." The present note addresses itself exclusively to the similarity or difference between public and private conformity, and not to the determination of private conformity as such.

Data

The conclusions of Dittes and Kelley in this respect can be applied in slightly modified form to data on the use of new drugs by physicians. Eighty-five percent of the general practitioners, internists, and pediatricians practicing in four selected cities were interviewed regarding their use of a certain widely used family of drugs, comprising several new variants which had made their appearance successively in the course of recent years. At the same time, the records of prescriptions written by these same doctors were examined in the local pharmacies for sampling dates extending over a period of 15 months. One may think of the physician's writing of prescriptions as his private behavior, and of his declarations in the course of an interview as the analogue of "public" expressions in the sense of the Dittes and Kelley experiment. So defined, "public" and "private" data are available on three items of behavior: (a) the date on which the doctor used "gammanym," the newest variant of the family of drugs, for the first time; (b) which of the three chief available variants he favored at the time the interviews were conducted; (c) which of the two chief variants then available he favored 15 months earlier.

Results and Discussion

EXISTENCE OF NORMS

In the fluid situation created by the recurrent appearance of new drugs, there is no established norm on record as to which of two or three competing variants a physician should prefer, nor as to the "right" date on which to introduce a new drug into one's practice. What the norm in these respects was at the time the interviews were conducted can, however, be inferred from the prevailing direction of the discrepancies between private performance and public accounts of behavior: (a) One-half of the physicians stated as the

Table 17.1.

Date of Introduction of a New Drug: Interval Between Interview Statements and Prescription Record

DATE ACCORDING TO INTERVIEW	PERCENTAGE OF DOCTORS ($N = 70$)
Follows prescription date by 2 months or more	24%
Falls within 1 month's distance of prescription date	27
Precedes prescription date by 2–7 months	25
Precedes prescription date by more than 7 months	24
	100%

date on which they first used the newest drug a date earlier—often many months earlier—than that established by the prescription search (Table 17.1). (*b*) Two-thirds of the physicians whose prescription record at the time of interviewing showed predominant use of the oldest drug stated that they preferred one of the newer drugs. Sixty percent of those whose current prescription record showed predominant use of the middle one of the three drugs stated that they preferred the newest (Table 17.2). (*c*) A substantial portion (29 percent) of the 52 doctors who, according to their prescription record, had prescribed predominantly the oldest variant 15 months before the interviews took place, failed to make any

Table 17.2.

Drug Variant Favored at Time of Interview

VARIANT FAVORED ACCORDING TO INTERVIEW STATEMENT	VARIANT FAVORED ACCORDING TO PRESCRIPTION RECORD		
	OLDEST	MIDDLE	NEWEST
Oldest	33%	8%	6%
Middle	25	32	18
Newest	42	60	76
Total	100%	100%	100%
N	(24)	(25)	(61)

Table 17.3.
Discrepancies in Date of First Prescription of a New Drug, by
Sociometric Status

INTRODUCTION DATE ACCORDING TO INTERVIEW STATEMENT	NUMBER OF DESIGNATIONS RECEIVED AS ADVISOR		
	NONE	ONE OR TWO	THREE OR MORE
Earlier than by prescription record	63%	33%	36%
Same as by prescription record[a]	26	33	21
Later than by prescription record	11	33	43
Total	100%	100%	100%
N	(35)	(21)	(14)

[a]Allowing a one-month tolerance.

mention of this drug when recounting the history of their use of drugs of this general kind.

From these results it may be concluded that there prevailed, at the time of the interviewing, norms in these communities of physicians which placed high value on (a) having introduced the newest drug early; (b) currently favoring the newest drug over its predecessors; (c) having favored the middle drug over the oldest 15 months earlier (i.e., before the appearance of the newest drug). Thus, with respect to all three items of behavior, the preponderant direction of the discrepancies between the prescription record and the interview statements is such that the interview statements make the doctor appear more up-to-date. This finding supports the inference that the prevailing norm in these medical communities at the time of interviewing was generally favorable to modernity, at least in the use of drugs. The findings to be reported below, however, are of interest even if the above three sets of discrepancies merely express three separate norms relating specifically to the use of the particular drugs in question.

CONFORMITY AND ACCEPTANCE IN THE GROUP

When the physician's standing in his medical community is taken into account, it is found that the discrepancies in the prevailing direction occur most frequently among the low-status physicians, who tend to make themselves appear more up-to-date than they really are. An individual's standing in the community of his colleagues is measured by the number of designations accorded him in response to the sociometric question: "When you need information or advice about questions of therapy, . . . on whom are you most likely to call?" It is chiefly those seldom or never named in answer to this question whose interview statements make them appear more up-to-date than their prescription record.

Table 17.3 shows this relationship for the date on which the doctor used the newest of the drugs for the first time. The contrast is quite marked, but is partly due to a ceiling effect: high status individuals did in fact tend to be more up-to-date in the timing of their first use of this new drug, and hence had less opportunity to deviate, in their interview statements, in the up-to-date direction. However, the phenomenon persists even when actual performance is held constant, as shown in Table 17.4. Doctors were first divided into two-month intervals according to their drug introduction date as established by the prescription search. Within each such two-month interval, the median interview statement as to the introduction date of the drug was then determined. Each doctor was then

Table 17.4.
Discrepancies in Date of First Prescription of a New Drug, in Relation to Sociometric Status, with Actual Performance Held Constant

PERCENTAGE OF DOCTORS WHO STATED A DRUG INTRODUCTION DATE EARLIER(LATER) THAN THE MEDIAN DATE STATED BY THOSE WHO ACTUALLY INTRODUCED THE DRUG SIMULTANEOUSLY WITH THEM	NUMBER OF DESIGNATIONS RECEIVED AS ADVISOR		
	NONE	ONE OR TWO	THREE OR MORE
Earlier than median	60%	45%	36%
Later than median	40	55	64
Total	100%	100%	100%
N	(35)	(21)	(14)

classified according to whether his own interview statement gave a date later or earlier than the median statement of doctors who actually introduced the drug within the same two-month interval as he did. It is seen that even when possible ceiling effects are eliminated by holding the date of introduction according to the prescription record constant, those of low standing in the group show a quite disproportionate tendency to report an introduction date which precedes that established from the prescription record.

Table 17.5 records the results obtained with respect to the second item of behavior: variant favored at the time the interviews were conducted. The necessity to control for actual performance here makes for very small base figures, and the results are somewhat less consistent than in Table 17.4, but they are substantially of the same order. Those of high standing in the group consistently up-date their behavior less than do those of low standing, although those of intermediate standing do not always fall into the expected

Table 17.5
Discrepancies in Drug Favored at the Time of Interviewing, in Relation to Sociometric Status

	NUMBER OF DESIGNATIONS RECEIVED AS ADVISOR		
	NONE	ONE OR TWO	THREE OR MORE
Percentage who stated they favored a *newer* variant than prescription record shows, among those who prescribed predominantly:			
the oldest variant	67% (12)	77% (9)	33% (3)
the middle variant	64% (11)	63% (8)	50% (6)
Percentage who stated they favored an *older* variant than prescription record shows, among those who prescribed predominantly:			
the middle variant	9% (11)	0% (8)	17% (6)
the newest variant	21% (24)	29% (14)	23% (13)

place. The two last rows of Table 17.5 show that this difference is specific to distortions in the direction of the norm; the relatively few distortions that occur in the opposite direction are, if anything, more prevalent among those of high standing.

Table 17.6 records the results for the third item of behavior: variant favored, among the two then available, 15 months prior to the time of interviewing. Once again, those of high standing in the community of colleagues only seldom reported having used, 15 months before the interviews took place, a newer drug than predominated among their recorded prescriptions, while those of low standing frequently made such reports.

Table 17.6

Discrepancies in Drug Favored 15 Months Prior to Time of Interviewing, in Relation to Sociometric Status

	NUMBER OF DESIGNATIONS RECEIVED AS ADVISOR		
	NONE	ONE OR TWO	THREE OR MORE
Percentage who stated they favored the newer variant, among those who prescribed predominantly the oldest	33% (24)	30% (20)	13% (8)

Discussion

Thus, with respect to all three items of behavior on which information is available, doctors of low standing in the community frequently reported, during an interview, more up-to-date behavior than is indicated by the prescription record, while doctors of high standing seldom did so. Since, as was shown above, the general norm favored being up-to-date in the three matters under investigation (and perhaps in other matters as well), these results seem to be close parallels to the corresponding findings of the Dittes and Kelley experiment.

One may note that the high-status doctors not infrequently deviated in their public (i.e., interview) statements from their prescription record in the "wrong" direction, that is, so as to appear *less* up-to-date than they actually were. It is not clear from the Dittes and Kelley report whether individuals who agreed with the group privately ever expressed disagreement in public. If not, the contrast may be due to the fact that in the present study the norm of the group was not "crystallized and registered," while the doctors' statements were subject to a certain amount of unmotivated error due to faulty recall, which played no part in the Dittes and Kelley experiment. It is also possible that there existed, uniquely among the high status individuals, a competing norm in favor of conservatism; but this seems an unlikely explanation in view of the simultaneous finding that high status individuals tended to be more up-to-date in fact than low status individuals, at least in the date of their introduction of the newest of the drugs.

REFERENCE

Dittes, J. E., and Kelley, H. H. 1956. Effects of different conditions of acceptance upon conformity to group norms. *Journal of Abnormal and Social Psychology* 53: 100–107.

18. **The effects of changes in roles on the attitudes of role occupants** Seymour Lieberman

Two groups of rank-and-file workers who underwent role changes in a factory situation completed questionnaires to determine attitudes toward management and the union. Workers promoted to foremen became more favorable

Reprinted with permission of the author and Plenum Publishing Corporation from *Human Relations* 9 (1956): 385–402.

toward management, whereas workers elected as union stewards became more favorable toward the union. At a later period those foremen and stewards who reverted back to their previous rank-and-file worker roles tended to revert to the attitudes they held prior to role change. Foremen who retained their foremen's positions retained or increased the favorable attitudes toward management they developed when they were first promoted.

Problem

One of the fundamental postulates of role theory, as expounded by Newcomb (1952), Parsons (1951), and other role theorists, is that a person's attitudes will be influenced by the role that he occupies in a social system. Although this proposition appears to be a plausible one, surprisingly little evidence is available that bears directly on it. One source of evidence is found in common folklore. "Johnny is a changed boy since he was made a monitor in school." "She is a different woman since she got married." "You would never recognize him since he became foreman." As much as these expressions smack of the truth, they offer little in the way of systematic or scientific support for the proposition that a person's attitudes are influenced by his role.

Somewhat more scientific, but still not definitive, is the common finding, in many social-psychological studies, that relationships exist between attitudes and roles. In other words, different attitudes are held by people who occupy different roles. For example, Stouffer et al. (1949) found that commissioned officers are more favorable toward the Army than are enlisted men. The problem here is that the mere existence of a relationship between attitudes and roles does not reveal the cause and effect nature of the relationship found. One interpretation of Stouffer's finding might be that being made a commissioned officer tends to result in a person's becoming pro-Army—i.e. the role a person occupies influences his attitudes. But an equally plausible interpretation might be that being pro-Army tends to result in a person's being made a commissioned officer— i.e., a person's attitudes influence the likelihood of his being selected for a given role. In the absence of longitudinal data, the relationship offers no clear evidence that roles were the "cause" and attitudes the "effect."

The present study was designed to examine the effects of roles on attitudes in a particular field situation. The study is based on longitudinal data obtained in a role-differentiated, hierarchical organization. By taking advantage of natural role changes among personnel in the organization, it was possible to examine people's attitudes both before and after they underwent changes in roles. Therefore, the extent to which changes in roles were followed by changes in attitudes could be determined, and the cause and effect nature of any relationships found would be clear.

Method: Phase 1

The study was part of a larger project carried out in a medium-sized Midwestern company engaged in the production of home appliance equipment. Let us call the company the Rockwell Corporation. At the time that the study was done, Rockwell employed about 4,000 people. This total included about 2,500 factory workers and about 150 first-level foremen. The company was unionized, and most of the factory workers belonged to the union local, which was an affiliate of the U.A.W., C.I.O. About 150 factory workers served as stewards in the union, or roughly one steward for every foreman.

The study consisted of a "natural field experiment." The experimental variable was a change in roles, and the experimental period was the period of exposure to the experimental variable. The experimental groups were those employees who underwent changes in roles during this period; the control groups were those employees who did not change roles during this period.

In September and October 1951, attitude questionnaires were filled out by virtually all factory personnel at Rockwell—2,354 workers, 145 stewards, and 151 foremen. The questions dealt for the most part with employees' attitudes and perceptions about the company, the union, and various aspects of the job situation. The respondents were told that the questionnaire was part of an overall survey to determine how employees felt about working conditions at Rockwell.

Between October 1951 and July 1952, 23 workers were made foremen and 35 workers became stewards. Most of the workers who became stewards during that period were elected during the annual steward elections held in May 1952. They replaced stewards who did not choose to run again or who were not reelected by their constituents. In addition, a few workers replaced stewards who left the steward role for one reason or another throughout the year.

The workers who became foremen were not made foremen at any particular time. Promotions occurred as openings arose in supervisory positions. Some workers replaced foremen who retired or who left the company for other reasons; some replaced foremen who were shifted to other supervisory positions; and some filled newly created supervisory positions.

In December 1952, the same forms that had been filled out by the rank-and-file workers in 1951 were readministered to:

1. The workers who became foremen during the experimental period ($N = 23$).
2. A control group of workers who did not become foremen during the experimental period ($N = 46$).
3. The workers who became stewards during the experimental period ($N = 35$).
4. A control group of workers who did not become stewards during the experimental period ($N = 35$).

Each control group was matched with its parallel experimental group on a number of demographic, attitudinal, and motivational variables. Therefore, any changes in attitudes that occurred in the experimental groups but did not occur in the control groups could not be attributed to initial differences between them.

The employees in these groups were told that the purpose of the follow-up questionnaire was to get up-to-date measures of their attitudes in 1952 and to compare how employees felt that year with the way that they felt the previous year. The groups were told that, instead of studying the entire universe of employees as was the case in 1951, only a sample was being studied this time. They were informed that the sample was chosen in such a way as to represent all kinds of employees at Rockwell—men and women, young and old, etc. The groups gave no indication that they understood the real bases on which they were chosen or that the effects of changes in roles were the critical factors being examined.[1]

Results: Phase 1

The major hypothesis tested in this study was that people who are placed in a role will tend to take on or develop attitudes that are congruent with the expectations associated with that role. Since the foreman role entails being a representative of management, it might be expected that workers who are chosen as foremen will tend to become more favorable toward management. Similarly, since the steward role entails being a representative of the union, it might be expected that workers who are elected as stewards will tend to become more favorable toward the union. Moreover, in so far as the values of management and of the union are in conflict with each other, it might also be expected that workers who are made foremen will become less favorable toward the union, and workers who are made stewards will become less favorable toward management.

Four attitudinal areas were examined: (1) attitudes toward management and officials of management; (2) attitudes toward the union and officials of the union; (3) attitudes toward the management-sponsored incentive system; and (4) attitudes toward the union-sponsored seniority system. The incentive system (whereby workers are paid according to the number of pieces they turn out) and the seniority system (whereby workers are promoted according to the seniority principle) are two areas in which conflicts between management and the union at Rockwell have been particularly intense. Furthermore, first-level foremen and stewards both play a part in the administration of these systems, and relevant groups hold expectations about foreman and steward behaviors with respect to these systems. Therefore, we examined the experimental and control groups' attitudes toward these two systems as well as their overall attitudes toward management and the union.

The data tend to support the hypothesis that being placed in the

1. Some of the top officials of management and all of the top officers of the union at Rockwell knew about the nature of the follow-up study and the bases on which the experimental and control groups were selected.

foreman and steward roles will have an impact on the attitudes of the role occupants. As shown in Tables 18.1 through 18.4, both experimental groups undergo systematic changes in attitudes, in the predicted directions, from the "before" situation to the "after" situation. In the control groups, either no attitude changes occur, or less marked changes occur, from the "before" situation to the "after" situation.

Although a number of the differences are not statistically significant, those which are significant are all in the expected directions, and most of the nonsignificant differences are also in the expected directions. New foremen, among other things, come to see Rockwell as a better place to work compared with other companies, develop more positive perceptions of top management officers, and become more favorably disposed toward the principle and operation of the incentive system. New stewards come to look upon labor unions in general in a more favorable light, develop more positive perceptions of the top union officers at Rockwell, and come to prefer seniority to ability as a criterion of what should count in moving workers to better jobs. In general, the attitudes of workers who become foremen tend to gravitate in a promanagement direction and the attitudes of workers who become stewards tend to move in a pro-union direction.

A second kind of finding has to do with the relative *amount* of attitude change that takes place among new foremen in contrast to the amount that takes place among new stewards. On the whole, more pronounced and more widespread attitude changes occur among those who are made foremen than among those who are made stewards. Using a p-level of .10 as a criterion for statistical significance, the workers who are made foremen undergo significant attitude changes, relative to the workers who are not made foremen, on 10 of the 16 attitudinal items presented in Tables 18.1 through 18.4. By contrast, the workers who are made stewards undergo significant attitude changes, relative to the workers who are not made stewards, on only 3 of the 16 items. However, for the steward role as well as for the foreman role, most of the differences found between the experimental and control groups still tend to be in the expected directions.

The more pronounced and more widespread attitude changes that occur among new foremen than among new stewards can probably be accounted for in large measure by the kinds of differences that exist between the foreman and steward roles. For one thing, the foreman role represents a relatively permanent position, while many stewards take the steward role as a one-shot job, and even if they

Table 18.1
Effects of Foreman and Steward Roles on Attitudes Toward Management

| | KIND OF CHANGE | | | | | |
	MORE FAVOR-ABLE TO MANAGE-MENT	NO CHANGE	MORE CRITICAL OF MAN-AGEMENT	TOTAL	N	p
	%	%	%	%		
1. *How is Rockwell as a place to work?*						
New foremen	70	26	4	100	23	N.S.‡
Control group*	47	33	20	100	46	
New stewards	46	31	23	100	35	N.S.
Control group†	46	43	11	100	35	
2. *How does Rockwell compare with others?*						
New foremen	52	48	0	100	23	<.05
Control group	24	59	17	100	46	
New stewards	55	34	11	100	35	N.S.
Control group	43	46	11	100	35	
3. *If things went bad for Rockwell, should the workers try to help out?*						
New foremen	17	66	17	100	23	N.S.
Control group	17	66	17	100	46	
New stewards	26	74	0	100	35	N.S.
Control group	14	69	17	100	35	

Table 18.1—Continued

| | KIND OF CHANGE | | | | | |
	MORE FAVOR- ABLE TO MANAGE- MENT	NO CHANGE	MORE CRITICAL OF MAN- AGEMENT	TOTAL	N	p
	%	%	%	%		
4. *How much do management officers care about the workers at Rockwell?*						
New foremen	48	52	0	100	23	< .01
Control group	15	76	9	100	46	
New stewards	29	62	0	100	35	N.S.
Control group	20	80	0	100	35	

*Workers who did not change roles, matched with future foremen on demographic and attitudinal variables in the "before" situation.

†Workers who did not change roles, matched with future stewards on demographic and attitudinal variables in the "before" situation.

‡3 > .10.

Table 18.2
Effects of Foreman and Steward Roles on Attitudes Toward the Union

| | KIND OF CHANGE | | | | | |
	MORE FAVOR- ABLE TO THE UNION	NO CHANGE	MORE CRITICAL TO THE UNION	TOTAL	N	p
	%	%	%	%		
5. *How do you feel about labor unions in general?*						
New foremen	30	48	22	100	23	N.S.
Control group*	37	48	15	100	46	
New stewards	54	37	9	100	35	< .05
Control group†	29	65	6	100	35	

Table 18.2—Continued

	KIND OF CHANGE					
	MORE FAVOR- ABLE TO THE UNION	NO CHANGE	MORE CRITICAL TO THE UNION	TOTAL	N	p
	%	%	%	%		
6. *How much say should the union have in setting standards?*						
New foremen	0	26	74	100	23	<.01
Control group	22	54	24	100	46	
New stewards	31	66	3	100	35	N.S.
Control group	20	60	20	100	35	
7. *How would things be if there were no union at Rockwell?*						
New foremen	9	39	52	100	23	<.05
Control group	20	58	22	100	46	
New stewards	14	86	0	100	35	N.S.
Control group	11	72	17	100	35	
8. *How much do union officers care about the workers at Rockwell?*						
New foremen	22	69	9	100	23	N.S.
Control group	15	78	7	100	46	
New stewards	57	37	6	100	35	<.05
Control group	26	68	6	100	35	

*Workers who did not change roles, matched with future foremen on demographic and attitudinal variables in the "before" situation.

†Workers who did not change roles, matched with future stewards on demographic and attitudinal variables in the "before" situation.

Table 18.3
Effects of Foreman and Steward Roles on Attitudes Toward
the Incentive System

| | KIND OF CHANGE | | | | | |
	MORE FAVOR-ABLE TO INCEN-TIVE SYSTEM	NO CHANGE	MORE CRITICAL OF IN-CENTIVE SYSTEM	TOTAL	N	p
	%	%	%	%		
9. *How do you feel about the principle of an incentive system?*						
New foremen	57	26	17	100	23	<.01
Control group*	15	52	33	100	46	
New stewards	17	54	29	100	35	N.S.
Control group†	31	40	29	100	35	
10. *How do you feel the incentive system works out at Rockwell?*						
New foremen	65	22	13	100	23	<.10
Control group	37	41	22	100	46	
New stewards	43	34	23	100	35	N.S.
Control group	40	34	26	100	35	
11. *Should the incentive system be changed?*						
New foremen	39	48	13	100	23	<.01
Control group	11	69	20	100	46	
New stewards	14	63	23	100	35	N.S.
Control group	20	60	20	100	35	

Table 18.3—Continued

	MORE FAVORABLE TO IN CENTIVE SYSTEM	NO CHANGE	MORE CRITICAL OF INCENTIVE SYSTEM	TOTAL	N	p
	%	%	%	%		
12. *Is a labor standard ever changed just because a worker is a high producer?*						
New foremen	48	43	9	100	23	<.01
Control group	11	74	15	100	46	
New stewards	29	57	14	100	35	N.S.
Control group	26	65	9	100	35	

*Workers who did not change roles, matched with future foremen on demographic and attitudinal variables in the "before" situation.
†Workers who did not change roles, matched with future stewards on demographic and attitudinal variables in the "before" situation.

want to run again their constituents may not re-elect them. Second, the foreman role is a full-time job, while most stewards spend just a few hours a week in the performance of their steward functions and spend the rest of the time carrying out their regular rank-and-file jobs. Third, a worker who is made a foreman must give up his membership in the union and become a surrogate of management, while a worker who is made a steward retains the union as a reference group and simply takes on new functions and responsibilities as a representative of it. All of these differences suggest that the change from worker to foreman is a more fundamental change in roles than the change from worker to steward. This, in turn, might account to a large extent for the finding that, although attitude changes accompany both changes in roles, they occur more sharply among new foremen than among new stewards.

A third finding has to do with the *kinds* of attitude changes which occur among workers who change roles. As expected, new foremen become more promanagement, and new stewards become more prounion. Somewhat less expected is the finding that new foremen become more antiunion, but new stewards do not become more antimanagement. Among workers who are made foremen, statisti-

Table 18.4
Effects of Foreman and Steward Roles on Attitudes Toward the Seniority System

	KIND OF CHANGE					
	MORE FAVOR- ABLE TO SENIOR- ITY SYSTEM	NO CHANGE	MORE CRITICAL OF SENIOR- ITY SYSTEM	TOTAL	N	p
	%	%	%	%		
13. *How do you feel about the way the seniority system works out here?*						
New foremen	0	65	35	100	23	<.05
Control group*	20	63	17	100	46	
New stewards	23	48	29	100	35	N.S.
Control group†	9	71	20	200	35	
14. *How much should seniority count during layoffs?*						
New foremen	9	52	39	100	23	<.10
Control group	24	59	17	100	46	
New stewards	29	48	23	100	35	N.S.
Control group	29	40	31	100	35	
15. *How much should seniority count in moving to better jobs?*						
New foremen	17	44	39	100	23	N.S.
Control group	20	54	26	100	46	
New stewards	34	46	20	100	35	<.05
Control group	17	34	49	100	35	

Table 18.4—Continued

	KIND OF CHANGE					
	MORE FAVOR- ABLE TO SENIOR- ITY SYSTEM	NO CHANGE	MORE CRITICAL OF SENIOR- ITY SYSTEM	TOTAL	N	p
	%	%	%	%		
16. *How much should seniority count in promotion to foreman?*						
New foremen	17	70	13	100	23	N.S.
Control group	15	52	33	100	46	
New stewards	31	35	34	100	35	N.S.
Control group	17	43	40	100	35	

*Workers who did not change roles, matched with future foremen on demographic and attitudinal variables in the "before" situation.

†Workers who did not change roles, matched with future stewards on demographic and attitudinal variables in the "before" situation.

cally significant shifts in an antiunion direction occur on four of the eight items dealing with the union and the union-sponsored seniority system. Among workers who are made stewards, there are no statistically significant shifts in either direction on any of the eight items having to do with management and the management-sponsored incentive system.

The finding that new foremen become antiunion but that new stewards do not become antimanagement may be related to the fact that workers who become foremen must relinquish their membership of the union, while workers who become stewards retain their status as employees of management. New foremen, subject to one main set of loyalties and called on to carry out a markedly new set of functions, tend to develop negative attitudes toward the union as well as positive attitudes toward management. New stewards, subject to overlapping group membership and still dependent on management for their livelihoods, tend to become more favorable toward the union, but they do not turn against management, at least not within the relatively limited time period covered by the present research project. Over time, stewards might come to develop somewhat hostile attitudes toward management, but, under the conditions prevailing at Rockwell, there is apparently no tendency for such attitudes to be developed as soon as workers enter the steward role.

Method: Phase 2

One of the questions that may be raised about the results that have been presented up to this point concerns the extent to which the changed attitudes displayed by new foremen and new stewards are internalized by the role occupants. Are the changed attitudes expressed by new foremen and new stewards relatively stable, or are they ephemeral phenomena to be held only as long as they occupy the foreman and steward roles? An unusual set of circumstances at Rockwell enabled the researchers to glean some data on this question.

A short time after the 1952 resurvey, the nation suffered an economic recession. In order to meet the lessening demand for its products, Rockwell, like many other firms, had to cut its work force. This resulted in many rank-and-file workers being laid off and a number of the foremen being returned to nonsupervisory jobs. By June 1954, 8 of the 23 workers who had been promoted to foreman had returned to the worker role, and only 12 were still foremen. (The remaining 3 respondents had voluntarily left Rockwell by this time.)

Over the same period, a number of role changes had also been experienced by the 35 workers who had become stewards. Fourteen had returned to the worker role, either because they had not sought reelection by their work groups or because they had failed to win reelection, and only 6 were still stewards. (The other 15 respondents, who composed almost half of this group, had either voluntarily left Rockwell or had been laid off as part of the general reduction in force.)

Once again, in June 1954, the researchers returned to Rockwell to readminister the questionnaires that the workers had filled out in

1951 and 1952. The instructions to the respondents were substantially the same as those given in 1952—i.e., a sample of employees had been chosen to get up-to-date measures of employees' attitudes toward working conditions at Rockwell, and the same groups were selected this time as had been selected last time in order to lend greater stability to the results.

In this phase of the study, the numbers of cases with which we were dealing in the various groups were so small that the data could only be viewed as suggestive, and systematic statistical analysis of the data did not seem to be too meaningful. However, the unusual opportunity to throw some light on an important question suggests that a reporting of these results may be worthwhile.

Results: Phase 2

The principal question examined here was: on those items where a change in roles resulted in a change in attitudes between 1951 and 1952, how are these attitudes influenced by a reverse change in roles between 1952 and 1954?

The most consistent and widespread attitude changes noted between 1951 and 1952 were those that resulted when workers moved into the foreman role. What are the effects of moving out of the foreman role between 1952 and 1954? The data indicate that, in general, most of the "gains" that were observed when workers became foremen are "lost" when they become workers again. The results on six of the items, showing the proportions who take pro-management positions at various points in time, are presented in Table 18.5. On almost all of the items, the foremen who remain foremen either retain their favorable attitudes toward management or become even more favorable toward management between 1952 and 1954, while the demoted foremen show fairly consistent drops in the direction of readopting the attitudes they held when they had been in the worker role. On the whole, the attitudes held by demoted foremen in 1954, after they had left the foreman role, fall roughly to the same levels as they had been in 1951, before they had ever moved into the foreman role.

The results on the effects of moving out of the steward role are less clear-cut. As shown in Table 18.6, there is no marked tendency for ex-stewards to revert to earlier held attitudes when they go from the steward role to the worker role. At the same time, it should be recalled that there had not been particularly marked changes in their attitudes when they initially changed from the worker role to the

Table 18.5

Effects of Entering and Leaving the Foreman Role on Attitudes Toward Management and the Union

	WORKERS WHO BECAME FOREMEN AND STAYED FOREMEN (N = 12)			WORKERS WHO BECAME FOREMEN AND WERE LATER DEMOTED (N = 8)		
	(w) 1951	(f) 1952	(f) 1954	(w) 1951	(f) 1952	(w) 1954
% who feel Rockwell is a good place to work	33	92	100	25	75	50
% who feel management officers really care about the workers at Rockwell	8	33	67	0	25	0
% who feel the union should not have more say in setting labor standards	33	100	100	13	63	13
% who are satisfied with the way the incentive system works out at Rockwell	17	75	75	25	50	13
% who believe a worker's standard will not be changed just because he is a high producer	42	83	100	25	63	75
% who feel ability should count more than seniority in promotions	33	58	75	25	50	38

steward role. These findings, then, are consistent with the interpretation offered earlier that the change in roles between worker and steward is less significant than the change in roles between worker and foreman.

A question might be raised about what is represented in the reversal of attitudes found among ex-foremen. Does it represent a positive taking-on of attitudes appropriate for respondents who are reentering the worker role, or does it constitute a negative, perhaps embittered reaction away from the attitudes they held before being demoted from the foreman role? A definitive answer to this question cannot be arrived at, but it might be suggested that if we were dealing with a situation where a reversion in roles did not constitute such a strong psychological blow to the role occupants (as was probably the case among demoted foremen), then such a marked reversion in attitudes might not have occurred. There were a number of reactions to demotion among the eight ex-foremen, as obtained from informal interviews with these respondents. Some reacted impunitively (i.e., they blamed uncontrollable situational determinants) and did not seem to be bothered by demotion. Others reacted extrapunitively (i.e., they blamed management) or intrapunitively (i.e., they blamed themselves) and appeared to be more disturbed by demotion. One way of testing the hypothesis that attitude reversion is a function of embitterment would be to see if sharper reversion occurs among extrapunitive and intrapunitive respondents. However, the small number of cases does not permit an analysis of this kind to be carried out in the present situation.

One final table is of interest here. Table 18.7 compares the attitudes of two groups of respondents: (1) the 12 employees who were rank-and-file workers in 1951, had been selected as foremen by 1952, and were still foremen in 1954; and (2) the 6 employees who were rank-and-file workers in 1951, had been elected as stewards by 1952, and were still stewards in 1954. At each time period, for each of the 16 questions examined earlier in Tables 18.1 through 18.4, the table shows (1) the proportion of foremen or future foremen who took a promanagement position on these questions; (2) the proportion of stewards or future stewards who took a promanagement position on these questions; and (3) the difference between these proportions. The following are the mean differences in proportions for the three time periods.

1. In 1951, while both future foremen and future stewards still occupied the rank-and-file worker role, the mean difference was only −.1 percent, which means that practically no difference in

Table 18.6

Effects of Entering and Leaving the Steward Role on Attitudes Toward Management and the Union

	Workers Who Were Elected Stewards And Were Later Reelected ($N = 6$)			Workers Who Were Elected Stewards But Were Not Later Reelected ($N = 14$)		
	(w) 1951	(s) 1952	(s) 1954	(w) 1951	(s) 1952	(w) 1954
% who feel Rockwell is a good place to work	50	0	0	29	79	36
% who feel management officers really care about the workers at Rockwell	0	0	0	14	14	0
% who feel the union should not have more say in setting labor standards	0	17	0	14	14	14
% who are satisfied with the way the incentive system works out at Rockwell	17	17	0	43	43	21
% who believe a worker's standard will not be changed just because he is a high producer	50	50	17	21	43	36
% who feel ability should count more than seniority in promotions	67	17	17	36	36	21

attitudes existed between these two groups at this time. (The minus sign means that a slightly, but far from significantly, larger proportion of future stewards than future foremen expressed a pro-management position on these items.)

2. In 1952, after the groups had been in the foreman and steward roles for about one year, the mean difference had jumped to +47.8 percent, which means that a sharp wedge had been driven between them. Both groups had tended to become polarized in opposite directions, as foremen took on attitudes consistent with being a

Table 18.7

Effects of Foreman and Steward Roles Over a Three-Year Period: Before Change in Roles, After One Year in New Roles, and After Two–Three Years in New Roles

% Who Take a Promanagement Position on the Following Questions:†	Before Change in Roles (1951)			After 1 Year in New Roles (1952)			After 2–3 Years in New Roles (1954)		
	Workers who became Foremen	Workers who became Stewards	D%*	Workers who became Foremen	Workers who became Stewards	D%*	Workers who became Foremen	Workers who became Stewards	D%*
Question 1.	33	50	−17	92	0	+92	100	0	+100
Question 2.	33	33	0	75	33	+42	67	17	+50
Question 3.	92	83	+9	100	100	0	100	50	+50
Question 4.	8	0	+8	33	0	+33	67	0	+67
Question 5.	67	100	−33	67	17	+50	33	17	+16
Question 6.	33	0	+33	100	17	+83	100	0	+100
Question 7.	8	0	+8	50	0	+50	58	0	+58
Question 8.	75	67	+8	75	50	+25	58	17	+41
Question 9.	33	83	−50	83	17	+66	83	0	+83
Question 10.	17	17	0	75	17	+58	75	0	+75
Question 11.	17	17	0	25	0	+25	67	0	+67
Question 12.	42	50	−8	83	50	+33	100	17	+83

Table 18.7 (continued)

Question 13.	58	50	+8	100	17	+83	100	17	+83
Question 14.	33	67	−34	50	17	+33	75	17	+58
Question 15.	33	0	+33	58	0	+58	67	0	+67
Question 16.	67	33	+34	67	33	+34	67	67	0
No. of Cases	12	6		12	6		12	6	
Mean D%			−0.1			+47.8			+62.4

*Percentage of workers who became foremen who take a promanagement position minus percentage of workers who became stewards who take a promanagement position.

†Question numbers refer to the question numbers of the attitudinal items in *Tables 18.1* through *18.4*.

representative of management, and stewards took on attitudes appropriate for a representative of the union.

3. In 1954, after the groups had been in the foreman and steward roles for two to three years, the mean difference was +62.4 percent, which means that a still larger gap had opened up between them. Although the gap had widened, it is interesting to note that the changes that occurred during this later and longer 1952 to 1954 period are not as sharp or as dramatic as the changes that occurred during the initial and shorter 1951 to 1952 period.

These findings offer further support for the proposition that roles can influence attitudes. The data indicate that changes in attitudes occurred soon after changes in roles took place. And inside a period of three years those who had remained in their new roles had developed almost diametrically opposed sets of attitudinal positions.

Discussion

A role may be defined as a set of behaviors expected of people who occupy a certain position in a social system. These expectations consist of shared attitudes or beliefs, held by relevant populations, about what role occupants should and should not do. The theoretical basis for hypothesizing that a role will have effects on role occupants lies in the nature of these expectations. If a role occupant meets these expectations, the "rights" or "rewards" associated with the role will be accorded to him. If he fails to meet these expectations, the "rights" or "rewards" will be withheld from him and "punishments" may be meted out.

A distinction should be made between the effects of roles on people's attitudes and the effects of roles on their actions. How roles affect actions can probably be explained in a fairly direct fashion. Actions are overt and readily enforceable. If a person fails to behave in ways appropriate to his role, this can immediately be seen, and steps may be taken to bring the deviant or nonconformist into line. Role deviants may be evicted from their roles, placed in less rewarding roles, isolated from other members of the group, or banished entirely from the social system.

But attitudes are not as overt as actions. A person may behave in such a way as to reveal his attitudes, but he can—and often does—do much to cover them up. Why, then, should a change in roles lead to a change in actions? A number of explanatory factors might be suggested here. The present discussion will be confined to two factors that are probably generic to a wide variety of situations. One pertains to the influence of reference groups; the other is based on an assumption about people's need to have attitudes internally consistent with their actions.

A change in roles almost invariably involves a change in reference groups. Old reference groups may continue to influence the role occupant, but new ones also come into play. The change in reference groups may involve moving into a completely new group (as when a person gives up membership in one organization and joins another one) or it may simply involve taking on new functions in the same group (as when a person is promoted to a higher position in a hierarchical organization). In both situations, new reference groups will tend to bring about new frames of reference, new self-percepts, and new vested interests, and these in turn will tend to produce new attitudinal orientations.

In addition to a change in reference groups, a change in roles also involves a change in functions and a change in the kinds of behaviors and actions that the role occupant must display if he is to fulfill these functions. A change in actions, let us assume, comes about because these actions are immediately required, clearly visible, and hence socially enforceable. If we further assume a need for people to have attitudes that are internally consistent with their actions, then at least one aspect of the functional significance of a change in attitudes becomes clear. A change in attitudes enables a new role occupant to justify, to make rational, or perhaps simply to rationalize his change in actions. Having attitudes that are consistent with actions helps the role occupant to be "at one" with himself and facilitates his effective performance of the functions he is expected to carry out.

The reference-group principle and the self-consistency principle postulate somewhat different chains of events in accounting for the effects of roles on attitudes and actions. In abbreviated versions, the different chains may be spelled out in the following ways.

1. Reference-group principle: A change in roles involves a change in reference groups . . . which leads to a change in attitudes . . . which leads to a change in actions.

2. Self-consistency principle: A change in roles involves a change

in functions . . . which leads to a change in actions . . . which leads to a change in attitudes.

In the first chain, a person's attitudes influence his actions; in the second chain, a person's actions influence his attitudes. Both chains might plausibly account for the results obtained, but whether either chain, both chains, or other chains is or are valid cannot be determined from the data available. A more direct investigation of the underlying mechanisms responsible for the impact of roles on attitudes would appear to be a fruitful area for further research.

But apart from the question of underlying mechanisms, the results lend support to the proposition that a person's attitudes will be influenced by his role. Relatively consistent changes in attitudes were found both among workers who were made foremen and among workers who were made stewards, although these changes were more clear-cut for foremen than for stewards. The more interesting set of results—as far as role theory in general is concerned—would seem to be the data on the effects of entering and leaving the foreman role. It was pointed out earlier that the foreman role, unlike the steward role, is a full-time, relatively permanent position, and moving into this position entails taking on a very new and different set of functions. When workers are made foremen, their attitudes change in a more promanagement and antiunion direction. When they are demoted and move back into the worker role, their attitudes change once again, this time in a more prounion and antimanagement direction. In both instances, the respondents' attitudes seem to be molded by the roles which they occupy at a given time.

REFERENCES

Newcomb, T. M. *Social Psychology*. New York: The Dryden Press, 1950; London: Tavistock Publications, 1952.

Parsons, T. *The Social System*. Glencoe, Ill.: The Free Press, 1951; London: Tavistock Publications Ltd., 1951.

Stouffer, S. A., Suchman, E. A., DeVinney, L. C., Star, S. A., and Williams, R. M., Jr. *The American Soldier: Adjustment During Army Life* (Vol. I). Princeton: Princeton University Press, 1949.

⚫D COMPLIANCE

One of the most startling aspects of compliance studies is the percentage of people who are compliant. In the Doob and Ecker study, for example, about a third of the people contacted agreed to submit to a 15–20 minute interview. The Freedman and Fraser results are even more surprising in that almost a quarter of the sample contacted by a complete stranger agreed to allow five or six men to enter their homes and have free access to the cupboards and storage areas for two hours. In the second Freedman and Fraser experiment the number of people who agreed to have a large sign placed on their front lawn is equally astonishing.

The growing interest in field experimentation introduces the problem of getting the undivided attention of people for studies that require persuasive communications and the like. Passersby on streets and other public areas frequently are not willing to be delayed, and those who are willing to stop and listen to an experimenter's spiel may well have particular personality characteristics. Whenever a subject population is restricted in some way, as when certain personality types are overrepresented, the experimenter must be careful in generalizing the conclusions of the experiment to the population at large.

Two methods for obtaining at least briefly attentive subjects are telephoning and door knocking. The telephone is particularly appealing, for, strictly speaking, subjects are as close as the nearest telephone. The door-to-door and telephone solicitation procedures offer several knotty problems to researchers, however. First, since the telephone is only an auditory communicative link, one's presentation is limited to auditory stimuli. Second, since the other person is unseen even rough subject classifications may not be possible. The door-to-door technique may also be vulnerable to subject selection bias in that some people may simply refuse to listen to the experimenter's spiel. Such flat refusals, however, are infrequent.

The second knotty problem relates to the ethical requirements one might care to impose on the use of such procedures. Data derived from telephone or door-to-door contact is not in the strict sense anonymous. Anonymity is not a problem if the experimenter tells the subject the true purpose of the contact, as in conducting an opinion survey. When the experiment calls for deception and manipulation of the independent variable, the problem becomes whether or not the subject should be dehoaxed—told the purpose, procedures, and perhaps the results of the study. It is possible, of course, that because the subject may become angry, hostile, or stressed, dehoaxing may be more harmful to him than simply allowing him to persist in his initial impression that the situation was exactly as represented.

Behavioral scientists have been wrestling with these problems for a long time. Many suggestions for conducting field experimentation have been offered, and many criticisms of such methods on ethical and moral grounds have appeared. These issues are not easy to deal with, and the least desirable solution is to throw the mantle of scientific respectability over a procedure by stating it is necessary for the pursuit of knowledge.

Bonafide situations possibly could be used for experimental purposes. For example, insurance company salesmen could be asked to use specific solicitation approaches. Insurance salesmen frequently receive lists of new arrivals in a community, and they usually call and attempt to "drop by to say hello." Such a situation might be adopted for a foot-in-the-door experiment. The salesmen might call persons, welcome them to the community, identify his company affiliation, and request answers to a few health-related questions, such as emergency poison treatments. A second group from his list could be called and, after similar company identification and welcoming statement, read the above questions with their answers as facts the family should know about. The salesmen would then call to request a house visit with each of these people plus a control group of persons not previously contacted.

The above situation includes groups of persons not previously contacted, those asked to comply with a minor request, and those given a little, perhaps useful, information. Obviously other conditions could be added. Subjects in this situation are placed in an identifiable, common, and legitimate persuasive situation; everyone knows that gimmicks are used every day to sell things. Such situations used for experimental purposes means, in effect, that persuasive techniques are made systematic to provide data. Of course, the salesman may benefit by developing new persuasive technologies, but things could go too far even in legitimate persuasive situations, and it is difficult to say when the line has been crossed. What would you think of conducting the Doob and Ecker experiment with Avon ding-dong ladies? It may well be that a straightforward field experiment such as that of Doob and Ecker would be the ethically preferable method.

19.   **Stigma and compliance**   Anthony N. Doob and Barbara Payne Ecker

Subjects in this experiment were 121 housewives who were asked either to fill out a 79-item questionnaire and return

Reprinted from the *Journal of Personality and Social Psychology* 14 (1970): 302–4. Copyright 1970 by the American Psychological Association, and reproduced by permission.

it through the mail or to submit to a 15–20-minute interview. For half of the subjects the person making the request was wearing a black eyepatch; for the other half, no eyepatch was worn. In the questionnaire condition, compliance was significantly higher when the requester was wearing the eyepatch; in the interview condition, the eyepatch had no effect on compliance. The results were explained in terms of two conflicting motives on the part of the subjects: a tendency to want to help the person who is stigmatized in some way and a difficulty and embarrassment in having to deal with someone who is stigmatized.

Previous research demonstrates that people do not feel comfortable in dealing with the physically handicapped. Richardson, Hastorf, Goodman, and Dornbusch (1961) found that groups of children from widely differing backgrounds thought that they would like a nonhandicapped child more than one handicapped in some way. Goffman (1963) stated: "In social situations with a person known or perceived to have a stigma . . . we are likely to experience uneasiness [p. 19]." Similarly, Kleck, Ono, and Hastorf (1966) found that when there were no pressures to do otherwise (such as to help the other person), subjects tended to terminate an interaction with a handicapped person sooner than they did with a nonhandicapped person. Presumably, this was a result of their feeling more uncomfortable in dealing with the handicapped. When, however, interaction between the two people was such that the subject perceived that he was helping the other by continuing the interaction, subjects stayed longer with a handicapped interviewer than with the nonhandicapped interviewer. Apparently there were two opposing tendencies: people often felt sorry for another person who was handicapped, while at the same time they were uncomfortable in dealing with such a person.

In the area of compliance, then, it would be argued that the kind of behavior requested would critically affect whether a person was more likely to comply with a handicapped than with a nonhandicapped person. Presumably, one important variable would be whether the subject thought that compliance would necessitate interaction with the person making the request. If he thought that he would have to interact with a handicapped person, he might be less likely to comply than if he thought that by complying he could avoid further contact.

The experiment described here represents an attempt to vary these two factors: the characteristics (i.e., stigma and no stigma) of the person making the request, and the implications of the request for future interaction (i.e., whether or not the subject thought that he would have to interact with the person making the request).

It seems likely that when someone is faced with a request from a stigmatized person where compliance would involve interaction, two contradictory forces would be working on him: a feeling that he should comply with the request because the requester is stigmatized; an avoidance response because he feels that the necessary interaction would be unpleasant for him. Since it is difficult to predict which of these two forces will be stronger, it is impossible to say whether there will be more compliance with the stigmatized requester than with the nonstigmatized requester. However, when the request is such that compliance does not involve the subject in future interaction, then only the first of these two factors should be operative: there should be more compliance when the request is made by a stigmatized person than when it is made by a normal person.

Method

Unfortunately, a number of practical considerations limited the choice of stigma to be used in this experiment. It had to be visible to the subject; it had to be relatively easy for the experimenter to put on and take off; and it had to be something that was essentially irrelevant to the particular task in hand. It was also necessary that the stigma seem permanent to the subject. It was decided to use an eyepatch: although it could be interpreted as temporary by some subjects, it is likely that they would feel some ambiguity about this.

PROCEDURE

Subjects were 121 housewives (or whoever answered the door) in a middle class area of Palo Alto, California. They were generally run in the middle of the afternoon on Mondays and Tuesdays, October through December. Because it was impractical to assign each subject randomly to an experimental condition, blocks of subjects (approximately four or five subjects were used from each block) were used as the unit of analysis. Thus the experimenter, an attractive 21-year-old girl, would drive to an area of Palo Alto and select and order the 4 blocks to be used. Each block was then randomly assigned to an experimental condition.

Under the pretense of a door-to-door survey, the girl would approach every second house on the block she had chosen and knock on the door. If someone answered, the subject was counted in the experiment. For half the subjects (questionnaire condition) she introduced herself by saying:

> Good afternoon. I represent a company called Industrial Research Associates. We conduct independent surveys for various industries in America. Right now we are conducting one trying to find out the differences between California homes and families and those in other parts of the country. Would you have 15 or 20 minutes to spare in the next few days to fill out this questionnaire for me? Just fill it out and mail it in the envelope provided. Thank you very much.

The subject was shown a 4-page questionnaire with 79 questions on it (e.g., Do you buy most of your gasoline for your car at one gas station? Do you have milk delivered to your home?) and a stamped, addressed envelope (addressed to a post office box in a neighboring town). The other subjects (interview condition) were given the same introduction but were asked, "Would you have 15 or 20 minutes to spare to answer a few questions for me?"

In both conditions, if any questions arose, the subject was quickly reassured that she was not being asked to buy anything and that no names were required. The experimenter answered questions about herself freely, saying that she was a student majoring in psychology and she was doing this job merely to earn money independent of her studies.

Half of the time she wore a black eyepatch completely covering one eye; the rest of the time she wore no eyepatch. Thus there were four conditions forming a 2 × 2 factorial design: Eyepatch or

214   *Compliance*

No Eyepatch × Request for Interview or Request to Fill Out a Questionnaire.

A subject was considered to have complied in the questionnaire conditions if she accepted the questionnaire and returned it through the mail filled out completely. A subject in the interview conditions was considered to have complied if she agreed to be interviewed and did not terminate the interview after the first few questions. Very early in the experiment it was found that if a subject agreed to be interviewed and had actually started answering questions, she would not terminate the interview before the experimenter finished. For reasons of efficiency, then, the experimenter usually interviewed the subject for only about five minutes. The experiment was run on seven separate days; for reasons independent of this experiment, the interview conditions were run only on six days. Either four or five subjects were run in each condition on each day. The number of subjects per cell varied from 26 (in the eyepatch-interview condition) to 35 (in the no-eyepatch–questionnaire condition).

The experimenter was obviously not blind to experimental condition, but was kept ignorant of the results until the end of the experiment.

Results

Because subjects were randomly assigned to condition by city block, that unit was used in analyzing these data. A percentage score for each condition for each day (i.e., the percentage of subjects in each condition who complied each day) was computed and used for analysis. There was essentially no difference between the eyepatch and no-eyepatch conditions in the interview condition (mean compliance rate in eyepatch condition = 33.7 percent; no eyepatch = 32.0 percent). In the questionnaire condition, however, there was quite a striking difference, with 69.2 percent of the subjects complying in the eyepatch condition and 40 percent complying in the no-eyepatch condition ($t = 3.51$, $df = 6$; $p < .02$). This result is due partly to the fact that the experimenter was more successful in getting subjects to accept the questionnaire in the eyepatch rather than in the no-eyepatch condition (87.2 percent versus 68.6 percent, $t = .70$), and partly to the fact that subjects in the eyepatch condition who accepted a questionnaire were more likely to fill it out than those subjects in the no-eyepatch condition who accepted the questionnaire (82.1 percent versus 57.1 percent, $t = 3.70$, $df = 6$, $p < .02$).

Discussion

It is clear that at least when compliance does not involve additional face-to-face contact, a stigmatized person is more likely to get compliance than a nonstigmatized person. This result is consistent with previous research (Freedman & Doob, 1968) in which subjects who perceived themselves as nondeviants complied more with deviant requesters than they did with nondeviant requesters. In that experiment, compliance did not involve future contact. The combination of these two results would argue that people who are nondeviant feel more pressure to comply when the other person is deviant either in an obvious physical sense (as in the present experiment) or in a more subtle, nonvisible sense (as in the Freedman & Doob experiment). However, when compliance does involve the nondeviant in future interaction with the deviant person, there is no such effect.

These results are analogous to those found in recent work on guilt and compliance (e.g., Carlsmith & Gross, 1969; Freedman, Wallington & Bless, 1967). In these experiments, guilt tended to increase compliance, but much less so (if at all) when compliance involved the possibility of interaction with the person who had been injured (Freedman et al., Experiments II and III).

REFERENCES

Carlsmith, J. M., and Gross, A. E. 1969. Some effects of guilt on compliance. *Journal of Personality and Social Psychology* 11: 232–239.
Freedman, J. L., and Doob, A. N. 1968. *Deviancy: The psychology of being different.* New York: Academic Press.
Freedman, J. L.; Wallington, S. A.; and Bless, E. 1967. Compliance without pressure: The effect of guilt. *Journal of Personality and Social Psychology* 7: 117–24.

Goffman, E. 1963. *Stigma.* Englewood Cliffs, N.J.: Prentice-Hall.

Kleck, R.; Ono, H.; and Hastorf, A. H. 1966. The effects of physical deviance upon face-to-face interaction. *Human Relations* 19: 425–36.

Richardson, S. A.; Hastorf, A. H.; Goodman, N.; and Dornbusch, S. M. 1961. Cultural uniformity in reaction to physical disabilities. *American Sociological Review* 26: 241–47.

20. Compliance without pressure: The foot-in-the-door technique   Jonathan L. Freedman and Scott C. Fraser

Two experiments were conducted to test the proposition that once someone has agreed to a small request he is more likely to comply with a larger request. The first study demonstrated this effect when the same person made both requests. The second study extended this to the situation in which different people made the two requests. Several experimental groups were run in an effort to explain these results, and possible explanations are discussed.

How can a person be induced to do something he would rather not do? This question is relevant to practically every phase of social life, from stopping at a traffic light to stopping smoking, from buying Brand X to buying savings bonds, from supporting the March of Dimes to supporting the Civil Rights Act.

One common way of attacking the problem is to exert as much pressure as possible on the reluctant individual in an effort to force him to comply. This technique has been the focus of a considerable amount of experimental research. Work on attitude change, conformity, imitation, and obedience has tended to stress the im-

Reprinted from the *Journal of Personality and Social Psychology* 4 (1966): 195–202. Copyright 1966 by the American Psychological Association, and reproduced by permission. These studies were supported in part by Grant GS-196 from the National Science Foundation.

portance of the degree of external pressure. The prestige of the communicator (Kelman & Hovland, 1953), degree of discrepancy of the communication (Hovland & Pritzker, 1957), size of the group disagreeing with the subject (Asch, 1951), perceived power of the model (Bandura, Ross & Ross, 1963), etc., are the kinds of variables that have been studied. This impressive body of work, added to the research on rewards and punishments in learning, has produced convincing evidence that greater external pressure generally leads to greater compliance with the wishes of the experimenter. The one exception appears to be situations involving the arousal of cognitive dissonance in which, once discrepant behavior has been elicited from the subject, the greater the pressure that was used to elicit the behavior, the less subsequent change occurs (Festinger & Carlsmith, 1959). But even in this situation one critical element is the amount of external pressure exerted.

Clearly, then, under most circumstances the more pressure that can be applied, the more likely it is that the individual will comply. There are, however, many times when for ethical, moral, or practical reasons it is difficult to apply much pressure when the goal is to produce compliance with a minimum of apparent pressure, as in the forced-compliance studies involving dissonance arousal. And even when a great deal of pressure is possible, it is still important to maximize the compliance it produces. Thus, factors other than external pressure are often quite critical in determining degree of compliance. What are these factors?

Although rigorous research on the problem is rather sparse, the fields of advertising, propaganda, politics, etc., are by no means devoid of techniques designed to produce compliance in the absence of external pressure (or to maximize the effectiveness of the pressure that is used, which is really the same problem). One assumption about compliance that has often been made either explicitly or implicitly is that once a person has been induced to comply with a small request he is more likely to comply with a larger demand. This is the principle that is commonly referred to as the foot-in-the-door or gradation technique and is reflected in the saying that if you "give them an inch, they'll take a mile." It was, for example, supposed to be one of the basic techniques upon which the Korean brainwashing tactics were based (Schein, Schneier &

Barker, 1961), and, in a somewhat different sense, one basis for Nazi propaganda during 1940 (Bruner, 1941). It also appears to be implicit in many advertising campaigns which attempt to induce the consumer to do anything relating to the product involved, even sending back a card saying he does not want the product.

The most relevant piece of experimental evidence comes from a study of conformity done by Deutsch and Gerard (1955). Some subjects were faced with incorrect group judgments first in a series in which the stimuli were not present during the actual judging and then in a series in which they were present, while the order of the memory and visual series was reversed for other subjects. For both groups the memory series produced more conformity, and when the memory series came first there was more total conformity to the group judgments. It seems likely that this order effect occurred because, as the authors suggest, once conformity is elicited at all it is more likely to occur in the future. Although this kind of conformity is probably somewhat different from compliance as described above, this finding certainly lends some support to the foot-in-the-door idea. The present research attempted to provide a rigorous, more direct test of this notion as it applies to compliance and to provide data relevant to several alternative ways of explaining the effect.

Experiment I

The basic paradigm was to ask some subjects (Performance condition) to comply first with a small request and then three days later with a larger, related request. Other subjects (One-Contact condition) were asked to comply only with the large request. The hypothesis was that more subjects in the Performance condition than in the One-Contact condition would comply with the larger request.

Two additional conditions were included in an attempt to specify the essential difference between these two major conditions. The Performance subjects were asked to perform a small favor, and, if they agreed, they did it. The question arises whether the act of agreeing itself is critical or whether actually carrying it out was necessary. To assess this a third group of subjects (Agree-Only) was asked the first request, but, even if they agreed, they did not carry it out. Thus, they were identical to the Performance group except that they were not given the opportunity of performing the request.

Another difference between the two main conditions was that at the time of the larger request the subjects in the Performance condition were more familiar with the experimenter than were the other subjects. The Performance subjects had been contacted twice, heard his voice more, discovered that the questions were not dangerous, and so on. It is possible that this increased familiarity would serve to decrease the fear and suspicion of a strange voice on the telephone and might accordingly increase the likelihood of the subjects agreeing to the larger request. To control for this a fourth condition was run (Familiarization) which attempted to give the subjects as much familiarity with the experimenter as in the Performance and Agree-Only conditions with the only difference being that no request was made.

The major prediction was that more subjects in the Performance condition would agree to the large request than in any of the other conditions, and that the One-Contact condition would produce the least compliance. Since the importance of agreement and familiarity was essentially unknown, the expectation was that the Agree-Only and Familiarization conditions would produce intermediate amounts of compliance.

METHOD

The prediction stated above was tested in a field experiment in which housewives were asked to allow a survey team of five or six men to come into their homes for two hours to classify the household products they used. This large request was made under four different conditions: after an initial contact in which the subject had been asked to answer a few questions about the kinds of soaps she used, and the questions were actually asked (Performance condition); after an identical contact in which the questions were not actually asked (Agree-Only condition); after an initial contact in which no request was made (Familiarization condition); or after no initial contact (One-Contact condition). The dependent measure was simply whether or not the subject agreed to the large request.

The subjects were 156 Palo Alto, California, housewives, 36 in each condition, who were selected at random from the telephone directory. An additional 12 subjects distributed about equally among the three two-contact conditions could not be reached for the second contact and are not included in the data analysis. Subjects were assigned randomly to the various conditions, except that the Familiarization condition was added to the design after the other three conditions had been completed. All contacts were by telephone by the same experimenter who identified himself as the same person each time. Calls were made only in the morning. For the three groups that were contacted twice, the first call was made on either Monday or Tuesday and the second always three days later. All large requests were made on either Thursday or Friday.

At the first contact, the experimenter introduced himself by name and said that he was from the California Consumers' Group. In the Performance condition he then proceeded:

> We are calling you this morning to ask if you would answer a number of questions about what household products you use so that we could have this information for our public service publication, "The Guide." Would you be willing to give us this information for our survey?

If the subject agreed, she was asked a series of eight innocuous questions dealing with household soaps (e.g., "What brand of soap do you use in your kitchen sink?") She was then thanked for her cooperation, and the contact terminated.

Another condition (Agree-Only) was run to assess the importance of actually carrying out the request as opposed to merely agreeing to it. The only difference between this and the Performance condition was that, if the subject agreed to answer the questions, the experimenter thanked her, but said that he was just lining up respondents for the survey and would contact her if needed.

A third condition was included to check on the importance of the subject's greater familiarity with the experimenter in the two-contact conditions. In this condition the experimenter introduced himself, described the organization he worked for and the survey it was conducting, listed the questions he was asking, and then said that he was calling merely to acquaint the subject with the existence of his organization. In other words, these subjects were contacted, spent as much time on the telephone with the experimenter as the Performance subjects did, heard all the questions, but neither agreed to answer them nor answered them.

In all of these two-contact conditions some subjects did not agree to the requests or even hung up before the requests were made. Every subject who answered the telephone was included in the analysis of the results and was contacted for the second request regardless of her extent of cooperativeness during the first contact. In other words, no subject who could be contacted the appropriate number of times was discarded from any of the four conditions.

The large request was essentially identical for all subjects. The experimenter called, identified himself, and said either that his group was expanding its survey (in the case of the two-contact conditions) or that it was conducting a survey (in the One-Contact condition). In all four conditions he then continued:

> The survey will involve five or six men from our staff coming into your home some morning for about two hours to enumerate and classify all the household products that you have. They will have to have full freedom in your house to go through the cupboards and storage places. Then all this information will be used in the writing of the reports for our public service publication, "The Guide."

If the subject agreed to the request, she was thanked and told that at the present time the experimenter was merely collecting names of people who were willing to take part and that she would be contacted if it were decided to use her in the survey. If she did not agree, she was thanked for her time. This terminated the experiment.

RESULTS

Apparently even the small request was not considered trivial by some of the subjects. Only about two-thirds of the subjects in the Performance and Agree-Only conditions agreed to answer the questions about household soaps. It might be noted that none of those who refused the first request later agreed to the large request,

Table 20.1

Percentage of Subjects Complying with Large Request in Experiment I

CONDITION	%
Performance	52.8
Agree-Only	33.3
Familiarization	27.8*
One-Contact	22.2†

NOTE: $N = 36$ for each group. Significance levels represent differences from the Performance condition.
*$p < .07$.
†$p < .02$.

although as stated previously all subjects who were contacted for the small request are included in the data for those groups.

Our major prediction was that subjects who had agreed to and carried out a small request (Performance condition) would subsequently be more likely to comply with a larger request than would subjects who were asked only the larger request (One-Contact condition). As may be seen in Table 20.1, the results support the prediction. Over 50 percent of the subjects in the Performance condition agreed to the larger request, while less than 25 percent of the One-Contact condition agreed to it. Thus it appears that obtaining compliance with a small request does tend to increase subsequent compliance. The question is what aspect of the initial contact produces this effect.

One possibility is that the effect was produced merely by increased familiarity with the experimenter. The Familiarization control was included to assess the effect on compliance of two contacts with the same person. The group had as much contact with the experimenter as the Performance group, but no request was made during the first contact. As the table indicates, the Familiarization group did not differ appreciably in amount of compliance from the One-Contact group, but was different from the Performance group ($\chi^2 = 3.70, p < .07$). Thus, although increased familiarity may well lead to increased compliance, in the present situation the differences in amount of familiarity apparently were not great enough to produce any such increase; the effect that was obtained seems not to be due to this factor.

Another possibility is that the critical factor producing increased compliance is simply agreeing to the small request (i.e., carrying it out may be necessary). The Agree-Only condition was identical to the Performance condition except that in the former the subjects were not asked the questions. The amount of compliance in this Agree-Only condition fell between the Performance and One-Contact conditions and was not significantly different from either of them. This leaves the effect of merely agreeing somewhat ambiguous, but it suggests that the agreement alone may produce part of the effect.

Unfortunately, it must be admitted that neither of these control conditions is an entirely adequate test of the possibility it was designed to assess. Both conditions are in some way quite peculiar and may have made a very different and extraneous impression on the subject than did the Performance condition. In one case, a housewife is asked to answer some questions and then is not asked them; in the other, some man calls to tell her about some organization she has never heard of. Now, by themselves neither of these events might produce very much suspicion. But, several days later, the same man calls and asks a very large favor. At this point it is not at all unlikely that many subjects think they are being manipulated, or in any case that something strange is going on. Any such reaction on the part of the subjects would naturally tend to reduce the amount of compliance in these conditions.

Thus, although this first study demonstrates that an initial contact in which a request is made and carried out increases compliance with a second request, the question of why and how the initial request produces this effect remains unanswered. In an attempt to begin answering this question and to extend the results of the first study, a second experiment was conducted.

There seemed to be several quite plausible ways in which the increase in compliance might have been produced. The first was simply some kind of commitment to or involvement with the particular person making the request. This might work, for example, as follows: The subject has agreed to the first request and perceives that the experimenter therefore expects him also to agree to the second request. The subject thus feels obligated and does not want to disappoint the experimenter; he also feels that he needs a good reason for saying "no"—a better reason than he would need if he had never said "yes." This is just one line of causality—the particular process by which involvement with the experimenter operates might be quite different, but the basic idea would be similar. The commitment is to the particular person. This implies that the increase in compliance due to the first contact should occur primarily when both requests are made by the same person.

Another explanation in terms of involvement centers around the particular issue with which the requests are concerned. Once the subject has taken some action in connection with an area of concern, be it surveys, political activity, or highway safety, there is probably a tendency to become somewhat more concerned with the area. The subject begins thinking about it, considering its importance and relevance to him, and so on. This tends to make him more likely to agree to take further action in the same area when he is later asked to. To the extent that this is the critical factor, the initial contact should increase compliance only when both requests are related to the same issue or area of concern.

Another way of looking at the situation is that the subject needs a reason to say "no." In our society it is somewhat difficult to refuse a reasonable request, particularly when it is made by an organization that is not trying to make money. In order to refuse, many people feel that they need a reason—simply not wanting to do it is often not in itself sufficient. The person can say to the requester or simply to himself that he does not believe in giving to charities or tipping or working for political parties or answering questions or posting signs, or whatever he is asked to do. Once he has performed a particular task, however, this excuse is no longer valid for not agreeing to perform a similar task. Even if the first thing he did was trivial compared to the present request, he cannot say he never does this sort of thing, and thus one good reason for refusing is removed. This line of reasoning suggests that the similarity of the first and second requests in terms of the type of action required is an important factor. The more similar they are, the more the "matter of principle" argument is eliminated by agreeing to the first request, and the greater should be the increase in compliance.

There are probably many other mechanisms by which the initial request might produce an increase in compliance. The second experiment was designed in part to test the notions described above, but its major purpose was to demonstrate the effect unequivocally. To this latter end it eliminated one of the important problems with the first study which was that when the experimenter made the second request he was not blind as to which condition the subjects were in. In this study the second request was always made by someone other than the person who made the first request, and the second experimenter was blind as to what condition the subject was in. This eliminates the possibility that the experimenter exerted systematically different amounts of pressure in different experimental conditions. If the effect of the first study were replicated, it would also rule out the relatively uninteresting possibility that the effect is due primarily to greater familiarity or involvement with the particular person making the first request.

Experiment II

The basic paradigm was quite similar to that of the first study. Experimental subjects were asked to comply with a small request and were later asked a considerably larger request, while controls were asked only the larger request. The first request varied along two dimensions. Subjects were asked either to put up a small sign or to sign a petition, and the issue was either safe driving or keeping California beautiful. Thus, there were four first requests: a small sign for safe driving or for beauty, and a petition for the two issues. The second request for all subjects was to install in their front lawn a very large sign which said "Drive Carefully." The four experimental conditions may be defined in terms of the similarity of the small and large requests along the dimensions of issue and task. The two requests were similar in both issue and task for the small-sign, safe-driving group, similar only in issue for the safe-driving petition group, similar only in task for the small "Keep California Beautiful" sign group, and similar in neither issue nor task for the "Keep California Beautiful" petition group.

The major expectation was that the three groups for which either the task or the issue were similar would show more compliance than the controls, and it was also felt that when both were similar there would probably be the most compliance. The fourth condition (Different Issue, Different Task) was included primarily to assess the effect simply of the initial contact which, although it was not identical to the second one on either issue or task, was in many ways quite similar (e.g., a young student asking for cooperation on a noncontroversial issue). There were no clear expectations as to how this condition would compare to the controls.

METHOD

The subjects were 114 women and 13 men living in Palo Alto, California. Of these, nine women and six men could not be contacted for the second request and are not included in the data analysis. The remaining 112 subjects were divided about equally among the five conditions (see Table 20.2). All subjects were contacted between 1:30 and 4:30 on weekday afternoons.

Two experimenters, one male and one female, were employed, and a different one always made the second contact. Unlike the first study, the experimenters actually went to the homes of the subjects and interviewed them on a face-to-face basis. An effort was made to select subjects from blocks and neighborhoods that were as homogeneous as possible. On each block every third or fourth house was approached, and all subjects on that block were in one experimental condition. This was necessary because of the likelihood that neighbors would talk to each other about the contact. In addition, for every four subjects contacted, a fifth house was chosen as a control but was, of course, not contacted. Throughout this phase of the experiment, and in fact throughout the whole experiment, the two experimenters not communicate to each other what conditions had been run on a given block nor what condition a particular house was in.

The small-sign, safe-driving group was told that the experimenter was from the Community Committee for Traffic Safety, that he was visiting a number of homes in an attempt to make the citizens more aware of the need to drive carefully all the time, and that he would like the subject to take a small sign and put it in a window or in the car so that it would serve as a reminder of the need to drive carefully. The sign was three inches square, said "Be a safe driver," was on thin paper without a gummed backing, and in general looked rather amateurish and unattractive. If the subject agreed, he was given the sign and thanked; if he disagreed, he was simply thanked for his time.

The three other experimental conditions were quite similar with appropriate changes. The other organization was identified as the Keep California Beautiful Committee, and its sign said, appropriately enough, "Keep California Beautiful." Both signs were simply black block letters on a white background. The two petition groups were asked to sign a petition which was being sent to California's United States senators. The petition advocated support for any legislation which would promote either safer driving or keeping California beautiful. The subject was shown a petition, typed on heavy bond paper, with at least 20 signatures already affixed. If she agreed, she signed and was thanked. If she did not agree, she was merely thanked.

The second contact was made about two weeks after the initial one. Each experimenter was armed with a list of houses which had been compiled by the other experimenter. This list contained all four experimental conditions and the controls, and, of course, there was no way for the second experimenter to know which condition the subject had been in. At this second contact, all subjects were asked the same thing: Would they put a large sign concerning safe driving in their front yard? The experimenter identified himself as being from the Citizens for Safe Driving, a different group from the original safe-driving group (although it is likely that most subjects who had been in the safe-driving conditions did not notice the difference). The subject was shown a picture of a very large sign reading "Drive Carefully" placed in front of an attractive house. The picture was taken so that the sign obscured much of the front of the house and completely concealed the doorway. It was rather poorly lettered. The subject was told that: "Our men will come out and install it and later come and remove it. It makes just a small hole in your lawn, but if this is unacceptable to you we have a special mount which will make no hole." She was asked to put the sign up for a week or a week and a half. If the subject agreed, she was told that more names than necessary were being gathered and if her home were to be used she would be contacted in a few weeks. The experimenter recorded the subject's response and this ended the experiment.

Table 20.2

Percentage of Subjects Complying with Large Request in Experiment II

ISSUE*	TASK[a]			
	SIMILAR	N	DIFFERENT	N
Similar	76.0†	25	47.8*	23
Different	47.6*	21	47.4*	19
	One-Contact 16.7 ($N = 24$)			

NOTE: Significance levels represent differences from the One-Contact condition.

[a]Denotes relationship between first and second requests.

*$p < .08$.

†$p < .01$.

RESULTS

First, it should be noted that there were no large differences among the experimental conditions in the percentages of subjects agreeing to the first request. Although somewhat more subjects agreed to post the "Keep California Beautiful" sign and somewhat fewer to sign the beauty petition, none of these differences approach significance.

The important figures are the number of subjects in each group who agreed to the large request. These are presented in Table 20.2. The figures for the four experimental groups include all subjects who were approached the first time, regardless of whether or not they agreed to the small request. As noted above, a few subjects were lost because they could not be reached for the second request, and, of course, these are not included in the table.

It is immediately apparent that the first request tended to increase the degree of compliance with the second request. Whereas fewer than 20 percent of the controls agreed to put the large sign on their lawn, over 55 percent of the experimental subjects agreed, with over 45 percent being the lowest degree of compliance for any experimental condition. As expected, those conditions in which the two requests were similar in terms of either issue or task produced significantly more compliance than did the controls (χ^2's range from 3.67, $p < .07$ to 15.01, $p < .001$). A somewhat unexpected result is that the fourth condition, in which the first request had relatively little in common with the second request, also produced more compliance than the controls ($\chi^2 = 3.40$, $p < .08$). In other words, regardless of whether or not the two requests are similar in either issue or task, simply having the first request tends to increase the likelihood that the subject will comply with a subsequent, larger request. And this holds even when the two requests are made by different people several weeks apart.

A second point of interest is a comparison among the four experimental conditions. As expected, the Same Issue, Same Task condition produced more compliance than any of the other two-contact conditions, but the difference is not significant (χ^2's range from 2.7 to 2.9). If only those subjects who agreed to the first request are considered, the same pattern holds.

Discussion

To summarize the results, the first study indicated that carrying out a small request increased the likelihood that the subject would agree to a similar larger request made by the same person. The second study showed that this effect was quite strong even when a different person made the larger request, and the two requests were quite dissimilar. How may these results be explained?

Two possibilities were outlined previously. The matter-of-principle idea which centered on the particular type of action was not supported by the data, since the similarity of the tasks did not make an appreciable difference in degree of compliance. The notion of involvement, as described previously, also has difficulty accounting for some of the findings. The basic idea was that once someone has agreed to any action, no matter how small, he tends to feel more involved than he did before. This involvement may center around the particular person making the first request or the particular issue. This is quite consistent with the results of the first study (with the exception of the two control groups which as discussed previously were rather ambiguous) and with the Similar Issue groups in the second experiment. This idea of involvement does not,

230   *Compliance*

however, explain the increase in compliance found in the two groups in which the first and second request did not deal with the same issue.

It is possible that in addition to or instead of this process a more general and diffuse mechanism underlies the increase in compliance. What may occur is a change in the person's feelings about getting involved or about taking action. Once he has agreed to a request, his attitude may change. He may become, in his own eyes, the kind of person who does this sort of thing, who agrees to requests made by strangers, who takes action on things he believes in, who cooperates with good causes. The change in attitude could be toward any aspect of the situation or toward the whole business of saying "yes." The basic idea is that the change in attitude need not be toward any particular issue or person or activity, but may be toward activity or compliance in general. This would imply that an increase in compliance would not depend upon the two contacts being made by the same person, or concerning the same issue or involving the same kind of action. The similarity could be much more general, such as both concerning good causes, or requiring a similar kind of action, or being made by pleasant, attractive individuals.

It is not being suggested that this is the only mechanism operating here. The idea of involvement continues to be extremely plausible, and there are probably a number of other possibilities. Unfortunately, the present studies offer no additional data with which to support or refute any of the possible explanations of the effect. These explanations thus remain simply descriptions of mechanisms which might produce an increase in compliance after agreement with a first request. Hopefully, additional research will test these ideas more fully and perhaps also specify other manipulations which produce an increase in compliance without an increase in external pressure.

It should be pointed out that the present studies employed what is perhaps a very special type of situation. In all cases the requests were made by presumably nonprofit service organizations. The issues in the second study were deliberately noncontroversial, and it may be assumed that virtually all subjects initially sympathized with the objectives of safe driving and a beautiful California. This is in strong contrast to campaigns which are designed to sell a particular product, political candidate, or dogma. Whether the technique employed in this study would be successful in these other situations remains to be shown.

REFERENCES

Asch, S. E. 1951. Effects of group pressure upon modification and distortion of judgments. In *Groups, leadership and men; research in human relations*, ed. H. Guetzkow, pp. 177–90. Pittsburgh: Carnegie Press.

Bandura, A.; Ross, D.; and Ross, S. A. 1963. A comparative test of the status envy, social power, and secondary reinforcement theories of identificatory learning. *Journal of Abnormal and Social Psychology* 67: 527–34.

Bruner, J. 1941. The dimensions of propaganda: German short-wave broadcasts to America. *Journal of Abnormal and Social Psychology* 36: 311–37.

Deutsch, M., and Gerard, H. B. 1955. A study of normative and informational social influences upon individual judgment. *Journal of Abnormal and Social Psychology* 51, 629–36.

Festinger, L., and Carlsmith, J. 1959. Cognitive consequences of forced compliance. *Journal of Abnormal and Social Psychology* 58: 203–10.

Hovland, C. I., and Pritzker, H. A. 1957. Extent of opinion change as a function of amount of change advocated. *Journal of Abnormal and Social Psychology* 54: 257–61.

Kelman, H. C., and Hovland, C. I. 1953. "Reinstatement" of the communicator in delayed measurement of opinion change. *Journal of Abnormal and Social Psychology* 48: 327–35.

Schein, E. H.; Schneier, I.; and Barker, C. H. 1961. *Coercive pressure.* New York: Norton.

■◐ ATTITUDE CHANGE

Attitude change studies are difficult to conduct in field settings. First, the experimenter must deliver a persuasive message to a subject in a way that does not arouse suspicion. Second, the measure of attitude change must be obtained, again without alerting the subject that he is under special scrutiny or that he is involved in an extraordinary situation.

The experiments reported in this section demonstrate three types of procedures that can be used for field studies on attitude change. The first experiment was conducted in an indoctrination type of setting in which persuasion attempts were made systematic for experimental purposes. Several interesting methodological aspects of this study should be considered; one is the detailed data breakdown procedure used. The effects of variety of subject characteristics on the net attitude change was determined by examining the data separately for groups that differed in years of education, initial attitude, evaluation of the persuasive message, and so on. In data analysis the data should be plotted or tabulated in a variety of ways that are theoretically or intuitively sensible. Such breakdowns and comparisons help the researcher to understand some of the complexities of the phenomenon he is studying. The first study also illustrates the camouflage techniques used to keep subjects from becoming sensitive to the relationship between message content and attitude measurement.

The Abelson and Miller study used the pollster or public opinion interviewer guise for an experimental situation. Whenever complex manipulations such as those reported in this reading are required, detailed pilot sessions are needed. Pilot studies usually involve trying all aspects of the experiment with only a few subjects. The effectiveness of the manipulations and the measurement procedures are determined during the pilot runs. In addition, the confederates are rehearsed and evaluated, and all the experimental materials, procedures, timing, and so on, are tried out. Usually the pilot subjects are interviewed in very great detail to determine if their perception of the situation was as the experimenter intended and to obtain any information that might permit the experimenter to improve the precision of his procedures.

The final reading in this section describes an experimental study using aggregate data. Hartmann distributed political leaflets that offered either a rational or an emotional appeal for voter support. Election returns were used as the dependent variable measurement, which revealed the greatest vote increases in areas exposed to the emotional appeal. Aggregate data procedures are fraught with potential problems. One must first assume that the samples are very well matched and that differences in grouped data do not simply reflect preexisting differences in the samples or differences in the effectiveness of the independent variable manipulation. In the Hartmann experiment, for example, one must assume that differences in the Socialist vote resulted from the different appeals or, more precisely, that Socialist voters in each of the experimental areas had comparable exposure to the appropriate leaflets. Since a person given a leaflet cannot be followed to the polls to ascertain his precise vote, the problem of spurious or artifactual findings is ever present. Confidence in the results of aggregate data may be gained by increasing the size of the sample, by careful group matching on various characteristics, and by replicating the experiment.

21. The effects of presenting "one side" versus "both sides" in changing opinions on a controversial subject. Carl I. Hovland, Arthur A. Lumsdaine, and Fred D. Sheffield

Men in training at an army camp during World War II were exposed to one-sided versus two-sided arguments regarding the estimated length of the war with Japan. The results indicated that for men who were already convinced of the point of view being presented and for poorly educated men one-sided arguments were more effective in changing attitudes than were two-sided arguments. For better educated men and those who were initially opposed to the presented view, two-sided arguments were most effective.

When the weight of evidence supports the main thesis being presented, is it more effective to present only the materials supporting the point being made, or is it better to introduce also the arguments of those opposed to the point being made?

The procedure of presenting only the arguments supporting a thesis is often employed on the grounds that when the preponderance of the evidence supports the point being made, the presentation of opposing arguments and misconceptions merely raises doubts in the minds of the audience. On the other hand, the procedure of presenting the arguments for both sides was defended on the grounds of "fairness"—the right of members of the audience to have access to all relevant materials in making up their minds.

From *Studies in Social Psychology in World War II,* Vol. III, *Experiments on Mass Communication* (Princeton, N.J.: Princeton University Press, 1949), pp. 201–27. Reprinted by permission of Princeton University Press.

Furthermore, there is reason to expect that those audience members who are already opposed to the point of view being presented may be distracted by "rehearsing" their own arguments while the topic is being presented and will be antagonized by the omission of the arguments on their side. Thus, presentation of the audience's arguments at the outset possibly would produce better reception of the arguments which it is desired to convey.

The present experiment was set up to provide information on the relative effectiveness of these two types of program content in changing the opinions of individuals initially opposing as compared with those favoring the position advocated in the program. Controlled variation of treatment was introduced by preparing two transcriptions with the same orientation message in alternative forms. In one form arguments were presented on only one side of the issue; in the other both sides were presented.

Methods of Study

1. THE TWO PROGRAMS USED

At the time the experiment was being planned (early 1945) the war in Europe was drawing to a close, and it was reported that Army morale was being adversely affected by overoptimism about an early end to the war in the Pacific. A directive was issued by the Army to impress upon troops a conception of the magnitude of the job remaining to be done in defeating Japan. This furnished a controversial topic on which arguments were available on both sides but where the majority of experts in military affairs believed the preponderance of evidence supported one side. It was therefore chosen as a suitable subject for experimentation.

Radio transcriptions rather than films were used, primarily because of the simplicity with which they could be prepared in alternative forms. The basic outline of the programs' content was prepared by the Experimental Section. All materials used were official releases from the Office of War Information and the War Department. The final writing and production of the programs were carried out by the Armed Forces Radio Service.

The two programs compared in this chapter were in the form of a commentator's analysis of the Pacific War. The commentator's conclusion was that the job of finishing the war would be tough and that it would take at least two years after VE Day. A brief description of the two programs follows.

Program I ("one side"): The major topics included in the program which presented *only* the arguments indicating that the war would be long were: distance problems and other logistical difficulties in the Pacific; the resources and stockpiles in the Japanese Empire; the size and quality of the main bulk of the Japanese Army that we had not yet met in battle; and the determination of the Japanese people. The program ran for about fifteen minutes.

Program II ("both sides"): The other program ran for about nineteen minutes and presented all of these same difficulties in exactly the same way. The difference of four minutes between this and the "one-sided" program was the time devoted to considering arguments for the other side of the picture—U.S. advantages and Japanese weaknesses such as our naval victories and superiority, our previous progress despite a two-front war, our ability to concentrate all our forces on Japan after VE Day, Japan's shipping losses, Japan's manufacturing inferiority, and the future damage to be expected from our expanding air war. These additional points were woven into the context of the rest of the program.

Before the preparation of these programs, pretests had been conducted in which men were individually interviewed on questions relating to the length of the war with Japan. The purpose of this was to discover what arguments were actually used by the soldiers who took the position that the war would soon be over. At the same time, the phrasing of questions for the final questionnaire to be used in the study was worked out. This qualitative pretest was followed by a quantitative pretest on 200 men to discover the approximate distribution of men's estimates of probable length of the war and the approximate frequency of the various arguments for and against a short or long war. The information thus gained was then used as a basis for preparing an outline of the factual material to be used in the program, greatest weight being given to the material relevant to countering the arguments most frequently offered by the men as a basis for expecting an early end to the war in the Pacific after VE Day.

In preparing the programs, the sequence and manner of presenting the various arguments was guided, in so far as possible, by principles thought to be those which would most effectively utilize the arguments on both sides so as to convince the men initially opposed to the orientation message. The major hypothesis governing the preparation of the presentation giving "both sides" was that those who were opposed would be stimulated by a one-sided argument to rehearse their own position and seek new ways of supporting it. A further aspect of this hypothesis was that those opposed to the position taken would discount a one-sided presentation as coming from a biased source that had failed to consider the arguments on the other side. The introduction of the arguments "on the other side" was designed to minimize such tendencies among those opposed. In line with these considerations, the following provisional rules or principles of presentation were formulated.

1. *All of the main arguments on the other side should be mentioned at the very outset.* This was designed to have the effect of indicating to the opposed members of the audience from the very beginning that their point of view and supporting arguments would not be neglected. As a consequence it was expected that they would be less likely to start rehearsing their own arguments to themselves, more likely to credit the presentation as having the authenticity that usually goes with unbiased interpretations, and less likely to have their own emotional motivations aroused against accepting the conclusion of the communication.

2. *Any appeals to the motives of the opposed audience members should be presented early.* On the assumption that appeals to motives are the most important determiners of opinion change, it seems likely that with opposed audience members the rational arguments would be more influential if the emotional appeal had already been made as far as possible. This timing would be less important with individuals already emotionally predisposed to accept the conclusion—the latter group would be highly receptive to the rational arguments that backed up their position.

3. *Opposed arguments that cannot be refuted should be presented relatively early.* Such arguments actually tend to weaken the conclusion, but they serve to satisfy the opposition and thus reduce antagonism. By highlighting them fairly early in the communication, the maximal advantage in reducing aggressive tenden-

cies is obtained, but they should also be expected to be remembered less at the conclusion of the communication.

4. *An attempt to refute arguments on the other side should be made only when an obviously compelling and strictly factual refutation is available.* Here the expectation is that any attempted refutation will have a tendency to antagonize the opposed members of the audience, and may motivate them to seek new arguments to support their position. Therefore, direct refutation should be considered only when it is based on factual evidence so strong that it will be accepted even by those who are opposed.

5. *An unrefuted opposed argument should be followed by an uncontroversial positive argument.* The inference here is that a negative argument can be offset by an equally strong or even stronger positive argument. It may even be true that the effect will often be greater if a refutable negative argument is left unrefuted in order not to arouse any antagonistic motivation—in order to avoid getting the opposed listener's "ego" involved—and is instead offset by a positive argument that is accepted as valid by the opposition. The order of negative, then positive, should serve to indicate that the negative point is being considered, but that despite this important point on the negative side, the positive point swings the balance in the direction of the conclusion endorsed. This sequence should take advantage of the appearance of impartiality and satisfy the opposition as to the correctness and relevance of their own considerations, but still leave the weight of evidence against their position.

6. *The timing in presenting counterarguments of the opposition should be: positive argument leading, objection raised by an opposed counterargument, and then positive argument offsetting the objection.* One purpose of this sequence is to state the negative argument exactly at the time that it is most likely to be aroused implicitly in the opposition group. They therefore should not be so likely to rehearse the argument in an antagonistic frame of mind, but instead be gratified to hear their own position voiced. At the same time their argument is presented in a context of doubt, and the argument that is favored by both primacy and recency is the positive argument that is used to refute or offset the negative counterargument.

7. *Any refutations, and those positive arguments which are potentially most antagonizing, should come late in the presentation.* This follows from the expectation that a potentially antagonizing refutation will elicit less antagonism if the opposition has already been changed in a positive direction by the preceding portions of the communications. If they have already been partly "won over" to the position of the communication, they may not be at all antagonized by an idea that would have aroused aggression at the outset.

8. *Members of the opposition should not be given a choice to identify themselves as such.* This principle is perhaps more difficult to utilize than the others. The basis for the principle is that a person is easier to change if he does not have his "ego" involved in supporting a particular point of view. If he feels that he belongs to a group that is being attacked by the communication, he is more likely to respond with aggressive resistance. Anything that can be done to present the communication as if it represented the views of each member of the audience, or to prevent the listeners from taking sides on the issue, should make those initially opposed more susceptible to change.

Not all of these "rules" could be adhered to strictly in the preparation of the actual scripts. However, an outline of the factual material to be presented was organized in such a way as to follow rather closely the implications of the first five rules, and in general to introduce the negative arguments at those points where, as determined by pretests, they seemed most likely to occur spontaneously to the opposed members of the audience. In these pretests, interviewers had actually presented the case for a long war in a face-to-face situation and had attempted to elicit counterarguments from interviewees who felt that the war would be short. In the final scripts used, refutations of the opposed arguments were in general avoided. Counterarguments rarely took the form of trying to *disprove* or *deny* the truth of an important argument; rather, the truth of the argument was admitted but its force was weakened by immediately bringing in additional relevant facts.

The outline of factual material thus organized was used by the script writers as the basis for preparing the program that used arguments on "both sides" of the question. The script for the "one-side" version was identical with that for "both sides" except for the omission of all facts or arguments supporting a short war, plus a very few wording changes necessary for transitional purposes.

At the time of preparing the scripts, the writer knew the purpose of the experiment and the actual wording of the main question to be used in measuring the effects of the transcriptions.

It should be pointed out that while Program II gave facts on *both sides* of the question, it did not give equal space to both sides, nor did it attempt to compare the case for thinking it would be a long war with the *strongest possible case* for believing it would be an easy victory and a short war. It took exactly the same stand as that taken by Program I—namely, that the war would be difficult and would require at least two years. The difference was that Program II mentioned the opposite arguments (e.g., U.S. advantages). In effect it argued that the job would be difficult, even when our advantages and the Japanese weaknesses were taken into account.

2. CONDUCT OF THE EXPERIMENT

The procedure was to give a preliminary "opinion survey" to determine the men's initial opinions about the Pacific War and then to remeasure their opinions at a later time, after the transcriptions had been played to them in the course of their orientation meetings. In this way the *changes* in their opinions from "before" to "after" could be determined. A control group, which heard *no* transcription, was also surveyed as a means of determining any changes in response that might occur during the time interval due to causes other than the transcriptions—such as the impact of war news from the Pacific.

Since the purpose of the study was to analyze differential effects of two kinds of content on individuals with differing initial opinions, it was desirable to obtain for analysis the maximum overall effects possible. For this reason the effects were measured immediately after the presentation of the programs. It is, of course, conceivable that the effects might have been even greater after a longer time interval, and further that with the longer time interval the pattern of effects might have been different from the immediate effects observed.

The preliminary survey was administered during the first week of April 1945 to eight Quartermaster training companies. One week later eight platoons, one chosen at random from each of the eight companies, heard Program I (which presented only one side) during their individual orientation meetings. Another group of eight platoons, similarly chosen, heard Program II (which presented both arguments). Immediately after the program the men filled out the second questionnaire, ostensibly for the purpose of letting the people who made the program know what the men thought of it. Included in this second questionnaire, with appropriate transitional questions, were some of the same questions that had been included in the earlier survey, asking the men how they personally sized up the Pacific War. A third group of eight platoons served as the control with no program. They filled out a similar questionnaire, during their orientation meeting, which, in addition to asking the same questions on the Pacific War, asked preliminary questions about what they thought of their orientation meetings and what they would like in future orientation meetings. For the control group, the latter questions—in lieu of the questions about the transcriptions—were represented to the men as the main purpose of the questionnaire.

While 24 platoons were used for this experiment, the units were at only about 70 percent of full strength at the preliminary survey and at the orientation meetings. The "shrinkage" was therefore quite large as to number of men present *both* times, and the sample available for "before-after" analysis was consequently small (a total of 625 men, with 214 in each experimental group and the remaining 197 men in the control group). In view of the rapidly changing picture in the Pacific, however, it was considered inadvisable to repeat the experiment at another camp.

3. ADMINISTRATION

For proper administration of the experiment there were three major requirements: presentation of the transcriptions under realistic conditions, preventing the men in the sample from realizing that the experiment was in progress, and getting honest answers in the questionnaires. For realism in presentation, the transcriptions for the experimental groups were incorporated into the training program and scheduled as part of the weekly orientation hour. This not only insured realistic presentation but also helped to avoid indicating that effects of the transcriptions were being tested.

The preliminary "survey." The preliminary "survey" had been presented as being part of a War Department survey "to find out how a cross section of soldiers felt about various subjects connected with the war," with examples being given of previous Research Branch surveys and how the findings had been used. Questionnaires were administered to all the men in a company at once, with the men assembled in mess halls for the purpose. The questionnaires were administered by "class leaders" selected and trained for the job from among the enlisted personnel working at the camp. In an introductory explanation of the survey the class leader stressed the importance of the survey and the anonymity of the answers. No camp officers were present at these meetings and the men were assured that the surveys went directly to Washington and that no one at the camp would get a chance to see what they had written. The questionnaire used in this preliminary "survey" consisted mainly of checklist questions plus a few questions in which the men were asked to write their own answers. The content of most of the questions was the point system for demobilization and the Army's plans for redeployment. This was a convenient context for the questions that formed the measuring instrument per se which dealt with the difficulty of defeating Japan. The questions about the point system and redeployment were not necessary for the actual experimental measurements but were used to give scope to the "survey" and to prevent a concentration of items dealing with material to be covered by the transcription. This was done partly to help make the survey seem realistic to the men but mainly to avoid "sensitizing" them to questions about the topic of the subsequently presented orientation material through placing too much emphasis on it in the survey.

The second questionnaire. To prevent the men from suspecting that an "experiment" was in progress because of the administration of two questionnaires within a short space of time, the second questionnaire differed from the first one both in its form and its announced purpose. Thus the first questionnaire was given as a general War Department "survey" while the second one was given during the orientation meetings to "find out what men thought of the transcriptions" (or, in the control group, "what they thought of their orientation meetings").

An additional difference in the administration of the two questionnaires, which was also designed to reduce the appearance of similarity, was that while the first had been given by company in mess halls, the second was administered by platoon in the men's barracks where the orientation meetings were held.

While the ostensible purpose in giving the men the second questionnaire was to get their opinion of the program, appropriate "tie-in" questions, such as whether or not they thought the commentator too optimistic or too pessimistic, were used to lead to the questions as to how long they thought the war would last and on the other topics concerning the difficulty of the job.

As in studies of opinion changes described in earlier chapters, it was considered necessary in the case of the present study to obtain opinions anonymously, and also to measure the effects of the program without awareness on the part of the men that an experiment was in progress. These precautions were dictated by the type of effect being studied—it was felt that if the men either thought their questionnaires were identified by name or if they knew they were being "tested," some men might give "proper" or otherwise distorted answers rather than answers expressing their true opinions in the matter.

Analysis of Results

The results to be presented are based on an analysis of the responses of men whose preliminary survey could be matched with the "after" questionnaire given in the orientation meetings. Although all of the questionnaires were anonymous, the "before" and "after" questionnaires of the same individual could be matched on the basis of answers to such personal-history questions as years of schooling, date of birth, etc., with handwriting serving as an additional factor among men whose personal history was similar.

1. OVERALL EFFECTS OF THE TWO PROGRAMS ON THE
   MARGINAL DISTRIBUTION OF ESTIMATES OF
   THE LENGTH OF THE WAR

As previously stated, the main question used to evaluate the effectiveness of the two programs was a question asking men for their estimates of the probable length of the war with Japan after VE Day. The wording of this question was the same in both the "before" and the "after" questionnaire and was as follows:

What is your guess as to how long it will probably take us to beat Japan after Germany's defeat? (Write your best guess below.)

About _____ from the day of Germany's defeat.

The men's answers to this question tended to be in half-year intervals and were accordingly coded by steps of one-half year each.

A marked overall shift in an upward direction in the distribution of estimates was obtained. The results are shown in Table 21.1, with the answers dichotomized into those estimating one-and-one-half years or less versus those estimating more than one-and-one-half years.

Table 21.1
Overall Effects of the Two Programs on Distribution of Estimated Length of War

| | PERCENTAGE ESTIMATING A WAR OF MORE THAN ONE-AND-ONE-HALF YEARS | | |
| | EXPERIMENTAL GROUPS | | |
	PROGRAM I "ONE SIDE"	PROGRAM II "BOTH SIDES"	CONTROL GROUP
Before	37%	38%	36%
After	59	59	34
Difference	22%	21%	−2%
Probability	<.01	<.01	

The effectiveness of both programs is revealed by the marked change shown for both experimental groups (with practically no change for the control group). However, no advantage for one program over the other for the audience as a whole is revealed.

While changes in overall frequencies of response, such as those shown above, are often useful in evaluating the effectiveness of a program in achieving its educational objective, they are not usually the most sensitive measure of effects. In the present case if the orientation objectives were specifically to prepare the men to expect a war of at least one-and-one-half years after VE Day, the above analysis does reveal the increase in the number of men holding this desired point of view. However, an analysis of this form often conceals other effects important for a more complete description of the changes that occur. Thus shifts occurring within the region below the point of dichotomy (e.g., from an estimate of six months to an estimate of one year) or within the region above this point (e.g., from two-and-one-half years to three years) are not revealed. A more sensitive analysis of the overall effects is described in the next section.

2. ANALYSIS IN TERMS OF NET PROPORTION WHO CHANGE

Since measurements on the same men were made both before and after the programs it was possible to get each man's individual change in estimating the length of the war. As already stated, the answers tended to be in terms of half-year units, so the minimum change occurring with a sizable frequency was a change of one-half year. Accordingly, the results were analyzed in terms of whether a man increased or decreased his estimate—from "before" to "after"—by one-half year or more. This analysis gets at individual shifts all along the time continuum, irrespective of whether they cross a particular cutting point along the marginal distribution.

Using this analysis procedure it was found that in all groups some men increased their estimates and others decreased their estimates. This is to be expected merely from the knowledge that most opinion questions are not perfectly reliable. In addition, a certain amount of "turnover" of opinion is expected because of various individual experiences during the interval between the two measurements.

The results showed, however, that in the control group the positive shifts (increased estimates) were about equal in number to the negative shifts, but that in both experimental groups the positive shifts greatly exceeded the negative shifts. These results are shown in Table 21.2.

Here the programs are seen to have resulted in a net proportion of *two-fifths* of the men increasing their estimates. On the basis of

Table 21.2

Effects of the Programs in Terms of Net Proportion Changing Their Estimates

| | PERCENTAGE WHO CHANGED THEIR ESTIMATE BY ONE-HALF YEAR OR MORE | | |
| | EXPERIMENTAL GROUPS | | |
KIND OF CHANGE	PROGRAM I "ONE SIDE"	PROGRAM II "BOTH SIDES"	CONTROL GROUP
No change	46%	45%	63%
Increased estimate	47	47	18
Decreased estimate	7	8	19
Net change (increase minus decrease)	40	39	−1
Net effect (experimental change minus control change)	41	40	
Probability*	<.01	<.01	

*The method for determining the significance level of the "net effect" utilizes the fact that the net *change* for each group is the difference between two mutually exclusive proportions in the same sample—namely, the proportion P_1 who gave an increased estimate and the proportion P_2 who gave a decreased estimate. The net *effect* is the difference between two such differences—i.e., the difference between the net change for an experimental group and that for the control group. Its standard error is given by the formula:

$$\text{Est. } \sigma_{\text{diff}-\text{diff}} = \sqrt{[P_1 + P_2 - (P_1 - P_2)^2]\left[\frac{1}{N_E} + \frac{1}{N_C}\right]}$$

where P_1 and P_2 are the above stated proportions computed for the experimental and control groups *combined,* and N_E and N_C are the N's for the experimental and control groups.

the analysis procedure used in Table 21.1 we could only have been sure that a net of around *one-fifth* was affected.

3. EFFECTS OF THE PROGRAMS ON MEN INITIALLY OPPOSING AND INITIALLY FAVORING THE COMMENTATOR'S CONCLUSION

The results already reported indicate no greater effectiveness of either program on the audience *as a whole*. However, as mentioned earlier, a critical feature in the theory underlying the experiment was the expectation of adverse effects of the "one-sided" program on men initially opposing the commentator's view that the war would take at least two years after VE Day. In line with the theory, therefore, the results were analyzed separately for men who initially opposed and those who initially favored the stand taken by the programs. The basis for distinguishing these two groups was whether their initial estimate of the length of the war in the "before" questionnaire was, respectively, less than two years, or was two years or more. The measure used in the analysis was the "net effect" described in the previous section for changes of one-half year or more.

The net effects of the two ways of presenting the orientation material are shown below for these two subgroups of men; those initially estimating a war of less than two years (the "opposed" group) and those initially estimating a war of two or more years (the "favorable" group). Control results are omitted for simplicity since the present concern is with comparing the two programs, both of which had the same control.

Figure 21.1 shows that the *net effects* were different for the two ways of presenting the orientation material, depending on the initial stand of the listener. The program giving some of the U.S. advantages in addition to the difficulties was more effective for men initially opposed, that is, for men who, contrary to the programs, expected a war of less than two years. On the other hand, the program giving the one-sided picture was more effective for men initially favoring the stand taken, that is, for the men who agreed with the point of view of the programs that the war would take at least two years. The initial division of opinion was roughly three men opposing to every man favoring the stand taken, but since the differential effect was greater in the latter group the overall net effects on the men as a whole were almost equal for the two programs.[1]

1. The statistical test used to assess the reliability of the differential effects is exactly analogous to that used in the previous section. In the above case, however, the control is not involved since the experimental subgroups can be directly compared.

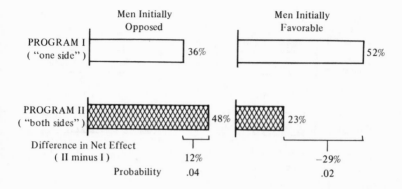

Figure 21.1
Differential effects of the two programs on men initially opposing and men initially favoring the commentator's position. See supplementary Table A for subgroup *N*'s and control results.

4. EFFECTS ON MEN WITH DIFFERENT AMOUNTS OF EDUCATION

In line with theoretical considerations it would be expected that the better educated men would be less affected by a conspicuously one-sided presentation and would conversely be more likely to accept the arguments of a presentation that appears to take all factors into account in arriving at a conclusion. On the other hand, the consideration of both sides of an issue could weaken the immediate force of the argument for the less well educated insofar as they are less critical and more likely to be impressed by the strength of the one-sided argument without thinking of objections.

When the results were broken down according to educational level, it was found that the program which presented both sides was more effective with better educated men and that the program which presented one side was more effective with less educated men. Figure 21.2 shows results comparing the effects on men who

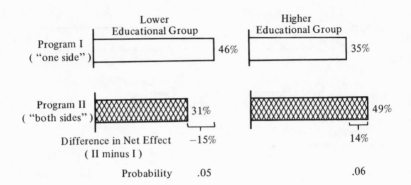

Figure 21.2
Differential effects of the two programs on men of different educational backgrounds.
See supplementary Table B for detailed computations.

did not graduate from high school with the effects on high school graduates. This breakdown by education divides the sample into approximately equal halves.

The above results show that the program giving both sides had *less* effect on the nongraduates but *more* effect on the high school graduates.

5. EFFECTS WHEN BOTH EDUCATION AND INITIAL ESTIMATES ARE CONSIDERED

The interesting question arises as to how initial position on the issue presented by the transcription is related to effects among men in each educational group. Definitive results on this point could not be obtained because of the small number of cases involved when the sample is broken into the eight subgroups required for this analysis. The data available are presented, however, to indicate the trends and to suggest a hypothesis deserving further study: that the argument giving both sides is more effective among the better educated regardless of initial position, whereas the one-sided presen-

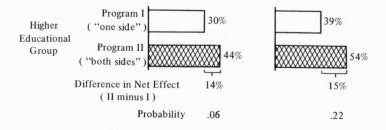

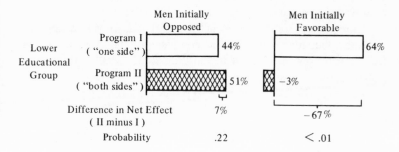

Figure 21.3
Differential effects of the two programs on men initially opposing and men initially favoring the commentator's position, shown separately for men with different education.
See supplementary Table C for detailed computations.

tation is primarily effective with those who are already convinced among the less well educated group (Figure 21.3).

The conclusions suggested by the pattern of results presented thus far may be summarized as follows: Giving the strong points for the "other side" can make a presentation more effective at getting across its message, at least for the better educated men and for those who are already opposed to the stand taken. This difference in effectiveness, however, may be reversed for the less educated men, and, in the extreme case, the material giving both sides may have a negative effect on poorly educated men already convinced of the major position taken by a program. From these results it would be expected that the total effect of either kind of program on the group as a whole would depend on the group's educational composition and on the initial division of opinion in the group. Thus, ascertaining this information about the composition of an audience might be of considerable value in choosing the most effective type of presentation.

6. MEN'S EVALUATION OF THE FACTUAL COVERAGE

One factor that should tend to make a presentation taking into account both sides of an issue more effective than a presentation covering only one side is that the men might believe the former treatment to be more impartial and authoritative.

In the present study, however, the group as a whole did not consider the factual coverage more complete in the program giving U.S. advantages in addition to the difficulties faced. This is illustrated below.[2]

PERCENT OF MEN SAYING THAT THE PROGRAM DID A
GOOD JOB OF GIVING THE FACTS ON THE PACIFIC WAR
Program I
("one side")   61%
Program II
("both sides")   54
PERCENT OF MEN SAYING THAT THE PROGRAM TOOK
ALL OF THE IMPORTANT FACTS INTO ACCOUNT
Program I
("one side")   48%
Program II
("both sides")   42

It can be seen above that the factual coverage was not considered better in the program giving U.S. advantages as well as the difficulties. The difference obtained was in the opposite direction, although

2. The *Ns* on which these percentages are based are 214 for Program I and 214 for Program II.

not reliably so. Essentially the same results were obtained for each of the two educational subgroups analyzed.

The explanation of this unexpected result apparently lies in the fact that both programs omitted any mention of Russia as a factor in the Pacific War, and *this omission seemed more glaring in the presentation that committed itself to covering both sides of the question.* This somewhat paradoxical conclusion is well supported by results to be shown shortly, and while it was not anticipated it is quite understandable in retrospect.

At the time that the Pacific War was chosen as the orientation subject for the experiment it was recognized that a weakness of this topic was that under existing informational policy no stand could be taken on the help to be expected from Russia. Thus maximum content difference between the two presentations could not be achieved because they *both* had to omit mention of an important argument on the "other side," namely, that Russia might enter the war against the Japanese. It was not anticipated, however, that this omission would be more noticeable in the program that otherwise covered both sides. That this actually happened was indicated by the men's answers to the "write-in" question: "What facts or topics that you think are important in the war with Japan are not mentioned in the program?" The percentages writing in that aid or possible aid from Russia was not mentioned are shown in Figure 21.4.

As shown above, almost twice as many men mentioned the omission of Russia in the program covering "both sides." The difference was even more pronounced among *groups that would be expected to be especially sensitive to this omission,* such as men who were initially optimistic about the length of the war, men with more education, and men who had indicated in the "before" questionnaire that they expected a great deal of help from Russia in the job against Japan.

7. RELATIVE EFFECTIVENESS OF THE TWO PROGRAMS
ON MEN MOST LIKELY TO NOTE THE OMISSION
OF THE TOPIC OF RUSSIAN AID

In the preceding section it was shown that the program giving "both sides" was *not* considered more adequate than the one-sided

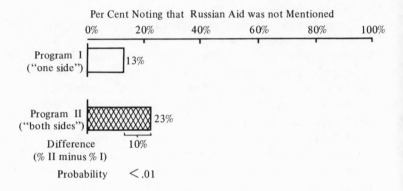

Figure 21.4
Frequency with which the omission of the topic of Russian aid was noted by the men.

program in its factual coverage and that it caused more men to note that Russia was not mentioned. The question now to be considered is whether this actually detracted from the effectiveness of this program that otherwise took all factors into consideration. A direct answer to this question cannot be given, but indirect evidence indicates that the omission did detract from this program's effectiveness.

The indirect evidence comes from a separate analysis of the results among men who initially opposed the point of view of the commentator. These were the men for whom the program giving both sides was more effective, even with the omission of the topic of Russian aid. The question is, would it have been still more effective if this topic could have been included? To get evidence on this question this subgroup of opposed men was further subdivided according to whether or not they were predisposed to note the omission of Russia. The logic of the analysis was that men especially sensitive to the omission (because they were opposed and thought Russia might help) would not accept the commentator's argument, whereas those men who were opposed to his position but did *not* have Russian aid as one of their own important arguments for a short war would show less detrimental effect of the omission. The following question in the "before" questionnaire was used to subdivide the initially opposed men into those anticipating and those not anticipating substantial aid from Russia.

> "How much help do you think America will get from other countries when it comes to the job of defeating the Japs?" (Check one)
> _____ very little
> _____ some, but not a great deal
> _____ a great deal (Which countries? _____)

The breakdown on this question among "opposed" men put about two-fifths of the men in the "sensitive" subgroup, that is, about two-fifths of the "opposed" men said they expected a great deal of help and *wrote in Russia* as one of the countries from which they expected a great deal of help.

When these subgroups of the "opposed" men were compared it was found that the men who counted on a great deal of help from Russia gave a relatively poorer evaluation of the factual coverage in the program giving "both sides" and were relatively less influenced in the direction of increasing their estimates of the probable length of the war.

The results for the men's evaluation of the factual coverage, based on two items, are shown in Figure 21.5.

The implication of the results in Figure 21.5 is that the authenticity of the program which presented both sides suffered from the omission of the subject of Russia. Men who counted on Russian aid had a lower evaluation of the factual coverage of this program than of the one-sided program.

The presumption from this indirect evidence is that if the program covering both sides had dealt with the subject of Russia, it might have been considered more complete in its factual coverage, particularly among men who expected Russian aid. This inference receives corroboration from the fact that in a fairly large-scale pretest of the two programs, conducted at a time when possible aid from Russia was a less important news topic, the program covering "both sides" had been found to be *reliably more accepted* in its factual coverage, just the reverse of the results shown earlier. This pretest was conducted with a sample of 347 Infantry reinforce-

A. Per cent saying program did "a very good job" of giving the facts.

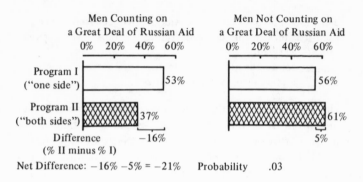

Men Counting on
a Great Deal of Russian Aid

Men Not Counting on
a Great Deal of Russian Aid

Program I
("one side") 53%

Program II
("both sides") 37%

Program I
("one side") 56%

Program II
("both sides") 61%

Difference   −16%
(% II minus % I)

5%

Net Difference: −16% −5% = −21%   Probability   .03

B. Per cent saying program "took all of the important facts into account."

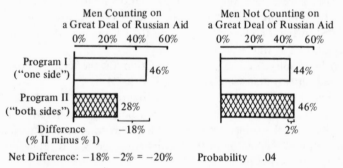

Men Counting on
a Great Deal of Russian Aid

Men Not Counting on
a Great Deal of Russian Aid

Program I
("one side") 46%

Program II
("both sides") 28%

Program I
("one side") 44%

Program II
("both sides") 46%

Difference   −18%
(% II minus % I)

2%

Net Difference: −18% −2% = −20%   Probability   .04

Figure 21.5
Differences in evaluation of factual coverage in the two programs, *among men opposed to the commentator's position,* comparing those who did and those who did not count on Russian aid.
For subgroup *N*s, see supplementary Table D.

ments in March 1945, and practically no difference was obtained between the two programs in the percentages of men noting the omission of Russian aid. In the present study, however, the pro-

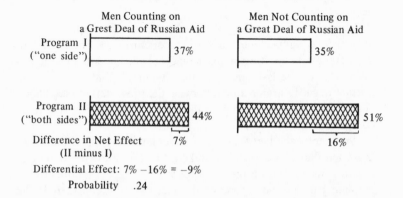

Men Counting on
a Grest Deal of Russian Aid

Men Not Counting on
a Great Deal of Russian Aid

Program I
("one side")   37%

35%

Program II
("both sides")   44%

51%

Difference in Net Effect   7%
(II minus I)

16%

Differential Effect: 7% −16% = −9%
Probability   .24

Figure 21.6
Differential relative effect of the two programs among men
initially opposed but differing as to whether they had counted
on a great deal of help from Russia.
See supplementary Table D for *N*s and control group results.

grams were played during the second week of April, about a week
after the Russians announced that they would not renew their non-
aggression pact with Japan.

Not only did the omission of the topic of Russia affect men's
evaluation of the factual coverage in Program II in the subgroups
above, but it may have reduced the effect of the program on the
men's estimates of the length of the war. This is suggested by an
analysis of the net effects of the programs on opinions of the men in
the same subgroups as those used in Figure 21.5. The results of this
analysis are shown in Figure 21.6.

These results are in line with the expectation that among the men
for whom the presentation with both sides is most effective (i.e., the
men initially opposing the idea of a two-year war) the advantage of
the "both-sides" presentation was less among those counting on a
great deal of help from Russia than among those not expecting
much help. The differential effect is too small to be reliable with

the small number of cases involved in the above subgroups, but they are consonant with the interpretation that the effects of the program giving some of the "other side" would have been even greater on those opposed to the stand taken if *all* of the other side could have been covered.

All of the results dealing with the omission of the topic of Russian aid seem to support one important conclusion, namely, that if a presentation supporting a particular conclusion attempts to take both sides of the issue into account, it must include *all* of the important negative arguments; otherwise the presentation may "boomerang" by failing to live up to the expectation of impartiality and completeness.

Apparently the fact that the commentator in giving "both sides" indicated that he was trying to take *all* factors into consideration in drawing his conclusion prepared the men to expect the inclusion of possible Russian aid as one of the factors to be considered. Thus the omission in the context of considering all factors stood out more than in the context of the one-sided program where only the difficulties were being considered. The general conclusion seems to be that a one-sided presentation in which the conclusion is stated in advance and the reasons for this conclusion are then given will be accepted as the argument for a given point of view without much loss of authenticity resulting from failure to cover the other side. However, if a presentation commits itself to taking everything into account, either by announcing this in advance or by actually covering parts of each side of the issue, it will seem less authentic than a single-sided presentation if any important facts known to the audience are not included in the discussion, and its effectiveness at changing opinions will be reduced among those who are most aware of the point omitted.

8. RELATION OF THE RESULTS TO THE CONTENTION THAT THE INITIALLY OPPOSED WILL BE NEGATIVELY AFFECTED

The results of this experiment have an obvious bearing on the frequently made assertion that "propaganda" merely reinforces the opinions already held, i.e., that those initially favoring a point of view tend to be made more favorable, whereas those initially opposed may tend to become even more opposed than at the outset (cf. e.g., Murphy et al., 1937, p. 874f and 963f). This would be predicted on the grounds that a person is receptive to arguments having the conclusion he himself has already reached, but that arguments counter to a strongly held opinion serve as the occasion for an individual to rehearse the arguments favoring his side, to think up new arguments to combat the ones presented, to "get his ego involved" in his position, and so forth.

In all of the results shown comparing the net effects of the programs on men "initially opposing" the point of view presented by the commentator, it will be observed that "opposed" men were influenced in the direction of the "message" presented rather than against it. Thus, regardless of educational level or expectation of aid from Russia, the "opposed" men were influenced to accept the point of view of the commentator with either program. This is definitely contrary to the contention that "propaganda" merely reinforces existing beliefs.[3]

It might be contended that in the results shown so far the men in the "opposed" group were not sufficiently opposed for the alleged phenomenon to be revealed. Thus the opposed group contained a sizable proportion who were close to the borderline of two years in their estimate of the length of the war and these could not be said to be very strongly opposed. But a finer breakdown of initial estimate reveals the same general result. This is shown below in Table 21.3, which shows net effects as a function of initial position for less broad categories than those used so far. The most opposed group possible with the coding used—that is, the group estimating a war of less than six months—is not shown because the number of cases was so small; only about 1 man in 20 fell in this category. However, even in this tiny group the results come out in the same direction. The results presented are for both programs combined.

It will be seen that the familiar "regression" phenomenon occurs

3. A word should also be said concerning the interpretations here placed on such expressions as "more opposed." The frequently stressed distinction between "intensity" of opinion and "content" or "direction" of opinion is relevant to this interpretation. Thus, changes in the direction of "more favorable" or "more opposed" might refer either to changes in the direction of a more extreme position on a content continuum, or to greater intensity of feeling on a given position, or both. However, the present discussion is limited to the former kind of change because of the absence of adequate measures of intensity.

Table 21.3
The Effects of Radio Transcriptions on Opinions about Duration of War, for Those with Various Initial Opinions

| | NET PERCENTAGE CHANGING ESTIMATE BY ONE-HALF YEAR OR MORE AMONG MEN WHOSE INITIAL ESTIMATE WAS: | | | |
	LESS THAN 1 YEAR	1 YEAR UP TO 1½ YEARS	1½ YEARS UP TO 2 YEARS	2 YEARS OR MORE
Net change in experimental groups	58%	53%	26%	2%
Net change in the control group	20	6	−12	−34
Net effects	38	47	38	36

in the control group, that is, because of the imperfect reliability of the question on length of the war the men who initially made long estimates tend to make shorter ones and the men who initially made short estimates tend to make longer ones. The changes due to regression as indicated by the changes in the control group must be subtracted from the changes in the experimental group to obtain the net effect of the program, shown in the third line of figures in Table 21.3.

It can be seen from the net effects shown in Table 21.3 that even with the finer breakdown of initial estimate, all of the subgroups were influenced in the direction of revising their estimates upward. This was true even of the men with the most extreme opposition— that is, men whose initial estimate was only one year or less.

It may be further argued that the contention that opposed men would be made more opposed applies not to the extremeness of their content position but rather to the intensity with which they hold their opinion or the extent of emotional involvement in supporting their point of view. No answer is available from the present study on this interpretation of degree of opposition because measurements of intensity of feeling independent of content were not feasible. To the extent, however, that intensity and content are correlated, the present study shows negative results regardless of how "opposition" is defined for the type of communication investigated.

This qualification concerning the type of communications investigated is made because it seems theoretically possible that opposition would be fostered with some kinds of "propaganda." This seems especially likely for face-to-face situations in which the communicator and the communicatee become involved in a give-and-take argument. In such a case the individual who constitutes the "audience" himself takes a stand and is likely to have more "ego involvement," actively to seek new arguments in support of his position, and so forth. A similar situation would be the debate form of communication in which there is a protagonist for each side of the issue. Exposure to debates has been shown to strengthen the initial opinions of those audience members initially expressing an opinion and to reduce the neutral, no-opinion category by shifting some people in one direction and others in the opposite direction (Millson, 1932). If the audience is initially divided in opinion on the issue, individual audience members would be expected to identify with the protagonist representing their own initial stand, and a situation similar to the face-to-face argument is created.

9. SUMMARY OF RESULTS

(1) Presenting the arguments on both sides of an issue was found to be more effective than giving only the arguments supporting the point being made, in the case of individuals who were *initially opposed* to the point of view being presented.

(2) For men who were *already convinced* of the point of view being presented, however, the inclusion of arguments on both sides was less effective, for the group as a whole, than presenting only the arguments favoring the general position being advocated.

(3) Better educated men were more favorably affected by presentation of both sides; less well educated men were more affected by the communication which used only supporting arguments.

(4) The group for which the presentation giving both sides was least effective was the group of poorly educated men who were already convinced of the point of view being advocated.

(5) An important incidental finding was that the absence of one relevant argument against the stand taken by the programs was more noticeable in the presentation using arguments on both sides than in the presentation in which only one side was discussed.

Furthermore, advantage of the program giving both sides among men initially opposed was less for those who regarded the omitted argument as an important one.

(6) Men who were initially very opposed to the point of view being presented—as measured by their deviation in *content* from the position taken by the communication—were nevertheless influenced to alter their opinion in the direction of the "message" rather than being shifted further in the direction of their initial opinion.

References

Millson, W. A. D. 1932. Problems in measuring audience reaction. *Quarterly Journal of Speech* 18: 621–37.

Murphy, G.; Murphy, L. B.; and Newcomb, T. M. 1937. *Experimental social psychology*. Rev. ed. New York: Harper.

See Supplementary Tables, pages 263–66.

Supplementary Table A

Breakdown of Changes in Estimates Among Men Initially Favoring and Men Initially Opposing the Stand Taken

	PROGRAM I "ONE SIDE"		PERCENT OF MEN PROGRAM II "BOTH SIDES"		CONTROL NO PROGRAM	
	INITIAL ESTIMATE		INITIAL ESTIMATE		INITIAL ESTIMATE	
	LESS THAN 2	2 OR MORE	LESS THAN 2	2 OR MORE	LESS THAN 2	2 OR MORE
No change	45	46	41	56	65	56
Revised estimate upward	50	36	58	16	22	5
Revise estimate downward	5	18	1	27	13	39
Net change (% up minus % down)	45	18	57	−11	9*	−34*
Control net change*	9	−34	9	−34		
Net effect (program net minus control)	36	52	48	23		
Number of cases in each subgroup†	152	45	150	55	140	41

*The net changes in the two subgroups of the *control* represent the familiar "regression" phenomenon due to unreliable test answers. (See p. 329ff, Appendix D.) The greater degree of regression in the subgroups estimating a war of two or more years is accounted for by the extent of their deviation from the average estimate of less than one-and-one-half years.

†The numbers of cases given here add to 583 instead of the total of 625 men studied because the analysis could not include the 42 individuals who failed to write legible estimates of the length of the war in either the "before" or the "after" survey. The omission of such individuals applies also to the three following tables.

Supplementary Table B
Breakdown of Change in Estimates Among Men with Differing Education

| | PERCENT OF MEN | | | | | |
| EDUCATION: | NONGRADUATES | | | HIGH SCHOOL GRADUATES | | |
PROGRAM:	I ("ONE SIDE")	II ("BOTH SIDES")	CONTROL	I ("ONE SIDE")	II ("BOTH SIDES")	CONTROL
No change	40	45	64	51	45	62
Revised estimate upward	54	44	19	40	50	17
Revised estimate downward	6	11	17	9	5	21
Net change	48	33	2	31	45	−4
Control net change	2	2		−4	−4	
Net effect (program net minus control)*	46	31		35	49	
Number of cases in each subgroup*	93	105	104	104	100	77

*See second footnote to Table A.

Supplementary Table C

Breakdown of Changes in Estimates in the Subgroups Separated Both According to Initial Estimate and According to Education

	PERCENT OF MEN							
EDUCATION:	NONGRADUATES				HIGH SCHOOL GRADUATES			
INITIAL ESTIMATE:	LESS THAN 2 YEARS		2 OR MORE YEARS		LESS THAN 2 YEARS		2 OR MORE YEARS	
PROGRAM:	I "ONE SIDE"	II "BOTH SIDES"	I "ONE SIDE"	II "BOTH SIDES"	I "ONE SIDE"	II "BOTH SIDES"	I "ONE SIDE"	II "BOTH SIDES"
No change	35	40	52	57	53	41	41	56
Revised estimate upward	59	60	39	3	43	56	32	32
Revised estimate downward	6	—	9	40	4	3	27	12
Net change	53	−60	30	−37	39	53	5	20
Control net change*	−9	9	−34	−34	9	9	−34	−34
Net effect	44	51	64	−3	30	44	39	54
Number of cases in each subgroup†	70	75	23	30	82	75	22	25

*The control net change used above to eliminate the effects of regression is the same as that used in Table A. This procedure assumes that regression was the same at the two educational levels, but it was considered a better estimate than could be obtained from the small separate subgroups of the control. In any case, chief interest is attached to the *differences* between the effects of the two programs; these differences are independent of the estimate of regression used.

†See second footnote to Table A.

Supplementary Table D
Breakdown of Changes in Estimates, Among Men Initially Opposed to the Stand Taken, for Those Who Had and Those Who Had Not Counted on a Great Deal of Help from Russia

	PERCENT OF MEN					
	MEN WHO HAD COUNTED ON A GREAT DEAL OF HELP FROM RUSSIA			MEN WHO HAD NOT COUNTED ON A GREAT DEAL OF HELP FROM RUSSIA		
	PROGRAM I "ONE SIDE"	PROGRAM II "BOTH SIDES"	CONTROL	PROGRAM I "ONE SIDE"	PROGRAM II "BOTH SIDES"	CONTROL
No change	46	48	66	45	34	64
Revised estimate upward	50	52	21	50	63	23
Revised estimate downward	5	0	13	5	2	13
Net change	45	52	8	45	61	10
Control net change	8	8		10	10	
Net effect (program net minus control)	37	44		35	51	
Number of cases in each subgroup	66	71	62	86	79	78

22.   Negative persuasion via personal insult   Robert P. Abelson and James C. Miller

A controlled experiment was performed in a field situation to test the hypothesis that an individual directly insulted by a communicator attempting to persuade him will show a boomerang effect by increasing the extremity of his initial attitude position. The field situation consisted of a park-bench discussion of a topical social issue, arranged by a public-opinion interviewer. Prepared experimental variations were introduced by one of the discussion partners, a confederate of the interviewer. In the critical variation, the confederate insulted the subject during discussion. In other variations, he tried to persuade but did not insult, or else simply gave certain arguments without intent to persuade. Attitude-change results supported the hypothesis of negative change in the insult condition. Other experimental variations were whether the insulter stayed or left following his last argument, and whether or not a crowd hostile to the insulter was present. No significant differences in attitude change were attributable to these variations. The mechanism for the obtained boomerang effect remains unexplained, although a social equity explanation has some plausibility.

In controlled experimental studies of attitude change, some degree of change in the direction advocated by the communicator is almost always observed, even under seemingly unfavorable conditions such as the use of communicators of very low credibility (Hovland, Janis & Kelley, 1953; Hovland, 1959; Cohen, 1964). It is ex-

Reprinted with permission of the authors and Academic Press, Inc. from the *Journal of Experimental Social Psychology* 3 (1967): 321–33.

tremely unusual for negative influence—the so-called boomerang effect—to occur, in which the mean attitude-change score differs significantly from zero in the direction *away* from the advocated position.

If the influence of persuasive communications in natural-field situations were always positive and never negative, one would be led to expect that social controversies would typically tend to resolve themselves by mutual compromise whenever audiences on opposing sides became exposed to each other's spokesmen. While such an outcome is by no means unheard of, it is obvious that there are a number of political and social issues for which considerable social disagreement persists in the face of repeated persuasive attempts by all participants. One is thus led to ask what social and attitudinal mechanisms might serve to freeze opinion bipolarity in large social groups. Abelson (1964), in discussing three possible mechanisms, tended to favor the boomerang effect as a strong explanatory principle. While it has been argued that boomerang effects are probably rare even in field situations (cf. McGuire, 1966, p. 490), it is nevertheless clear that chronic bipolarity of opinion could readily be accounted for if mutual repulsion of opinions were found to occur between opposing partisans under certain circumstances during social controversy.

What might be the circumstances that could result in negative persuasion? One interesting possibility is that when a speaker insults the listener during a persuasive attempt, the listener will react "negatively" not only in terms of his feelings toward the speaker but in terms of attitude change. This possibility has significance in field applications. Coleman (1957, p. 10), in a classic monograph reviewing psychological and sociological factors common to a number of disparate community controversies, pointed out that "A . . . change in the nature of issues as a controversy develops is the shift from *disagreement* to *antagonism*. A dispute which began dispassionately, in a disagreement over issues, is characterized suddenly by personal slander, . . . by the focusing of direct hostility." Coleman went on to discuss a number of mechanisms by which personal antagonisms typically arise, and the effects of antagonisms in rendering conflicts independent of specific issues. Although he did not comment directly on the matter, it seems a plausible conjecture that the targets of personal insults subsequently adopt more extreme attitude positions on the issues with which the insults were associated.

The study to be reported in this paper was an attempt to discover whether, in fact, a boomerang effect could be produced by slanderous argumentation. Strict experimental procedures were employed in a natural field situation in an effort to avoid the possibly over-constrained, polite atmosphere of the experimental laboratory. As previously noted, boomerang effects are very infrequent in the laboratory. The only previous studies deliberately designed to find a boomerang effect are those of Cohen (1962) and Berscheid (1966), although there have been scattered and largely unanticipated post hoc findings of boomerang effects in particular experimental subgroups (e.g., Kelley & Volkhart, 1952; Mann, 1965).

The hypothesis of the present study was not that personal insult is the only way to produce a boomerang effect, but merely that it is one of the effective ways. That insults should have negative persuasive effectiveness is by no means a foregone conclusion, however. Insults have previously been found to have certain limited positive effects in attitude-change research by Weiss and Fine (1956) and by Norman Miller.[1] Weiss and Fine found that insulted subjects were more likely to accept later communications urging a punitive point of view toward juvenile delinquents. Miller found a slight facilitating effect of a snide reference to obesity on the subsequent persuasibility of overweight women, as though guilt prodded them into obliging docility. However, the insult in this latter study was delivered "accidentally," and the communicator could not be held accountable for it. In the Weiss and Fine study, the communicator was presumably completely unaware of the prior insult. In the present study, the insults were designed to come directly and intentionally from the communicator.

While a boomerang effect from intentional personal insults seems intuitively plausible, it is not obvious what the psychological mechanism might be (if indeed the effect occurs). In considering possible mechanisms, it is important to select those which might explain neg-

1. "Defaming and agreeing with the communicator as a function of communication extremity, emotional arousal, and evaluative set." (Unpublished manuscript.)

ative attitude change, not merely zero change. The present study, designed primarily to verify the hypothesized boomerang effect in a natural field situation, was also intended as a preliminary probe of two possible boomerang mechanisms: a social equity mechanism, and an imagined supporter mechanism.

The social equity mechanism might operate as follows. Participation in a communication situation represents a social investment (cf. Homans, 1961), a willingness to expose one's views to challenge, in return for which a certain level of social reward in the form of social acceptance or approval is considered appropriate. If social equity is violated by virtue of gratuitous insults from the other party, the victim attempts to redress the inequity in some fashion, very possibly by withdrawing his investment and adopting a more extreme version of his original position. It is as though the victim says, "I'll show you. If you're going to insult me when I give you a chance to change my opinions, I not only won't change them, I'll make them more objectionable to you."

This theoretical derivation is much more loose and informal than in other, more clear-cut recent applications of social equity theory (Adams, 1965), and it is not completely clear what experimental manipulations would be germane to these conjectures. One seemingly important variable is whether the communicator remains in the social situation after his insulting argumentation. Reprisal by boomeranging would seem to make less sense for the victim if his tormentor has left the scene. Accordingly, we arranged in our experiment for the insulter to leave immediately after his performance for half the subjects, and to remain on the scene for the other half. This manipulation was intended as a tentative exploration of the social equity explanation.

The imagined supporter mechanism involves a completely different kind of explanation. In giving his insults during persuasive argument, the attacker conveys the impression that people arguing his particular side of the issue are obnoxious individuals. The victim, harassed and confronted with an obviously bad opinion model, may cast about in his memory for a good opinion model, a reference person whose views may be adopted the more effectively to ward off hostile arguments. The chances are that his "imagined supporter" will be someone whose views are well crystallized and highly polarized, i.e., someone probably more extreme in his opinions than the victim himself. It is as though the victim says, "Well, if a lout like you has those opinions, they can't be right. The good people I know don't believe those things at all. In fact, I can recall someone proving the exact opposite."

In an attempt to test the "imagined supporter" mechanism, an experimental condition was designed in which the victim could be provided with a determined group of onlookers whom the victim could easily imagine to be extreme partisans on his side of the issue. This condition was applied for half the subjects, while for the other half there were no onlookers.

In sum, then, the present experimental study was designed to test whether personal insults during persuasion would in fact produce a boomerang effect, and, if so, to explore two possible explanatory mechanisms. Irrespective of the explanatory mechanism, a demonstration of the occurrence of such an effect would counterbalance the dominant impression of universally pliant communication audiences in laboratory attitude-change studies, and would fill an important missing link in the understanding of bitter community controversies. Additionally, the procedures by which we were able to introduce the appropriate experimental manipulations in a field situation are of special methodological interest, particularly in view of the potential artifacts which may sometimes endanger the validity of laboratory studies (cf. Aronson & Carlsmith, 1967).

Method

SUBJECTS

Subjects were 80 persons, of heterogeneous ages and backgrounds, sitting on park benches in Washington Square Park in New York City on weekend afternoons in the summer of 1963. They were selected by a confederate of the experimenter who sat down near them, posing as another park inhabitant. The only criterion used in selecting the subjects was that they appear intelligent enough to understand the procedure, which was a two-person debate format staged by a "roving reporter." Thirty other persons declined to participate when approached.

General Procedure. The subject was approached by the experimenter, who announced that he was from "Survey Research Associates" and wished to interview him on the issue of discrimination against Negroes in employment. This was an extremely salient issue at the time, since several well-publicized sit-ins protesting discrimination in the building trades had just occurred in New York City, and the "March on Washington" was imminent. The experimenter's credibility as an interviewer was enhanced by the equipment he carried: clipboard, microphone, and tape recorder.

In order to obtain a preliminary indication of the subject's position on the issue, he or she was asked: "What do you think of the recent demonstrations by Negroes against job discrimination; do you favor them or not?" If the subject indicated a generally favorable attitude toward the demonstrations, objecting, if at all, only in cases of property damage and work interference, he was interviewed further. If he had broad objections or was generally opposed to the demonstrations, he was dropped from the experiment. This was done in order to allow the subsequent presentation by the confederate of a uniform set of statements opposing efforts to gain job equality.

Subjects who were accepted were asked to indicate their agreement or disagreement, on a 30-point scale, with the following statement: "The demonstrations against job discrimination, even the peaceful ones, are hurting the Negro's chances for job equality." This was used as the premeasure against which the effect of the discussion with the confederate was evaluated by administering the same statement again at the end of the procedure.

At this point, while the subject was checking his response to the initial statement, the experimenter looked to other people sitting nearby, explaining that he would like to get as many reactions as possible during his survey. He then asked the confederate if he would be willing to express his opinion on the problem of job discrimination. When the confederate indicated his willingness to do so, the same question and statement were administered to him that had been administered to the subject, and he presumably checked a point along the same scale. The scales were printed on 5×8 cards, four on each side of the card, eight scales in all. Both "subjects" were encouraged to hold their cards so that the other could not see their responses.

The central part of the procedure consisted of a series of six questions asked by the experimenter of both participants, three in which the subject answered first (1, 3, and 5) and three in which the confederate answered first (2, 4, and 6). These questions covered a broad range of issues involved in the job discrimination problem, e.g., the importance of the problem itself, the role of fair employment laws in helping the Negro, the effectiveness of such laws, their consequences on job conditions, job training, etc. Each time that both participants answered the question, they were asked to check along the scale whether they agreed or disagreed with what the other had said. The confederate had been given a series of prepared statements which he presented throughout the experiment. All of these statements were notably anti-Negro, but they embodied a sufficient assortment of other ideas to permit considerable potential variation in agreement. (For example: "Forced integration in employment will undoubtedly lead to friction on the job, which makes it economically unsound.")

In the final step of the procedure, the subject was asked to respond again to the initial statement (concerning the alleged deleterious effects of antidiscrimination demonstrations), indicating "how you feel now about the issue."

EXPERIMENTAL CONDITIONS

The basic design was a 2 × 2 × 2 factorial: Insulting vs. Neutral remarks; Opponent leaves vs. Opponent stays; Crowd present vs. No crowd. In addition, there were two "No persuasive intent" control conditions (to be explained below).

To each of these 10 conditions, 8 subjects were assigned. Randomization of these assignments was achieved with the aid of a random sequence on a perforated roll in the confederate's pocket. After the experimenter had insured that a particular subject was acceptable, the confederate covertly exposed the next experimental assignment and set himself to behave accordingly. (Except for the "No persuasive intent" conditions, it was not necessary for the confederate to signal the experimenter about the assignment, but only to carry out his own part at the appropriate time.) It was not feasible to determine the Crowd conditions in this manner, however. Instead, all Crowd present subjects were run on particular randomly determined days and all No crowd subjects on the remaining days.

In the Neutral remarks variation, the confederate simply presented his six prepared statements, each beginning with a neutral comment to the effect that he was interested in the subject's comments, that he had listened carefully, or that he had heard them before. In the Insulting remarks variation he preceded all of his statements with insults to the subject. He had a list of five standard insults from which he could draw the one which seemed the most appropriate for each statement, provided that he used the majority of them for each subject. They were: (1) "That's ridiculous"; (2) "That's just the sort of thing you'd expect to hear in this park"; (3) "That's obviously wrong"; (4) "That's terribly confused"; and (5) "No one really believes that." In practice, he used all five insults for all subjects, for it was found that they were general enough that they could be said in a natural way almost regardless of what the subject had said.

In the Opponent leaves variation, the confederate delivered a plausible excuse and rushed off immediately following the subject's reply to his sixth statement. In the Opponent stays variation, he delivered the same excuse, but did not leave until after both he and the subject had checked their final attitude scales.

In the Crowd present variation, the "crowd" was actually a group of from three to five persons (usually four: two men, two women) who were also confederates of the experimenter. They were instructed both in how to approach the interview (they either came up singly or in pairs, stopping 15 feet from the experimenter, enquiring what was happening, and then gathering closer to watch), and in what to say in response to the confederate's statements. They had a standard list of comments to make about his statements. (1) "Oh, no!"; (2) "That's absurd"; (3) "I disagree"; and (4) "tut-tut-tut." In practice these tended to be the main comments, although occasionally a similar one was added. To avoid direct social reinforcement of the real subject's statements, the crowd assumed an air of silent attentiveness when the subject was speaking.

For purposes of assessing attitude change due solely to the content of the confederate's six statements as distinct from the effects of the confederate as persuasive communicator, the No persuasive intent variation was added, for which a slightly different procedure was used. When the confederate was initially asked if he would be willing to express his opinions on the issue of job discrimination, he indicated that he would be willing but that he had not followed the issues very closely and, in fact, had been out of the country during most of the demonstrations and felt he had better not comment. He was then asked if he would consent to play the role of someone (actually several people) who had given opinions—that is, to read a series of statements which the interviewer had collected in the course of his survey. This would allow the interviewer to get the reaction of the other person (the subject). This the confederate consented to do, and proceeded to read the statements without responsibility for them, but in much the same forceful vocal fashion as in the experimental conditions (omitting the preliminary insults or neutral comments). All of the remaining parts of the procedure were the same for the No persuasive intent control variation as for the experimental variations, except that no crowd was ever used. Thus there were but two cells involving this variation: No persuasive intent–Opponent leaves and No persuasive intent–Opponent stays.

Results

AGREEMENT WITH OPPONENT'S STATEMENTS

Following each of the confederate's six anti-Negro statements, the subject had rated his agreement or disagreement on a 30-point scale. The greatest disagreement was scored 1 and the greatest agreement 30, with the neutral point between 15 and 16. Table 22.1 displays the mean agreement scores for each condition, averaged first over the six statements and then over the eight subjects. A separate statement-by-statement analysis reveals nothing not contained in the summary analysis.

At the time the ratings were made, the Opponent leaves vs. Opponent stays variation had not yet been introduced. Thus no systematic differences in mean agreement can accrue to that variable, and the essential facts are revealed more clearly when Table 22.1 is collapsed into 5 cells rather than 10.

The strong effect of Insulting remarks can be interpreted as

Table 22.1
Agreement with the Opponent's Statements

Conditions	No Crowd	Crowd Present
Insulting remarks		
Opponent leaves	7.56 (7.41)[a]	4.21 (4.56)
Opponent stays	7.25	4.92
Neutral remarks		
Opponent leaves	16.04 (16.03)	9.73 (8.17)
Opponent stays	16.02	6.60
No persuasive intent		
Opponent leaves	10.71 (11.31)	
Opponent stays	11.92	

[a]Figures in parentheses represent averages over the two Opponent conditions. Each such mean is based on $N = 16$.

evidence of the effective "take" of the insult manipulation. Much more disagreement with the confederate's brief speeches occurred when these incorporated insults, and it therefore seems safe to infer that this experimental variation succeeded in offending the target subjects. The strong effect on agreement due to the Crowd variation may be taken to suggest that the crowd performs a supportive function. When there is a crowd present to register disapproval of the confederate's remarks, the subject tends to disagree more strongly in his ratings of those remarks. Whether the social support provided by the crowd is of the specific sort contemplated by the "imagined supporter" hypothesis, however, cannot be judged from the agreement data.

It is interesting that the mean agreement for the Neutral remarks–No crowd cell lies on the agreement side of the scale, although barely so. Apparently, subjects lacking social support did not typically feel so deeply about the attitude issue as to reject the mediocre opposition arguments when these were presented earnestly and politely. For the No persuasive intent cell, with the arguments simply read without personal responsibility for them, the mean agreement score of 11.31 is significantly below ($p < .05$) the mean of 16.03 for the Neutral remarks–No crowd cell, but not quite significantly higher than the mean of 7.41 for the Insulting remarks–No crowd cell.

Table 22.2
Attitude-Change Scores

CONDITIONS	NO CROWD	CROWD	MEAN[a]
Insulting remarks			−1.81
Opponent leaves	−1.25	−1.75	
Opponent stays	−3.12	−1.12	
Neutral remarks			−1.19
Opponent leaves	−1.00	−2.00	
Opponent stays	.00	−1.75	
No persuasive intent			+.44
Opponent leaves	.38	—	
Opponent stays	.50	—	

[a]Each cell mean based on $N = 8$.

BOOMERANG EFFECTS

Agreements with the interview topic statement, "The demonstrations against job discrimination, even the peaceful ones, are hurting the Negro's chances for job equality," were also scored on a scale from 1 to 30. Higher scores were assigned to the agreement (i.e., anti-sit-in) side, and then the after-discussion scores were subtracted from the before-discussion scores. A negative change score thus indicates a boomerang effect, with the subject's becoming more opposed to the anti-sit-in, anti-fair-employment position advocated by the confederate. Table 22.2 displays the mean change scores in the ten experimental conditions.

As predicted, the average persuasive effect was consistently negative in the Insulting remarks conditions. The differences between the average effect (−1.81) in the four experimental cells involving insults and in the two No persuasive intent control cells (+.44) yields a statistically significant result ($t = 1.79$, $p < .05$). The average effect in the four Insulting remarks cells is significantly different also from zero ($t = 2.49$, $p < .05$), i.e., a reliable group boomerang effect occurred. Out of 32 insulted subjects 15 displayed attitude change in the negative direction, 13 no change, and 4 in the positive direction.

The picture of the results becomes less sharp when the four Neutral remarks conditions are also considered. In three of the four cells, the average attitude change was negative. The average effect (-1.19) in the four experimental cells without insults is not significantly different either from the control cells ($t = 1.24$) or from the base-line of zero ($t = 1.44$), nor is it significantly less negative than the average effect of -1.81 in the Insulting remarks cells.

Neither experimental variation conjectured to be crucial to the boomerang effect yielded significant main effects or interactions. The Crowd present variation, supposed to provide "imagined supporters" and thus a larger boomerang effect for the victim of insults, instead produced (nonsignificantly) less boomerang than the No crowd variation for Insulting remarks and (nonsignificantly) more boomerang for Neutral remarks. The Opponent leaves variation, supposed to undercut the possibility of social retribution and thus to reduce the boomerang effect for the victim of insulting remarks, did produce a (nonsignificant) lessening in the No crowd variation, but not in the Crowd present variation.

Discussion

We have demonstrated the primary effect hypothesized at the outset; namely, that personal insults during intended persuasion produce a boomerang effect. We regard this demonstration as more convincing by virtue of its occurrence in the field than a corresponding laboratory demonstration would have been.

It should not be supposed, however, that our procedural innovations were easy to effect. A complicated scenario was involved, with deft performances required by the experimenter, the confederate, and the crowd. There was no indication that any of our subjects regarded the "debate" as suspicious or unnatural; yet it was certainly a novel experience calling forth a variety of reactions from the subjects and a number of necessary adjustments by the experimental players. Thus there was inevitably considerable variation in how well the procedure "came off." Additional sources of variation were age, sex, and personality differences among subjects, and hour-by-hour variations in the surrounding park environment.[2]

2. The park is notorious for its Greenwich Village "types" and its sometimes noisy atmosphere. (The police had once unsuccessfully attempted to ban folk-singing there, following complaints from some of the more staid

The pattern of results among the several experimental cells bears explanation even in the absence of statistical reliability for various differences. In particular, the Crowd present variation produced unexpected results. The "imagined supporter" hypothesis requires that a boomerang effect occur only when the subject is insulted. However, with a crowd present there was at least as much boomerang effect under Neutral remarks as under Insulting remarks. Informal observations made by the experimenter perhaps explain why this was so. The subjects in the Crowd present variation appeared more relaxed and self-confident. After a brief initial period of nervous attentiveness to the crowd's reactions,[3] subjects appeared reassured by the crowd's hostility to the opponent and began to "play to the crowd," basking in the presumption of right-mindedness. They did not even seem to care very much when they were being insulted, adopting a patronizing tone toward the out-numbered and presumably desperate opponent. In effect, this behavior may be interpreted as social conformity in which the subject takes his cues from the crowd. The crowd disagrees with the opponent's remarks, and hence subjects disagree significantly more in their ratings of those remarks than do subjects in the No crowd condition. The crowd makes it obvious that the opponent's point of view is odious, and thus subjects show a slight tendency toward negative attitude change irrespective of the other experimental variations.

These outcomes are obverse to those observed by Kelley and Woodruff (1956) in an experiment on the persuasive effects of applause. In their study, applause by an audience enhanced susceptibility to the persuasive communication. Here, opprobrium expressed by a "crowd" enhanced rejection of the persuasive communication. However, the crowd in our experiment did not seem

---

sitters, strollers, and neighborhood residents.) The only extremely unusual incident interfering with our experiment occurred during a pilot run, when a psychotic woman seized the experimenter's microphone and began "broadcasting." However, there were a variety of small distractions during the regular runs, including an occasional real spectator or two.

3. In a pilot experiment, we had employed a "crowd" instructed to remain completely silent throughout the discussion. We found that subjects became quite tense during this procedure. Most subjects seem both to desire and to expect some kind of feedback from the crowd.

to function as a spur to the rehearsal of an extreme attitude position solely by the victim of insult, as postulated in the "imagined supporter" hypothesis. At this point it is not clear whether this hypothesis is a poor one or whether the chosen experimental manipulations were inadequate to test it.

The evidence in favor of the "social equity" line of explanation is no more than minimal. If in Table 22.2 attention is confined to the No crowd cells (on the grounds that the presence of the crowd induces conformity effects overriding all else), one notes that the Opponent stays vs. Opponent leaves variation at least operates in the appropriate direction. When the subject is insulted, the boomerang effect tends to be stronger when the opponent stays than when he leaves, although the difference is not significant.

In his study of a boomerang effect, Cohen (1962) discussed a "bargaining" explanation of his outcome. A person might move his attitude position further away from that of a resistant or hostile opponent in anticipation of future interaction in which a tough "bargaining position" might prove useful. Cohen tried to rule out this possibility by making clear to his subjects that they were very unlikely to encounter the opponent again. In the present study, the same implication was quite obvious. The opponent was a total stranger who had announced his intention even in the Opponent stays condition to hurry off immediately at the conclusion of the procedure, presumably to vanish forever in the vast anonymity of New York City. In neither study was there an experimental variation offering the prospect of further interaction with the opponent. If the boomerang effect is envisioned as a kind of unthinking "tit-for-tat" maneuver to redress a violation of social equity, it is not obvious that the expectation of further interaction with the opponent would at all increase the effect. On the other hand, if a more self-conscious effort at social bargaining is involved, then an Opponent comes back variation might have produced an even stronger boomerang effect for us. Anticipating that further research is necessary, we feel it important to note that the different shadings of interpretation of the boomerang mechanism are further complicated by the unknown effects of the presence of the experimenter. To the extent that the subject orients his final responses in terms of the perceived demands of the experimenter, the influence of the opponent's parting behavior is attenuated.

One of the many other empirical issues left open is the question of the permanence of negative attitude change following personal insult. One might suspect that the effect is so closely tied to a particular social situation that any attitude change would soon decay if the situation were not reinvoked.[4] Even were this the case, however, it would still be possible to understand the dynamics whereby a social controversy could escalate out of control through rapid successive cycles of insult and return insult. Any social mechanism that tended to reinstitute personal affronts would presumably also tend to sustain abnormal extremity of attitude positions on both sides of the controversy. However, our experimental situation, although field-based, was not directly designed to investigate long-range escalation of controversy. Thus we have succeeded only in isolating one small piece of a much larger and more interesting picture.

4. In a later experiment, we repeated the insult manipulation in a field setting that did not permit assessment of the effects until three weeks later. University students fulfilling an unpopular physical-education obligation were interviewed individually in a gymnasium office by the experimenter, who posed as an advanced physical-education student from a nearby teachers' college. In the Insulting Remarks condition, subjects were ridiculed for neglecting their physical condition and for their overly casual attitudes toward physical fitness. As a precaution against the arousal of suspicion that the interview was part of an experiment, no measures of any kind were obtained during this session. Instead, a questionnaire was mailed three weeks later as part of a regular University Health procedure for keeping in touch with student attitudes.

The insults produced a negative mean change on attitudes toward physical fitness programs, but this mean change was small and not significantly different from zero or from the mean change in the control group. Evidently, whatever boomerang effect may have been produced during the interview was not of sufficient permanence to be strongly manifest three weeks later.

REFERENCES

Abelson, R. P. 1964. Mathematical models of the distribution of attitudes under controversy. In *Contributions to mathematical psychology,* ed. N. Frederiksen and H. Gulliksen, pp. 142–60. New York: Holt, Rinehart & Winston.

Adams, J. S. 1965. Inequity in social exchange. In *Advances in experimental psychology,* ed. L. Berkowitz, vol. 2, pp. 267–97. New York: Academic Press.

Aronson, E., and Carlsmith, J. M. 1967. Experimentation in social psychology. In *Handbook of social psychology*, ed. G. Lindzey and E. Aronson, Cambridge: Addison-Wesley.

Berscheid, Ellen. 1966. Opinion change and communicator-communicatee similarity and dissimilarity. *Journal of Personality and Social Psychology* 4: 670–80.

Cohen, A. R. 1962. A dissonance analysis of the boomerang effect. *Journal of Personality* 30: 75–88.

Cohen, A. R. 1964. *Attitude change and social influence.* New York: Basic Books.

Coleman, J. S. 1957. *Community conflict.* Glencoe, Ill.: Free Press.

Homans, G. 1961. *Social behavior: its elementary forms.* New York: Harcourt, Brace & World.

Hovland, C. I. 1959. Reconciling conflicting results derived from experimental and survey studies of attitude change. *American Psychologist* 14: 8–17.

Hovland, C. I.; Janis, I. L.; and Kelley, H. H. 1953. *Communication and persuasion.* New Haven: Yale University Press.

Kelley, H. H., and Volkhart, E. H. 1952. The resistance to change of group-anchored attitudes. *American Sociological Review* 17: 453–65.

Kelley, H. H., and Woodruff, C. L. 1956. Members, reactions to apparent group approval of a counternorm communication. *Journal of Abnormal and Social Psychology* 52: 67–74.

McGuire, W. J. Attitudes and opinions. 1966. *Annual Review of Psychology* 17: 475–514.

Mann, L. 1965. The effects of emotional role playing on smoking attitudes and habits. Unpublished doctoral dissertation, Yale University.

Weiss, W., and Fine, B. J. 1956. The effect of induced aggressiveness on opinion change. *Journal of Abnormal and Social Psychology,* 52: 109–14.

23. **A field experiment on the comparative effectiveness of "emotional" and "rational" political leaflets in determining election results** George W. Hartmann

During the election campaign of 1935, the city of Allentown, Pennsylvania, was divided for experimental purposes

Reprinted with permission from the *Journal of Abnormal and Social Psychology* 31 (1936): 99–114.

into three types of wards: (1) an emotional area in which all the resident adults received leaflets written in vigorous advertising style urging support of the Socialist ticket; (2) a rational region, in which a more academic type of persuasion was used; and (3) a control district where nothing was distributed. The increase in the minority party vote was greatest in the emotional wards, next largest in the rational wards, and lowest in the control wards. These facts may constitute a significant beginning for an experimentally grounded political psychology and pedagogy.

Political psychology as a separate branch of scientific inquiry is all but nonexistent. As an art or practice, however, it has long ranked among the essentials of statecraft and is now a powerful and flourishing factor in the intricate world of affairs. Dictatorships and democracies make different, but apparently equally extensive, use of it in the process of molding public opinion and shaping attitudes. Like all technologies, political psychology may be employed for a variety of ends—it is a tool skill for attaining efficiently the goals established by some sort of systematic or unformulated political philosophy.

By the very nature of the field which gives it its name, political psychology is bound to have close relations with advertising and salesmanship, two regions of modern commercial life in which applied psychology has been conspicuously influential. The practices of publicity, propaganda, and intentional indoctrination are the very lifeblood of political activity and other institutional behavior—remove them and the human interests supporting even the worthiest of movements lose most of their power to affect the course of group conduct or even to maintain their own coherence. He who lacks control over the required stimuli cannot obtain the desired responses.

Despite the serious need for an organized corpus of knowledge about political psychology—which in this generation of large-scale conflict promises to become the most important single division of social psychology—the phrase itself is barely found in current usage. The available information and techniques comprising it are loosely distributed in incoordinated fragments among experienced politicians, reflective journalists, and copywriters, curious social scientists and an occasional laboratory man whose versatility or heterodoxy have allowed him to be sensitive to a broader range of interests. This is a strange circumstance when one recalls that American political parties, machines, and individual candidates annually spend unascertained millions either to get or to hold public office with its associated benefits. A substantial fraction of this sum is undoubtedly sheer waste, not only from the standpoint of positive social gain, but even from the point of view of the seekers for power, irrespective of motive. If the direct and indirect expenditures involved in incessant campaigning were correctly totaled, they would probably approach in the aggregate the amount spent on public education in the United States. To enhance the efficiency of the latter process we have developed an army of educational psychologists and allied specialists, but neither the professions nor the universities recognize such an individual as the political psychologist.

However, if psychologists on the basis of Strong's law can recommend that the small businessman spread his modest budget for a little advertising over a number of periodicals rather than concentrating all in one journal, why should they not be able to guide a minority political party in using its limited funds to secure the maximum number of votes? The social utility in both cases may be low, but it is surely no lower in the competitive political field of a democracy than in the competitive business sphere of our economic system. The politician would like to know more exactly the relative vote-getting strength of an equal expenditure of time, money, and effort on newspaper, billboard, radio, personal interview, and speechmaking publicity, but the psychologist has given him little or no help in this or related matters. So far as the writer knows, the present study is the first experimental attempt to develop a *rapprochement* between the two fields of endeavor on other than insecure laboratory analogies.

Both Gestalt theory and the doctrine of the "total situation" have shown that the capacity of apparently "identical" stimuli to evoke certain desired responses is dependent upon the setting, context, or manner in which they occur. Will an appeal, request, or command to vote for a certain party, policy, issue, or individual be more influential when it accompanies or follows a logical exposition of the case or when it appears with or after an emotional approach to the unanalyzed existing loyalties of the voter? The question as phrased implies an extreme dichotomy and opposition between the two types of mental process, whereas it is more likely that the real contrast is between two appeals containing various combinations of rationality and emotionality. The contrast here proposed is between a complex fusion of excitement, resentment, vague enthusiasms, strongly aroused fears and hopes, and a calm, orderly, and restrained presentation of either concrete proposals or abstract objectives. It does not take a high degree of psychological sophistication to bet (other things being equal) on the greater strength of the emotional attack with any random sample of the American population. However, it is important to remember that this prediction rests exclusively upon theoretical and empirical considerations, and not upon the measured findings of any deliberately devised experiment on the problem of political behavior under complex motivation. It is this kind of confirmation which the investigation here reported seeks to supply.[1]

Method

The possibility of a really effective test was provided by the local and state elections held in Pennsylvania on November 6, 1935. At the time, many municipal and county offices were to be filled, as well as two important statewide judgeships. Because it met certain extraneous considerations, such as ease of access for the experimenter, the use of voting machines, which are generally believed to enhance, if they do not guarantee, the accuracy of the poll, etc., the city of Allentown in Lehigh County was chosen as the scene of operations. For a similar variety of reasons the Socialist Party in that community was made the beneficiary of the special appeals whose relative potency was being measured. The local Democratic

1. Similar researches could be built around such pairings as the relative effectiveness of constructive vs. destructive political appeals, emphasis upon ideas versus personalities, the use of praise and blame, the strength of group versus self-interests, material versus spiritual incentives, and even the specific advantages of placards with and without the portraits of candidates. Our existing knowledge of these matters is exceedingly shaky.

and Republican parties were so closely matched that any publicity which would have favored one rather than the other would have created an intolerably delicate situation for an experimenter whose motives could hardly have been made clear or acceptable to a suspicious populace.[2] The Socialist Party, on the other hand, was admirably suited to this purpose, since it was universally agreed that its candidates were not likely to win in this area; its exaltation of principles and ideals over individual standard bearers made possible more sharply defined contrasts without the danger of wounding personal feelings.

The next task was the construction of the contrasting leaflets. This was much harder than anticipated because a search through Socialist propaganda literature gave types of printed appeals which were too mixed and impure in style, content, and length to meet the prescribed conditions. Consequently, the experimenter wrote the texts for three pairs of emotional and rational leaflets of the desired brevity. These were submitted to 30 rank-and-file adults in Allentown; the pair finally used was the pair overwhelmingly adopted by them as the most liked. Inspection showed that the rejected leaflets had a more involved sentence structure, heavier vocabulary burden, and lower persuasiveness than those retained. Six competent psychologists agreed that in the pair finally selected, one—the academic test involving some reflective judgment—was predominantly reasonable in character, and the other—an intimate family letter—mainly sentimental.

Five thousand copies of each of the two appeals were printed on heavy white paper in identical typography in the form of a four-page (one sheet folded) leaflet, the cover pages bearing the titles, "Try this test on yourself" (= rational) and "Will you answer this letter?" (= emotional), respectively. The two inside pages are reproduced below. The last or back page simply bore a straight-forward list of the party candidates with the respective city, county, and state offices opposite their names.

> You've heard of intelligence tests, haven't you? Well, we have a little examination right here which we are sure you will enjoy taking, even if you didn't care much for school when you were a youngster.

2. The present writer was the 1935 Socialist candidate whose vote appears in the tables below. This union of psychologist and politician explains how the present study came into being.

The beauty of this test is that you can score it yourself without any teacher to tell you whether you passed or failed.

This is how it works. First read each one of the seven statements printed below. If you *approve* the idea as it stands, *underline* the word AGREE; if you *disapprove* of the idea, underline the word DISAGREE. Simple, isn't it? All right, then. Get your pencil ready. All set? Go!

1. We would have much cheaper electric light and power if this industry were owned and operated by the various governmental units for the benefit of all the people. AGREE—DISAGREE.

2. No gifted boy or girl should be denied the advantages of higher education just because his parents lack the money to send him to college. AGREE—DISAGREE.

3. The Federal Government should provide to all classes of people opportunity for complete insurance at cost against accident, sickness, premature death and old age. AGREE—DISAGREE.

4. All banks and insurance companies should be run on a non-profit basis like the schools. AGREE—DISAGREE.

5. Higher income taxes on persons with incomes of more than $10,000 a year should be levied immediately. AGREE—DISAGREE.

6. The only way most people will ever be able to live in modern sanitary homes is for the government to build them on a non-profit basis. AGREE—DISAGREE.

7. Many more industries and parts of industries should be owned and managed co-operatively by the producers (all the workers) themselves. AGREE—DISAGREE.

Have you answered them all? Fine. Now go back and count the number of sentences with which you AGREED. Then count the number with which you DISAGREED. *If the number of agreements is larger than the number of disagreements, you are at heart a Socialist*—whether you know it or not!

Now that you have tested yourself and found out how much of a Socialist you really are, *why don't you try voting for the things you actually want?* The Republicans and Democrats don't propose to give these things to you, because a mere look at their records will show that they are opposed to them. Do you get the point?

HELP BUILD THE AGE OF PLENTY!

VOTE: SOCIALIST   X

Allentown, Pennsylvania
November 1, 1935

Dear Mother and Father:

We youngsters are not in the habit of giving much thought to serious things. You have often told us so and we admit it.

But while we like to play football and have a good time dancing and cause you a lot of amusement as well as worry with our "puppy loves," we sometimes think long and hard. You ought to know what many of us young folks are quietly saying to ourselves.

Our future as American citizens in 1940 looks dark. We want jobs—and good jobs, too—so that we can help in the useful work of the world. But we know that many of our brightest high school and college graduates find it absolutely impossible to get any kind of employment. We also know that this condition is not temporary, but that it will last as long as we stick to harmful ways of running business, industry and government.

We want to continue our education, but we haven't the heart to ask you to make that sacrifice. With Dad working only part time on little pay and Mother trying to make last year's coat and dress look in season, we feel we ought to pitch in and help keep the family's neck above water. But we can't. The world as it is now run has no use for us.

Many of our teachers know what is wrong, although we can see that most of them are afraid to say what they really think. Luckily, the text books and school magazines keep us in touch with new ideas, and we have learned how to read between the lines of the ordinary newspaper. Please don't be frightened if we tell you what we have decided!

We young people are becoming Socialists. We have to be. We can't be honest with ourselves and be anything else. *The Socialist Party is the only party which is against all wars*—and we have learned from our history courses what awful wars have taken place under both Republicans and Democrats. We refuse to be slaughtered (like Uncles Bob and Charles were in 1918) just to make profits for ammunition manufacturers.

The Socialist Party seeks to create a world in which there will be no poverty. In our science classes we learn how power machinery and other modern inventions make it possible for all of us to have enough of all the goods and services we need. Yet look at our town with its unpainted shacks, suffering parents, half-starved children! We might have everything, but we continue to live on next to nothing.

288 *Attitude Change*

It is all so unnecessary. You have had to lead a poor workingman's life, because you and most of the workers and farmers of this country have regularly voted for either the Republican or Democratic parties, between which there is no real difference. These old machines are not for us.

The youth of 1935 want to Build a Better America, in which there will be no poverty, no fear of unemployment, no threat of war. We ask you to follow the lead of the Socialist Party this year because that is the most direct way for you to *help hasten the day when Peace and Plenty and lasting Prosperity will be the lot of all men.* Good parents such as you desire these things for us. But we can never have them as long as you are controlled by your old voting habits.

We are profoundly earnest about this. Our generation cannot enjoy the beauty and justice of the *New America* if you block our highest desires. There was a time when you too were young like us. We beg you in the name of those early memories and spring-time hopes *to support the Socialist ticket in the coming elections!*

Your Sons and Daughters

VOTE: SOCIALIST ☒

Composition of the Testing Population

Having settled upon the differential stimuli, the next step was the mapping out of the city into experimental and control areas. The variations in the size of the wards, density of population, assessed real estate valuation, previous voting habits, and presumptive socioeconomic status made the problem of establishing "comparable" groups unexpectedly difficult. While it is not pretended that all the obstacles were overcome, a feasible apportionment consisted in matching wards 2, 9, and 10 (= the emotional) with wards 3, 4, 5, and 7 (= the rational); the remaining 12 wards (there are 19 in all) were simple controls. The two experimental regions consequently had the nature of adjacent islands in a large control sea. Table 23.1 contains some of the relevant data concerning these three areas which may be used in interpreting the results.

Application of the Stimulus Patterns

The stimulation plan consisted in distributing the two sets of leaflets in their assigned districts so that every family residing therein would be affected. The distributors were interested adults, all party members, who discharged their task by giving the recipient the leaflet with a polite request that it be read when convenient. If no one was at home to receive the leaflet in this manner, it was simply thrust under the door. About half of the prospective voters were given the leaflet in person; the other half presumably found it upon returning home. The material was all distributed between Monday and Thursday of the week preceding Election Day. Apart from a few radio talks, which affected the entire city uniformly, no other campaign activity or proselytizing was carried on during this season.

Results

The reaction to such stimulation with a specific purpose can be tested only at the ballot box, i.e., the final measure of belief or conviction is the readiness and willingness to act. Here we need to know not only the present vote, but also the baseline or reference vote of the preceding year. This has to be calculated in terms of percentages because of the fluctuating participation of the electorate in successive years. Schematically, a clear-cut check would be provided if in 1934 the Socialist vote in Allentown as a whole were 4 percent of the total for all parties and if in 1935 it were 5 percent in the rational wards, 6 percent in the emotional wards, and 3 percent in the control wards (assuming statistically reliable differences). This comparison made it necessary to contrast figures for the statewide heads of the tickets which in 1934 were the governor and in 1935 the judge of the Supreme Court. Other offices fluctuate slightly from the figures for the party candidates for these leading positions. Table 23.1 contains the necessary data for an appraisal of the effect of the two kinds of propaganda.

The first item to be noted is that the total vote cast increased by 3,594, or 16.69 percent, from 21,533 in 1934 to 25,127 in 1935. This decided increase in public participation is a fact which complicates the remaining calculations. The official Allentown registration list contained 34,424 names—17,236 Democrats, 15,001 Republicans, and 187 Socialists. The Socialists polled about three and a half times as many ballots as they had registered adherents, while the other two parties received from two-thirds to four-fifths of their overt registration. This is a common American phenomenon, since economic discretion probably causes many Socialist sympathizers to enroll on the other lists. Even in the nearby city of Reading, which has had Socialist administrators and consequently greater party prestige, the Socialist vote normally trebles its registration.

The second fact to be observed is that the Socialist vote in Allentown as a whole (and even in the control wards where there was no definite activity) rose proportionately more than did that of the other parties.[3] With about 17 percent more general participation in 1935 than in 1934, the total Socialist vote increased 30.86 percent, the Republican 19.79 percent, and the Democrat 13.10 percent, indicating a relative loss for the last party despite an absolute gain. The crucial detail for our purpose is that the Socialist vote in the emotional wards rose 50 percent, in the rational 35.42 percent, and in the control 24.05 percent—all differences large enough to be reliable even though no single adequate measures of this are applicable. This is wholly in harmony with the predicted outcomes and is a gratifying confirmation of the general hypothesis. The relations may be seen more clearly from an inspection of Figure 23.1.

Although the use of percentages rather than absolute figures may create a faulty emphasis, these diagrams nevertheless portray best the main finding of this study, viz., that specific revealed propaganda definitely accelerates a tendency already present. This general secular trend, of course, may in turn be due to widespread contributory propaganda of a more diffuse sort.

The efficacy of these two leaflets may be brought out more fully by comparing the actual with the predicted increases of each party's

3. Does this mean that the larger the total participation in balloting, the greater will be the relative minority vote? Is it not possible that the customary nonvoters are more plastic in their political convictions, and that they contain a proportionately larger number of protest and opposition voters who usually refrain from exercising the franchise because of a sense of futility? In this case, only severe social crises will bring them out. Cf. the extraordinary high rate of suffrage utilization in Germany from 1918 to 1933.

Table 23.1
Comparative Increase in Voting Behavior Under Differential Stimulation

WARD	VOTE FOR GOVERNOR, 1934			VOTE FOR SUPREME COURT JUDGE, 1935			ASSESSED VALUATION PER CAPITA	INHABITANTS PER ACRE
	DEMO-CRAT	REPUB-LICAN	SOCIAL-IST	DEMO-CRAT	REPUB-LICAN	SOCIAL-IST		
RATIONAL								
3	384	378	4	518	496	14	$1,663.64	32.51
4	402	347	10	374	381	8	2,786.19	44.08
5	283	209	14	320	321	19	3,094.01	40.70
7	484	556	20	575	650	24	1,478.73	41.40
	1553	1490	48	1787	1848	65	2,070.12(Mean)	38.44(Mean)
Percent of Party Total	14.38	14.56	9.62	14.63	15.08	9.95		
Raw increase				234	358	17		
Percentage increase				15.07	24.03	35.42		
EMOTIONAL								
2	497	311	30	541	302	33	1,581.26	29.44
9	618	284	16	666	337	29	851.69	43.89
10	1188	623	64	1282	828	103	615.82	38.37
	2303	1218	110	2489	1467	165	871.72(Mean)	37.28(Mean)
Percent of Party Total	21.32	11.90	22.04	20.37	11.97	25.27		
Raw increase				186	249	55		
Percentage increase				8.08	20.44	50.00		

Table 23.1 (continued)

WARD CONTROL								
1	502	408	25	512	422	39	$941.34	11.82
6	591	177	23	782	114	18	624.80	15.97
8	1383	1371	101	1635	1835	110	721.53	24.06
11	1264	2358	28	1430	2648	47	1,202.87	20.23
12	605	419	51	665	606	49	1,089.54	3.36
13	748	1206	19	730	1399	22	1,264.51	18.83
14	577	208	48	626	277	64	704.56	6.35
15	507	436	25	551	472	32	1,021.68	2.01
16	341	·186	13	468	268	22	556.76	4.85
17	160	408	1	167	428	2	2,380.04	2.24
18	67	158	—	83	171	1	447.78	10.50
19	200	190	7	291	303	17	773.89	13.42
	6945	7525	341	7940	8943	423	946.19 (Mean)	7.58 (Mean)
Percent of Party Total	64.30	73.54	68.34	65.00	72.96	64.78		
Raw increase				995	1418	82		
Percentage increase				14.33	15.86	24.05		
Party Total	10,801	10,233	499	12,216	12,258	653	1,088.08 (City Mean)	10.17 (City Mean)
Percent of all ballots	50.16	47.52	2.32	48.62	48.78	2.60		
Raw increase				1415	2025	154		
Percentage increase				13.10	19.79	30.86		

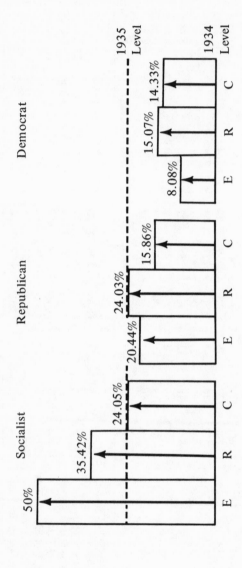

Figure 23.1
Rough schema indicating differential gains in voting preference under various types of stimulation. Although all parties received more votes in 1935 than in 1934, the Socialists gained relatively more in the areas where emotional (E) and rational (R) appeals were used; (C) stands for control district.

total vote in the various regions under consideration. This has been done in Table 23.2.

If the Actual/Expected ratio is 1.00, this means that the two values coincide; if it is less it means that the party involved obtained less than its proportionate share; if more than 1.00, the party affected gained unduly. Since they are based upon the same raw data, these computations tell essentially the same story conveyed by Figure 23.1. The increase in the Socialist vote in the rational and emotional areas was about two or three times, respectively, its probable gain if these stimuli had been omitted.

In order to correct for the inevitable exaggerative effect which such phrases as "percent of gain" evidently produce, Table 23.3 has been prepared. This should effectively dispel the spurious impression of a landslide suggested by some types of comparison.

Table 23.2

How the Three Parties Fared in Three Differently Treated Areas

PARTY	DISTRICT	1934 VOTE	1935 VOTE	EX- PECTED IN- CREASE	ACTUAL IN- CREASE	A-E	A/E
Socialist							
	Rational	48	65	8	17	9	2.13
	Emotional	110	165	18	55	37	3.06
	Control	341	423	57	82	25	1.44
	Entire City	499	653	83	154	71	1.86
Democrat							
	Rational	1553	1787	259	234	− 25	.94
	Emotional	2303	2489	384	186	− 198	.48
	Control	6945	7940	1159	995	− 164	.86
	Entire City	10801	12216	1803	1415	− 388	.78
Republican							
	Rational	1490	1848	249	358	109	1.44
	Emotional	1218	1467	203	249	46	1.23
	Control	7525	8943	1256	1418	138	1.13
	Entire City	10233	12258	1708	2025	317	1.17

NOTE: The Expected Increase column is obtained by multiplying the 1934 vote by the coefficient of increase in public participation, viz., 16.69.

Table 23.3
Percent Which Socialist Vote Is of Total for All Parties in
Different Sections of Allentown

	1934	1935
Control wards	2.30	2.44
Rational wards	1.55	1.76
Emotional wards	3.03	4.00
Entire City	2.32	2.60

If we select the most favorable showing—that made in the emotional district—we see that the effect of the leaflet has been to make 1 voter out of every 25 support the Socialist ticket where before only 1 person in 33 had done so. Had no leaflets been distributed at all, the entire Socialist vote presumably would have been 619 (i.e., 499 plus 499 × 24.05, the control rate of increase); if the superior emotional leaflet had been spread evenly throughout the town, the probable total would have been 749 (i.e., 499 plus 499 × .50); actually, under the mixed conditions obtaining where most of the community was the control, the total was 653.

Because of the selective treatment which these leaflets received, they may be presumed to be above the average of their kind. Nevertheless, even these relatively good broadsides have an efficiency of but .5 percent, since it took 10,000 leaflets to produce 72 additional votes in the emotional and rational wards combined. Moreover, about half of these added votes were in the bag anyhow because of the general situation. It may be estimated that 1 person in 200 who would not otherwise have voted Socialist was impelled to do so by virtue of the motivation directly traceable to these leaflets. Since it took an absolute commercial minimum of one cent per leaflet for printing and delivery, it will be seen that even this cheap form of legitimate political propaganda costs about three dollars for each additional party voter it secures. To be sure, this stimulation probably has some deferred propaganda value in the sense that cumulative increments at some later date may be made to function more readily because of the summation of stimuli involved.

About two weeks after Election Day, personal interviews were arranged with 45 householders (22 men and 23 women) chosen at

Table 23.4
Responses Obtained in Follow-up Interviews for Determining
the Impressiveness of Two Types of Campaign Literature

QUESTION (GIVEN ORALLY)	REPLY
1. Do you remember receiving any Socialist literature recently?	29 out of 45 answered Yes
2. What was its nature?	8 out of 12 in the emotional wards said, "An open letter"; only 7 out of 33 in the rational wards knew it was a pamphlet or folder, and only 1 said it contained "questions"
3. Did the literature you read influence you to vote for any Socialist candidates?	4 said it made them split their votes, for the first time; no effect on others.
4. What did you think of the Socialist literature you saw?	24 said they were "not interested"; 6 said it contained "good principles"; 4 said "very good"; 2 said they would never read any Socialist material; 1 said it was "too deep, he couldn't understand it"; 8 others expressed some degree of favor

random from different streets in the rational and emotional districts. It seemed desirable to supplement the objective record of the polls with some qualitative clues as to the way in which the personalities of the voters had been affected by these appeals. Four simple questions were asked of each interviewee, with the results shown in Table 23.4.

Incomplete as this evidence is, it shows plainly the greater impressive and retentive effect of the sentimental appeal. It is axiomatic that a piece of printed salesmanship must be attended to and remembered before the message it contains can achieve the end desired by the purveyor. This the emotional leaflet did much more decisively than the rational one, even though both produced more pure goodwill than immediately significant action. As soon as reasonable certainty was attained on these points, the interviews were discontinued, since additional cases did not promise to yield any new information.

Although this study bears the formal pattern of the familiar between-group experiment, it rests upon an exceedingly imperfect matching of the contrasted populations. The mean density of population in the emotional and rational wards was purposely kept practically identical, but the latter region has more than twice the per capita real estate valuation of the former (tax exempt property is excluded in these calculations). In matching for one factor, we have unmatched for another. Are not the preexisting attitudes of prospective Socialist voters strongly affected by their economic status?

The answer, of course, is a qualified yes, but this does not mean that there is an inverse relation between receptivity to the Socialist appeal and financial well-being. Observation indicates that the correlation is zero or slightly positive. Both the well-to-do and the poor may be persuaded to vote Socialist, although they may respond differentially to a specific approach. The control group occupies the same financial level as the emotional population, but because of the absence of stimulation no comparable voting increase occurred. To be sure, the rational group did not gain as much as the emotional one, but this was not due to its superior economic position—these people were simply bombarded with an inferior instrument.[4] Absolute assurance that this interpretation is correct can be obtained only by reversing the appeals in another community.

Admittedly, pure experimental conditions are hard to maintain in a study of this sort, but it is an unscientific counsel of despair to refrain from using to best advantage whatever approximations thereto one can achieve. Election results are not the outcomes of single stimulation—they resemble more a complex resultant of intricate forces. Thus, energetic Socialist propaganda would undoubtedly call forth more effort from the other parties, but that would probably occur only where they sensed a genuine threat to their position, which was not the case in this city.

4. As a matter of fact, the per capita valuation per resident is a misleading index to the apparent wealth of the rational group. These wards are in the downtown business section where rented apartments above the ground floors are the commonest type of housing. The buildings are largely owned by persons living in the control wards.

Conclusions

There seems to be no escape from the decision that the emotional political appeal is a better vote-getting instrument than the rational approach, at least in the sense in which these terms describe the essential difference between the two leaflets reproduced above. The sentimental open letter integrates itself easily with such strong permanent central attitudes as parental affection and the desire for a better life. It employs a familiar literary form, is concrete in imagery, breathes sincerity, and is not obviously or even basically untrue. It is interesting because it digs deeply into the inner personality and links Socialism with some vital needs.

The intelligence test, on the other hand, is straightforward, matter of fact, and unexpectedly maneuvers the reader into an acknowledgment that he is more of a Socialist than he realizes.[5] Save for a faint inferiority feeling which this form may create, these features are positive advantages, although they evidently do not outweigh the factors of strength in the other leaflet.

From a certain point of view, this investigation may be considered a research in political pedagogy. Thorndike has repeatedly insisted that "education is a process of changing human beings for the better," and much of current educational technique consists in discovering and applying ways for making these modifications more efficiently. Political propaganda for good or ill does more to influence people's knowledge and attitudes in the field of the social sciences than all the formal educational apparatus of our time. Since so many desirable social changes are not made because the public refuses to admit that they would constitute an improvement, it is important for educational statesmanship to know what *means* of persuasion will increase the probability of realizing these *ends*. The present problem is just one aspect of this larger issue.

5. The seven propositions which appear in this appeal are items favored by a definite majority of sample Pennsylvania populations. Hence, the high probability of obtaining a preponderance of Agrees from a new random selection. Otherwise, they would have been too risky to use. With many individuals, of course, these statements definitely prejudice the case against rather than for.

■■ RUMORS

Although we generally seem to believe that rumors become highly distorted as they are communicated through a social group, evidence from several field studies has indicated that rumors are frequently transmitted with little if any distortion. Caplow's (1947) study of rumor transmission in army regiments during World War II indicated that rumors are recirculated through the social network and therefore subject to repeated correction. Distortion, he found, occurred where numerical statements were involved. Similarly, Schachter and Burdick found that planted rumors were not distorted in transmission. They found, though, that new rumors emerged when the group was exposed to an unprecedented and undefined event.

Field studies of rumor transmission are conducted of necessity on closed groups, such as schools, military installations, and companies where rumors recirculate and are subject to repeated correction of both the details and the source of the message. Laboratory studies of serially transmitted messages suggest, however, that rumors that move through open groups may become highly distorted.

Two methodological aspects of the reading in this section are of interest. First, the experiment demonstrates the one-shot nature of many field experimental situations. If the study had been poorly planned and rehearsed, the entire subject population could have been lost. If errors are made in studies that are only brief interludes in single subjects' lives, the study can be easily repeated simply by finding a few more people in some other location. When an experimenter requires a unique situation, such as a closed group of mutually acquainted persons, mistakes are costly because the experimental population may be destroyed. Thus in such research endeavors procedure planning and rehearsal of the experimenter's agents are critical.

The experiment also illustrates the use of increasing depth interviewing for dependent variable measurement. In this procedure information related to the independent variable manipulation is obtained from subjects by increasing the specificity of the questions. Thus interviewers in the Schachter and Burdick study started by asking the girls if anything unusual had happened that day. If this open-ended question did not elicit mention of the relevant event, more pointed questions were asked. Increasing the salience of the independent variable manipulation in an interview without giving away the experiment is not easy to accomplish.

The problems of reliability and validity emerge in any coding or classifying of subject behavior. Reliability refers to the consistent repeatability of a measuring instrument. A thermometer placed in ice water should read 0°C. each time it is read. If the thermometer reads 0°C. today, 7°C. tomorrow, and 3°C. the day after we would reject the instrument as unreliable. Coders, observers, questionnaires, interviewers, and the like also are measurement instruments. A "piece" of verbal or nonverbal behavior should be classified in the same way by different observers (interjudge reliability) as well as by the same observer at different times (intrajudge reliability).

Reliability does not imply that the instrument is measuring what we think it is measuring. Just as an IQ test should measure intelligence, observers who code a behavior as aggressive should be measuring aggression and not voice characteristics or race or social position in life. It is thus quite possible for judges to agree on the coding of a behavior that in actuality is totally invalid. In the Schachter and Burdick experiment, for example, judgments had to be made on which rumors were new and which were variations or distortions of planted rumors, and the new rumors had to be categorized by favorableness to the target girl. Judges can agree that a rumor is unfavorable when actually it reflects the admiration of the other girls. A rumor that the girl was being disciplined for attending a wild party the previous night could fall into either category, depending on the norms and values of the subject population. Interjudge reliability, then, is a necessary but not sufficient condition for concluding that the categories are veritable.

REFERENCE

Caplow, T. 1947. Rumors in war. *Social Forces* 25: 298–302.

24.   A field experiment on rumor transmission and distortion
Stanley Schachter and Harvey Burdick

Current notions of the determinants of rumor spread and distortion were tested in a field experiment. It has been hypothesized that rumors will spread when there is (*a*) a state of cognitive unclarity about (*b*) an important issue which is (*c*) common to all or most members of a group. Evidence is presented indicating that under conditions of widespread cognitive unclarity there is far more transmis-

Reprinted from the *Journal of Abnormal and Social Psychology* 50 (1955): 363–71. Copyright 1955 by the American Psychological Association, and reproduced by permission.

sion of a planted rumor and far more speculation involving new rumors when the issue is important than when it is relatively unimportant.

In distinct contrast to expectations created by studies using the technique of serial reproduction, there is absolutely no indication of distortion of the planted rumor. Several factors are suggested which may account for this difference between laboratory and field situations.

Rumor is usually characterized as an unreliable, sometimes wildly distorted form of communication which spreads rapidly and mysteriously to almost all available members of a population. The conception of distortion and exaggeration as characteristic of such forms of communication arises largely from generalization of findings in studies of perception and memory using the technique of serial reproduction (Allport & Postman, 1947; Bartlett, 1932). The impression of widespread and rapid diffusion is, with the exception of numbers of dramatic anecdotes, relatively undocumented, for there have been few studies of the spread of rumor.

The results of the few systematic studies which have been published are peculiarly at variance with the conception of rumor outlined above. In Table 24.1 the results of four such studies are outlined. In the first three of these studies (Black et al., 1950; Festinger et al., 1950; Schall et al., 1950), rumors were planted and then by means of systematic interviewing or participant observation of the relevant population, it was possible to make reasonably accurate estimates of the extent of rumor spread. For the 13 planted rumors reported in these 3 papers, an average of only 5 percent of the relevant population per rumor actually heard the rumor. An average of about 3 percent per rumor is reported as having told the rumor. In addition, the authors are familiar with two other studies using planted rumors; these have remained unpublished because of complete failure of the rumors to spread. The present paper is prompted, in part, by sheer exasperation at the growing number of such abortive studies.

Whether such results should be attributed to experimental failure or accepted as evidence that our notions about rumor are much

Table 24.1
Rumor Spread in Four Studies of Rumor

Study	Number of Rumors	Population × No. of Rumors	Percentage of Population Per Rumor Who Heard Rumor	Percentage of Population Per Rumor Who Told Rumor
Back et al. (1950)	9	55 × 9	5.9*	4.2*
Festinger, Schachter, and Back (1950)	2	100 × 2	5.1	2.5
Schall, Levy, and Tresselt (1950)	2	10 × 2†	0	0
Festinger, Cartwright, et al. (1948)	1	100 × 1	59.0	21.2

*From information reported in the publication, it is impossible to compute the exact figures. The figures reported are maximum possible estimates.

†Rumors were planted in two different groups, but N is reported for only one of these groups. It is assumed that the groups were roughly the same size.

exaggerated is equivocal. Comparison of these studies with reports of spontaneously arising rumors is difficult, for so few of the studies concerned with spontaneous rumors present any accurate estimate of the extent of rumor spread. One exception is the study of Festinger, Cartwright, et al. (item 4 in Table 24.1) of a spontaneous rumor concerning Communist activity in a housing project. Fifty-nine percent of the interviewed population reported having heard the rumor, 21 percent reported having told the rumor—considerably greater percentages than those reported in any of the studies employing planted rumors. However, since this single study was conducted specifically because the authors' attention was drawn to an already widespread rumor, it is impossible to make any guesses as to the extent to which such results may be typical of spontaneously arising rumors.

The limited data available on rumor distortion are similarly at odds with current expectations. In the two studies (Black et al.,

1950; Festinger et al., 1950) listed in Table 24.1 in which the senior author participated, and is, therefore, familiar with data not reported in the published papers, there was almost no evidence of any distortion or modification of the planted rumors. In the Festinger et al. (1948) study rumor spread was tested by a recognition question which made it impossible, of course, to evaluate distortion.

Such results as these are so puzzlingly at odds with current notions of the nature of rumor that one is forced to examine critically the studies here reviewed as well as to reexamine our current conceptions of rumor. We will consider first the problem of the spread of rumor and reserve for consideration in a later section of this paper the problem of rumor distortion.

In an attempt to formalize the conditions of rumor spread, Allport and Postman (1947, p. 34) propose as "the basic law of rumor" that "the amount of rumor in circulation will vary with the importance of the subject to the individuals concerned times the ambiguity of the evidence pertaining to the topic at issue." A similar proposition is the "principle of cognitive unclarity" by Festinger et al. (1948, p. 484). "Rumors will tend to arise in situations where cognitive regions especially relevant to immediate behavior are largely unstructured." Both formulations agree in identifying cognitive unclarity or ambiguity and importance or relevance as key determinants of the origin and spread of rumor. The latter formulation is somewhat more specific in its treatment of the "importance" variable, relating it to areas with relevance for immediate behavior. We shall use the term in this sense.

It is probably wise, too, to make explicit what is undoubtedly implicit in both formulations—that the state of cognitive unclarity about an important issue be common to all or a major part of the population under consideration. Our apparent insistence on this factor arises from consideration of the pattern of communication which rumor customarily follows. In most social communication there is a back and forth exchange between two or more people and little further relaying of the contents of such conversations. The form of communication called rumor is characterized by a chain pattern of communication. A communicates an item to B, B communicates the item to C, C to D, and so on. In such a pattern, possession of the item of information seems to create a force to communicate it further. If one presumes that one kind of situation giving rise to such forces to communicate may be characterized by cognitive unclarity about an important issue, it seems clear that these conditions must hold for all or a large portion of the group in order that the rumor spreads. Otherwise, this chain pattern of communication will be quickly interrupted,[1] and, unless there are particularly persistent rumor mongers involved, there will be little spread of the rumor.

Though none of the studies outlined in Table 24.1 attempted a direct test of the relationship of unclarity and importance to rumor spread, the technique employed in almost all of these studies assumed an acceptance of these hypotheses concerning the determinants of rumor spread. Usually the experimenters attempted to identify areas which seemed important and about which there may have been some ambiguity and then to plant rumors relevant to these areas. Since none of these studies collected evidence which would allow proper evaluation of the extent to which these conditions were satisfied, it would seem a fruitless sort of postmortem to examine the details of these studies in terms of the postulated determinants of rumor spread.

Rather than attempt to explain such failures of rumor spread in terms of a conceptualization which is still largely untested, it would seem more worthwhile to proceed to a direct test of the conceptualization. The present study is a field experiment designed to test some of these ideas of the determinants of rumor spread. A situation which plausibly can be described as involving cognitive unclarity about an important issue is experimentally manipulated, and rumors relating to the issue are systematically planted.

Method

BACKGROUND

The study was conducted in a girls' school. Three months before this study was conducted, two of the teachers in the school decided

1. This seems to be the case with most of the rumors listed in Table 24.1. In the Festinger, Schachter, and Back study, 71 percent of all communications were initiated by the 4 percent of the population with whom the rumors were originally planted. In the Back et al. study an estimated minimum of 26 percent of all communications was initiated by the 4 percent of the population with whom the rumors were planted.

to conduct a demonstration experiment on rumor mongering. The procedure they adopted was similar to that employed in most studies in which planted rumors are used. Two girls were let in on the secret, instructed how to proceed, and during the course of one day planted the rumor with some 10 to 15 girls.

The rumor concerned the school's Christmas play. There had been some friction between the teacher directing the play and the girls involved, and there had been a series of quarrels and petty incidents concerning casting, rehearsals, and the like. The rumor was that the Christmas play had been canceled. Some of the girls with whom the rumor was planted were involved in the play; others were not.

The results again were nil; there seems to have been virtually no spread of the rumor. The two girls who had planted the rumor and several of the teachers acted as participant observers and were unable to report a single act of communication. As a demonstration, the experiment was an unfortunate failure; but it does serve as a casual additional control for the present study since precisely the same girls were the subject population for the attempt at rumor spreading described in this paper.

POPULATION

The school in which the study was conducted is a small, exclusive, girls' preparatory day school. The school is both a primary and secondary school and has 12 grades with 1 class of about 18 students constituting each grade. The school day begins at 8:25 and ends at 4:00; the girls do not return home during this period. Most of this time is occupied with standard class work, but each grade has a 1-hour lunch period and a 15-minute recess at 10:15 during which time the girls meet together in the lunchroom. Most of the girls have a one-hour study period and an hour of gym. During recess, at lunch, and in gym periods the girls are free to communicate with one another. There is a five-minute interval between class periods, during which time the girls change classrooms and are again free to communicate and socialize.

The experiment proper was conducted in the upper six grades of the school—the standard junior high school and high school grades. The age range of the girls concerned was between 12½ and 17½.

307 SCHACHTER/BURDICK   TRANSMISSION AND DISTORTION

There were three experimental conditions: (*a*) The cognitive unclarity–rumor (CU-R) condition—a situation of cognitive unclarity was manipulated, and a rumor was planted. (*b*) The cognitive unclarity (CU) condition—a situation of cognitive unclarity was manipulated, and no rumor was planted. (*c*) The rumor (R) condition—a rumor was planted, but no situation of cognitive unclarity was created.

Six classes containing a total of 96 students were involved in the study. Two classes were assigned to each experimental condition so that in each condition there was one of the older three classes and one of the younger three classes.

PRODUCING A SITUATION OF COGNITIVE UNCLARITY

On the day of the study, between 8:25 and 8:35, the principal of the school went into four different classrooms. In each class, she interrupted the work, stood in front of the class, pointed a finger at one girl, and announced, "Miss K., would you get your hat, coat, and books, please, and come with me. You will be gone for the rest of the day." Then, without a word, she and the girl walked out of the room together. Such an action was completely unprecedented in the experience of the girls. To insure that the event remained a complete mystery, the entire staff of the school had been instructed to reply to any questions about the event that "they knew nothing about it."

The girls taken from each of the four classes had been selected on the basis of their sociometric status and their academic and disciplinary records. All four girls were matched on these three criteria. They were chosen so as to fall between the 50th and 75th percentile in grade average and in the number of sociometric choices they received from their classmates. In addition, none of the girls had a disciplinary record. These girls, then, were fairly average members of their classes, reasonably popular and with fair grades. None of them knew anything about the study before they were taken from class.

Was the manipulation effective in producing the desired constellation of variables? As part of the standard data collecting procedure, the teachers in the school had all been instructed to keep a record of all questions addressed to them about the manipulation. They were asked to record who spoke to them, when, and the content of the question or remark. There were 62 girls in the 4 classes from which the principal had removed 1 student. The teachers reported a total of 198 questions, plus the report of one harried teacher, unable to keep up with the curiosity of the girls, that "everyone in the class asked me what had happened," and of another that "half the class asked questions." Virtually every girl in the classes affected made inquiries of one or more of her teachers, and almost all questions were of the sort, "What happened to Miss K.?" "Why did the principal take Miss K. out of class?" "What's going on?" etc. We assume from the nature of these questions, which were largely expressions of curiosity, puzzlement, and attempts to get information, that the manipulation did produce a state of cognitive unclarity common to all or most of the girls involved. Evidence relevant to the importance variable will be presented in a later section.

It should be pointed out that this manipulation has undoubtedly produced more than a simple state of cognitive unclarity. The event was novel and dramatic, and there can be little doubt that it produced surprise and excitement as well as considerable curiosity and unclarity as to what was going on. We have abstracted from this constellation the element of cognitive unclarity, and the nature of the questions asked the teachers would seem to justify this characterization, but it is likely that the effects of the manipulation on rumor transmission are in part attributable to the additional elements involved.

PLANTING THE RUMOR

The rumor was planted with two girls from each of four different classes. Two of these classes were from the four in which the situation of cognitive unclarity was produced; in the remaining two classes there had been no such manipulation. The eight girls with whom the rumor was planted were also matched in terms of their sociometric, academic, and disciplinary records.

A day or two before the study took place, various teachers made appointments for 8:15 on the morning of the study to see each of the eight girls with whom the rumor was to be planted. Ostensibly, the purpose of these appointments was to discuss academic progress, next year's program, etc. This was routine procedure. Each of these interviews followed an identical pattern. After six or seven minutes of discussing the matter for which the appointment had presumably been arranged, and immediately before terminating the interview, each teacher said, "By the way, some examinations have been taken from the office. Do you happen to know anything about this?" No such thing had taken place, and, of course, all of the girls interviewed denied any knowledge of the affair. The interview was so timed that each of the girls returned to her classroom before the principal entered any of the rooms.

The rumor planted in this way was intentionally chosen so as not to be an immediate explanation for the "cognitive unclarity" manipulation. It could, however, be readily linked to the morning's events as a tentative sort of explanation. The rationale for this choice is the following. One of our interests was the origin of new rumors. It seemed preferable to entrust the job of planting the rumor to teachers rather than making confederates of a number of girls and thereby imposing on them the difficult job of maintaining a standard pattern of behavior throughout the day. It seems a reasonable hunch that a clearly explanatory rumor originating from an authority figure, such as a teacher, would tend to inhibit the kind of speculation from which new rumors arise.

DATA COLLECTED

Three types of data were collected.

1. Sociometric data: Three weeks before the study took place all of the girls involved answered a sociometric questionnaire. The school was planning a school fair for which the girls were to work together at planning exhibits, running shows, etc. The sociometric questionnaire was linked to this affair and read: "As you know, we are hoping to hold the school fair early in the fall. We would like you to work with girls you enjoy being with. If you will list your five best friends we will try to arrange it."

2. Teachers' observations: As previously mentioned, all of the teachers kept a record of comments addressed to them concerning the manipulation.

3. Standardized interview: At 2 in the afternoon, toward the end

of the school day, a team of 20 interviewers took over the school lunchroom in order to interview all of the girls involved in the study. The interviewing schedule was so arranged that an entire class was interviewed at the same time in order to prevent any communication among the girls about the nature of the interview. The classes were scheduled and brought down to the interview room in a fashion which prevented any communication among classes.

The interview was a standardized, open-end instrument designed to get information about what the girls had heard about the situation created by the cognitive unclarity manipulation, with whom they had talked about this, whether or not they had heard the planted rumor, from whom they had heard it and to whom they had told it, and how much time they had spent discussing all of these matters during the day.

At the end of the day, after all of the girls had been interviewed, a general assembly was called for all of the classes involved in the study. The study was explained in complete detail at this gathering. The four girls who had been taken from their classes (and who had spent the day, in the company of the principal, on a tour of the University of Minnesota campus) returned to school in time for the assembly and were the heroines of the next two days.

Results

1. KNOWLEDGE OF THE RUMOR AND THE COGNITIVE
UNCLARITY MANIPULATION

Table 24.2 presents data on the percentage of girls who in their interviews reported that they had heard the planted rumor and the percentage of girls indicating that they knew that the principal had removed girls from their classrooms. In this and in several of the following tables, data are reported for each of the classes individually as well as for the two classes in each condition combined. Thus, the symbol CU-R1 stands for one of the two classes in the CU-R condition, CU-R2 for the other class in this condition, and so on. The symbol CU-R1 + CU-R2 stands for the two classes in the condition combined.

It is clear from Table 24.2 that virtually every girl had heard the planted rumor. Only 1 of the 96 girls interviewed reported that she

Table 24.2
Knowledge of the Rumor and the Cognitive Unclarity Manipulation

CONDITION	N	PERCENT KNOWING OF CU MANIPULATION	PERCENT KNOWING RUMOR
CU-R1	18	100	100
CU-R2	15	100	100
CU-R1 + CU-R2	33	100	100
CU1	18	94	100
CU2	11	100	100
CU1 + CU2	29	97	100
R1	18	94	94
R2	16	100	100
R1 + R2	34	97	100

had not heard the rumor. In terms just of having heard the rumor, there are no differences between conditions. Similarly, almost all of the girls, including those in the R condition, were aware that girls had been taken out of their classes. Only two girls reported that they knew nothing about this. Eighty-five percent of the girls interviewed linked the planted rumor, in some fashion, to the manipulation.

Clearly, there had been considerable communication not only within classes but between classes. The CU girls had all heard the planted rumor. Almost all of the R girls were aware that the principal had removed girls from other classes. The unexpected volume and generality of communication make it necessary to recharacterize the three experimental conditions.

The fact that the planted rumor is widely known in both the CU-R and the CU conditions essentially reduces these two to the same condition—a situation of cognitive unclarity about an important issue, with a widely spread, planted rumor. The R condition is recharacterized as a state of cognitive unclarity about a relatively unimportant issue. Though all of the girls in this condition are aware that for some mysterious reason the principal has taken girls out of other classes, they have almost no sociometric connections with these girls. They are familiar with the faces, but indifferent to the girls. Though the manipulation poses the possibility of real changes in the relationship between the girls removed from class and their immediate classmates, no such problems exist for girls in the R condition.

Several sources of data support this recharacterization of the R condition. Previously, inferences were made about the success of the attempt to create a cognitively unclear situation from the *nature* of the questions asked the teachers. Tentative inferences relating to the importance variable may be drawn from the *number* of such questions. Virtually all subjects in all conditions knew about the cognitive unclarity manipulation. Presumably only those girls who seriously cared about the event would have attempted to glean information from the teachers. The teachers reported well over 200 questions from the 62 girls in the CU-R and CU conditions. They reported only 1 question from the 34 girls in the R condition.

The amount of time the girls spent speculating and discussing the manipulation may also be considered as an indication of the importance of the event. In their interviews, after they had indicated that they were aware of the manipulation and had discussed it, the girls were asked, "Could you say just how much time you've spent talking about this today? Try to make an accurate guess." Girls in the CU-R and CU conditions estimated an average of almost 1 hour and 40 minutes; girls in the R condition estimated an average of 20 minutes. The difference is significant at better than the .001 level of confidence.[2]

2. It could, of course, be argued that rather than indicating that the issue was unimportant in the R condition, the number of questions to the teachers and the amount of time spent talking might indicate that there was less cognitive unclarity in the R condition. Such might indeed be the case if girls in the R condition were either (*a*) more prone to link the rumor to the manipulation and to believe that the girls taken from class had stolen the examinations or, (*b*) had some other generally accepted and credited explanation for the manipulation. The data reveal, however, that there are no between-condition differences in the extent to which the rumor is linked to the manipulation or in the degree to which it is believed that the planted rumor conclusively explains why the girls were removed from class. Further, the great majority of Ss in the R condition indicated in their interviews that they had no real idea as to why the girls had been taken from class.

Clearly these last two bits of data must be qualified by the fact that girls in the R condition necessarily learned of the events of the cognitive unclarity manipulation somewhat later than the girls in the other conditions and consequently had less time to discuss and ask questions of the teachers. However, the interviews indicate that almost all of the girls in the R condition had learned of this event by the 10:15 morning recess. Since previous to this time the girls were free to communicate to one another and to the teachers only in the two five-minute periods between classes, it is clear that this factor alone cannot account for the major differences between conditions.

Supporting evidence free of this time factor can be derived from the indications of saliency of issue in the standardized interviews with each girl. The interview was so constructed that the first question relevant to the manipulation of cognitive unclarity was a recall question and the following questions were recognition questions. After a few icebreaker questions the girl was asked: "In most schools things are pretty much the same from day to day, but sometimes things do happen that are out of the ordinary. Would you say that anything unusual happened today?" If in response to this question she failed to mention the experimental manipulation, she was asked, "Some of the other girls we've spoken to have told us that this morning some girls were called out of class by the principal. Have you heard anything about this? What have you heard?" It is assumed that the cognitive unclarity manipulation is more salient and more important for those girls who mention it on the recall question than for those who first mention it on the recognition question. Ninety-three percent of the girls in the CU-R condition mentioned the incident in answer to the recall question; 76 percent of the girls in the CU condition mentioned it to the recall question; and only 26 percent of girls in the R condition responded to the recall question by describing this event.

Such evidence supports the recharacterization of the experimental conditions. The three conditions are characterized by an equal degree of cognitive unclarity, for the event was the same mystery to all the girls. The issue involved, however, was relatively unimportant to the R condition classes and extremely important to the CU-R and the CU classes.

2. TRANSMISSION OF THE PLANTED RUMOR

Our conceptualization suggests that the force to communicate a relevant rumor should vary with the degree of importance of the issue concerning which there is ambiguity. It should be anticipated then that there will be far more transmission and discussion of the rumor in the CU-R and CU conditions than in the R condition. Table 24.3 presents the relevant data.[3]

Table 24.3
Mean Number of Subjects to Whom Communications Concerning the Rumor Were Initiated

CONDITION	N	MEAN NO. OF GIRLS TO WHOM RUMOR WAS TRANSMITTED
CU-R1	16	3.19
CU-R2	13	2.46
CU-R1 + CU-R2	29	2.86
CU1	18	2.22
CU2	11	2.36
CU1 + CU2	29	2.28
R1	16	1.38
R2	14	.79
R1 + R2	30	1.10

The data in Table 24.3 are derived from the responses of the girls to the interview questions concerning their knowledge of the rumor, from whom they had heard it, and to whom they had communicated it. The figures reported are the averages, for each class and condition, of the number of different girls to whom each girl is reported as *initiating* a communication concerning the rumor. There is an average of more than twice as many transmissions of the

3. In order to make the data of all six classes completely comparable, the data for the girls whom the rumor was originally planted are not included in this table. In the CU-R condition, these 4 girls initiated communications concerning the rumor with an average of 7.00 girls; in the R condition, they averaged 6.00 girls.

rumor in both the CU-R or CU conditions than in the R condition. The difference between CU-R and R conditions is significant at better than the .01 level of confidence; between CU and R conditions at the .03 level of confidence. There is no significant difference between CU-R and CU conditions.

Transmission of the rumor was widespread in CU-R and CU classes and relatively restricted in the R condition classes. Seventy-eight percent of the girls in CU-R and CU conditions initiated one or more communications concerning the rumor; only 40 percent of the girls in the R condition did so. Since we know that virtually all of the girls heard the rumor, it would seem that knowledge of the rumor creates far stronger forces to communicate and discuss it when the issue to which it is relevant is important than when it is unimportant. Some caution, however, must be observed in weighing this interpretation. It was previously suggested that the dramatic nature of the manipulation probably produced surprise and excitement as well as a state of cognitive unclarity. It would seem a reasonable guess that such factors would operate more strongly for the girls who were immediate witnesses of the event than for those girls who heard about the incident but were not present. The CU-R and CU conditions, then, may differ from the R condition not only in the importance of the event, but in the effects produced by being witness to the manipulation. Though we do believe that importance is the crucial variable in accounting for the differences between conditions, it is clear that, within the present design, this conclusion must be tempered by the existence of these additional factors.

It is to be expected, too, that the importance of the issue varied within class and condition. For some girls the issue may have been extremely important and for others trivial. One criterion for distinguishing among the girls on this dimension would be the nature of their relationship to the girls who are taken out of class by the principal. Plausibly, this should be a more important event for those who are good friends of the girl removed from class than for those who are not, and the friends should be expected to communicate the rumor more.

Since almost all sociometric choices were within class, the following means are based on just the four classes in the CU-R and CU conditions. Girls who on their sociometric have given one of their choices to the girl taken out of their class by the principal initiated communications concerning the rumor to an average of 3.10 different girls. Girls who did not make this sociometric choice initiated only 2.00 communications of the rumor. This difference is significant by *t* test at the .08 level of confidence.

3. ORIGIN OF NEW RUMORS

The same factors which promote the spread of the planted rumor should presumably stimulate the kind of speculation and guesswork from which new rumors arise, and it should be anticipated that there will be greater diversity and circulation of new rumors in those conditions where the issue is most important. Relevant evidence is presented in Table 24.4.

In column 3 of Table 24.4 are reported the percentages of girls in each of the classes who in their interviews reported that they discussed some rumor related to the cognitive unclarity manipulation other than the planted rumor. Some 70 percent of the girls in the CU-R and CU conditions reported discussing other rumors; less than 15 percent of the girls in the R condition did so. The

Table 24.4
The Prevalence and Variety of New Rumors

CONDITION	N	PERCENTAGE OF GIRLS REPORTING NEW RUMORS	NUMBER OF DIFFERENT RUMORS
CU-R1	18	72.2	16
CU-R2	15	80.0	15
CU-R1 + CU-R2	33	75.8	
CU1	18	72.2	14
CU2	11	54.6	5
CU1 + CU2	29	65.5	
R1	18	5.6	1
R2	16	25.0	2
R1 + R2	34	14.7	

difference between either CU-R or CU condition and R condition is significant at better than the .001 level of confidence. The difference between CU-R and CU conditions is not significant. Clearly the greater the importance of the issue, the greater the circulation of new rumors.

Not only is there greater circulation of rumors other than the planted rumor in the two high importance conditions but there is greater diversity of new rumors as well. In column 4 of Table 24.4 are listed the number of different rumors in circulation in each of the classes. There is an average of over 12 different rumors per class reported in the CU-R and CU conditions and of 1.5 different rumors per class in the 2 R condition classes.

In terms of our previous reasoning it might be anticipated that "good friends" would tend to circulate new rumors more than would those girls who do not choose sociometrically the girls taken out of class by the principal. Though friends circulated an average of 1.55 new rumors and nonfriends an average of 1.32, a slightly smaller proportion of friends transmitted such new rumors. Sixty-eight percent of friends reported discussing rumors other than the planted rumor and 74 percent of the nonfriends did so. Neither of these differences is significant.

There is, however, a difference between these two groups in the kind of rumor which they report having discussed. It is possible to categorize the various rumors circulated in terms of the optimism or pessimism of the explanation offered for the removal of the girl from class. Some of these rumors were distinctly favorable to this girl, e.g., "She's a great beauty and has been invited to tea at the principal's house." Other rumors were more unfavorable, "She's being disciplined for going to a wild party last weekend." Still other rumors were neutral in tone, "She's going to attend a lecture." Table 24.5 presents the percentage of each type of rumor transmitted by friends and nonfriends. Of the total number of rumors transmitted by friends 52 percent are favorable and 29 percent unfavorable. Nonfriends transmitted 34 percent favorable rumors and 56 percent unfavorable. Of the friends who did transmit rumors 76.2 percent transmitted one or more favorable rumors. Of nonfriends who transmitted rumors, 47.8 percent transmitted 1 or more

Table 24.5
Friendship and New Rumors

Group	N	Number of Times New Rumors Transmitted	Percentage of New Rumors Which Were:		
			Favor- able	Neutral	Unfa- vorable
Friends	31	48	52	19	29
Nonfriends	31	41	34	10	56

favorable rumors. This difference is significant at close to the .10 level of confidence. Though there is no difference between friends and nonfriends in the extent to which they transmit rumors other than the planted rumor, there is a tendency for friends to transmit predominantly favorable rumors and for nonfriends to transmit predominantly unfavorable rumors.

DISTORTION OF THE PLANTED RUMOR

The interview of each girl was examined for indications of distortion of the planted rumor. In no one of the 96 interviews is there any indication of distortion. In every case, the planted rumor was reported to the interviewer in essentially the form in which it was originally planted with no instance of embellishment or variation. Though many new and bizarre rumors did spring up, the planted rumor itself came through a day's discussion intact. This finding is consistent with the results of two of the studies (Black et al., 1950; Festinger et al., 1950) discussed in the introduction to this paper where also there was no indication of distortion of the planted rumors. Caplow (1947) too, in a study of rumors in war reports "the veracity of rumors did not decline noticeably during transmittal." Though he notes the existence of tendencies to distortion, his major impression is that of a marked lack of distortion.

Such findings, of course, are in direct contrast to the widespread impression of rumor as an unreliable and sometimes fantastically distorted form of communication. These results suggest that experiments such as those of Bartlett (1932) and Allport and Postman

(1947) are questionable laboratory paradigms of the field situation of rumor transmission. This is not meant, in any way, to question the results of these laboratory and classroom experiments as such, but to suggest that the results of these studies are not immediately applicable to field situations in which rumor or transmission is a voluntarily initiated action subject to a variety of corrective tendencies, rather than an experimentally induced communication with no possibility of correcting exaggerations, distortions, or omissions during the course of transmission.

Caplow in discussing the discrepancy between his findings and those reported in the Allport and Postman experiments suggests two mechanisms by which distortion may be eliminated or prevented during the course of transmission of a rumor. (a) "A rumor is usually heard more than once, and usually transmitted more than once by each individual in the channel. This re-circulation tends to eliminate variation. . . ." (b) Persons associated with previous inaccuracies or exaggerations tend to be excluded from the developing channels of rumor transmission (Caplow, 1947, p. 301).

Other factors which may account for the differences between the field studies discussed and the Allport-Postman experiments are: (a) The complexity of the material transmitted. In the laboratory experiments, the material transmitted is customarily the content of highly detailed and complicated pictures or stories. In the field studies the planted rumors have usually been relatively simple, uncomplicated, and with a minimum of irrelevant detail. Plausibly, the process of leveling (the omission of details in serial reproduction) will be most apparent when highly detailed and complicated material is transmitted.

(b) The nature of the force to communicate. In the laboratory experiments, subjects communicate the contents of picture or story only to follow the experimenter's instructions. In the field studies, subjects communicate only on their own initiative. Presumably, subjects will transmit a rumor on their own initiative only when the content of the rumor is of some interest to them. Higham (1951) in a study using the technique of serial reproduction has maintained that there is less distortion when subjects are ego involved and interested in the content of their communication.

REFERENCES

Allport, G. W., and Postman, L. 1947. *The psychology of rumor.* New York: Holt.

Back, K.; Festinger, L.; Hymovitch, B.; Kelley, H. H.; Schachter, S.; and Thibaut, J. W. 1950. The methodology of studying rumor transmission. *Human Relations* 3: 307–17.

Bartlett, F. C. 1932. *Remembering.* London: Cambridge University Press.

Caplow, T. 1947. Rumors in war. *Social Forces* 25: 298–302.

Festinger, L.; Cartwright, D.; Barber, K.; Fleischl, J., Gottsdanker, J.; Kaysen, A.; and Leavitt, G. 1948. A study of a rumor: its origin and spread. *Human Relations* 1, 464–85.

Festinger, L.; Schachter, S.; and Back, K. 1950. *Social pressures of informal groups.* New York: Harper.

Higham, T. M. 1951. The experimental study of the transmission of rumor. *British Journal of Psychology* 42: 42–55.

Schall, H. M.; Levy, B.; and Tresselt, M. E. 1950. A sociometric approach to rumor. *Journal of Social Psychology* 31: 121–29.

INDEX

in future replications, 151
"Cooperation" operationally defined, 71, 93
Courtesy expectation not supported, 105
Credibility, low, and attitude change, 267
Crime reporting, 63, 69
  with and without confronting thief, 64
Criminal record effect on job opportunities, 35
Criteria for selection of alternatives, 127
Crowd conditions, 273–280
  and social conformity, 279
  supportive function, 276
Culture, controlled experimental, 169, 171–178

Davidson, 119
Dealer and seller
  distance, 160, 162, 164
  eye contact, 160, 161, 164
Debates
  and initial opinion strengthening, 261
  as procedural format, 271
  and reduction of no-opinion category, 261
Debriefing, 101
Deception, 34
  and economic harm, 35
Decision making
  and similarity of alternatives, 136, 137
  stressful for humans, 136
Dehoaxing, 210
Delinquency, apparent, 178
Denial strategy in intervention situations, 61
Dependence perceived as caused by external vs. internal factors, 166
Dependent variable, 5
Deprivations accruing to non-

sanctioned, 33
Descriptive numbers and apparent differences, 47
Deutsch and Gerard, 219
Development of theory, function of, 9
Deviant requesters and compliance, 216
"Differential deterrence," 32
Differential treatment of foreign and compatriot strangers, 70–97
Diffuse action and involvement mechanism, 231
Directions, asking for, 73–75
Direct or fully personal contact, 45
Discrepancy, stated vs. actual, 170
Discrimination, 25–45
Disparity and age, 58
Dissonance, 121, 122, 129–136
  arousal of, and compliance, 218
  in choice between two equally attractive objects, 111
  increasing amount of, 125
Dissuasion techniques, 45
Distortion, 130
  in numerical statement rumors, 300
Dittes and Kelley, 179, 180, 185, 186
Doob and Gross, 46
Doob and Ecker, 209, 211

East Side Restaurant Survey of New York City, 45
Education level and opinion change, 249, 250
Ehrlich, Guttman, Schonbach and Mills, 120
Elimination from analysis, 55
Emotional contrast and dissonance-like effects, 111
Empirical investigation of verbal attitudes/actual behavior discrepancies, 39
Enlisted men, 187
Environment engineering, 13

as psychological blow, 202
Role theory, 206
  postulates, 187
Rosenthal, 158
Rubin, 34
Rumors
  "basic law," 305
  origin of new, 317
  planting, 309, 310
  spontaneously arising, 304
Rumor studies results, 303
Rumor spread
  and commonness of issue to
    group members, 302
  and importance of issue, 302, 313,
    314, 316
  and state of cognitive unclarity,
    302
Rumor transmission
  and closed vs. open groups, 300
  and distortion, 300, 302-305, 319
  and the nature of the force to
    communicate, 320
  and repeated correction by
    recirculation, 300, 320
  in World War II army, 300
Salesman influence on purchases
  and claim to similar relationship
    to product, 143-146, 150-152
Salzinger and Pisoni, 22
Sampling considerations, 73
Sanders, 94
Sarbin and Allen, 47
Schachter and Burdick, 300, 301
Schachter, Willerman, Festinger
  and Hyman, 152
Schall et al., 303
Schein, Schneier and Barker, 219
Schopler and Bateson, 166
Schopler and Mathews, 166
Schwartz, 33
Self-identification of opposite
  opinion holders avoided, 240
Self-report studies, 2
Sensitization by first measurement

as problem, 108
"Sensitizing," avoidance of, 243
Serial reproduction technique
  and characterization of rumor,
    303
  and ego involvement, 320
Sherif and Sherif, 169
"Shock" and recovery, 22
Shopper activity, 11-14
Shop size, 159, 163, 164
Similarity perception of recipient
  to model
  and ability level, 145
  and adoption of model's
    preference, 145
  and "anxiety," 145
  and attraction to communicator,
    144
  and change toward communicator
    144
Situation as behavior determinant, 2
Situational factors
  and cooperation, 93
  and differentiation of experi-
    mental encounters, 72
  and treatment of foreigners, 71
Skinnerian view, 16
Small request compliance and subsequent larger request compliance, 217-232
Social class differences and treatment of foreigners, 71, 94-96
Social comparison theory, 144, 152
  Festinger, 145
Social equity mechanism explored
  as possible boomerang
    mechanism, 270
Social inhibitions, 62, 66, 69
Socialist appeal, receptivity to,
  and financial well-being,
    298
Socialist party, principles and
  ideals vs. standard
  bearers, 286
Socialist vote in excess of

302-S978s

164031

AUTHOR
Swingle, Paul G.

TITLE   Social psychology in natural settings.

DATE DUE	BORROWER'S NAME
	Myra P. Bragg 87538
10 01 1	
10 31 1	Myra P Bragg 87538

302-S978s   164031